URGENT COPY

Books by Anthony Burgess

(*in the order in which they were written*)

Novels

A VISION OF BATTLEMENTS

THE LONG DAY WANES

THE RIGHT TO AN ANSWER

THE DOCTOR IS SICK

DEVIL OF A STATE

A CLOCKWORK ORANGE

THE WANTING SEED

HONEY FOR THE BEARS

NOTHING LIKE THE SUN

TREMOR OF INTENT

ENDERBY

Nonfiction

RE JOYCE

THE NOVEL NOW

URGENT COPY

CONTENTS

PER LILIANA

la revestita carne alleluiando

Acknowledgments

These pieces first appeared in the following periodicals: *The Times*, *The Times Literary Supplement*, the *Spectator*, the *American Scholar*, the *Hudson Review*, the *New York Times*, *Horizon*, *Encounter*, the *Journal of Contemporary History*, *Commonweal*, *Book World*. I am most grateful for the permission of the editors to reprint.

A.B.

Foreword

MOST of the essays in this book were written because I was asked to write them. Writing them, I was in the position of a carpenter commissioned to make a table or cupboard of a specified size, and to do the job as quickly as is consistent with efficiency. In this respect, these writings are different from the seventeen novels and three books of literary exegesis that I have produced. One doesn't usually work to a deadline with a book, and hence one thinks one is taking more trouble than with journalism. This isn't necessarily true. Some fine nervous prose can be jerked out by deadlines. Fine nervous music also: think of Mozart composing the Overture to *Don Giovanni* while the audience was coming in. What I mean is, I suppose, that there is a disparity of function between the essay in a magazine and the essay in a book: the book's way is an expansive one, while the magazine's is contractive. One isn't apologizing for the quality so much as the lack of quantity—in the individual essay, I mean. The assumption is that a literary essay is better if it is longer. This, of course, is arguable.

Anyway, one tends to be a little apologetic at putting pieces of journalism in a book. Sufficient unto the day is the newspaper thereof, as J. J. O'Molloy says, and hard covers are supposed to be there to eternize great thoughts and glorious language. However permanent the subject of a journalistic essay, the writer is aware of the need to infuse topicality, to suggest—if he can—that what he is writing has news-value. Thus, the name of a forgotten politician will rest, like a bit of uncollected rubbish, in the corridors of an essay on Milton. Ernest Newman, in a Sunday article on Wagner, referred to chromaticism without a key-centre as one of the 'many doors that Richard opened'. The reference is to a pop-song of the nineteen fifties called 'Open the door, Richard'. I have excised from the following articles odd gibes at contemporary bellwethers and teen-age idols, but I am not sure whether I have done the right thing. It is cheating to pretend that the pieces are something that they are not: the ephemeral is part of their fabric.

The reader will also notice occasional sneers at writers who slap articles between hard covers and call them Collected Essays. The sneering was done before I myself thought of so dignifying my journalism, but I have not tried to rub out the facial gesture. It is best to see it now as an apologetic grimace, tinged with irony, on behalf of a whole profession that finds it hard to pay bills when first presented. Let the reader make no mistake about it. Professional writing is an unremunerative calling. The major rewards, when they come at all, come on the margins. The novelist survives because of film options and television adaptations. Criticism itself is a secondary vocation—it is a field where the don, the staff-man and the novelist meet—and, in Britain anyway, it is very ill-paid.

If one does a lot of magazine work (and I have done a great deal in the last ten years), there is a danger that this secondary occupation may look—especially to the person who doesn't read many books—like a primary one. The title of journalist is probably very noble, but I lay no real claim to it. I am really, I think, a novelist and a musical composer *manqué*: I make no other pretensions. I find it hard to evaluate the new books I read and, as I get older, I find even the act of reading difficult. This is because a fair-sized area of my brain is concerned with working out new novels, and other people's ima-ginative writings get in the way of this. When a girl student wrote to me to ask how one set about becoming a critic, I had to reply that first one had to write two or three novels, and then an editor rang up and asked if one would care to do a little reviewing. The whole business is beautifully exhibited in Cyril Connolly's *Enemies of Promise*, even to the stock locutions that editors use.

Whether novelists are really qualified to judge other people's books is hard to say. It was again Cyril Connolly who exhibited, with his usual clarity and good sense, the nexus between primary and secondary vocation. He said that everybody who has written a book knows how difficult it is to do, and hence is favourably disposed to anyone who has written even a very bad one. Book-writing is hard on the brain and excruciating to the body: it engenders tobacco-addiction, an over-reliance on caffeine and dexedrine, piles, dyspepsia, chronic anxiety, sexual impotence. Behind the new bad book one is asked to review lie untold misery and a very little hope. One's heart, stomach and anal tract go out to the doomed aspirant.

On the whole, I think I have been kinder and more cautious to other authors than, for the good of the art of writing, I ought to have been. Critics who know everything about books except how to write them—there are several of these around in London and New York, and far too many in Paris—have a sharp-eyed fierceness which, although possibly really a sublimation of sheer howling jealousy, is generally taken to be essential to good criticism. It is noteworthy, and it has been frequently noted, that the verb 'criticize' has, in the market-place, a wholly pejorative denotation, as in 'Oh, don't keep on criticizing all the bloody time.'

I fear that there is very little criticism of this kind in, I see it now, this over-bland compilation. Bitchings and sneerings can be very enjoyable and are true market-place criticizing, but my temperament cannot encompass such tabascoid poignancy. I have been the victim of a good deal of it myself, and I am inclined to think that it is ultimately self-destructive: it hardens all within and petrifies the feeling. Nevertheless, it is generally liked, and to those in search of destructive entertainment I apologize for being so white-sauce-like and reasonable.

I have had difficulty in finding a title for this book. I thought of *Conflict and Confluence*, which is the title of the final essay, but that would sound over-instructive. I thought also of *Homage to Qwert Yuiop*, whose name is blazoned on the second bank of the typewriter console: I owe a great deal to typewriters, though—like a farmer—I daren't make individual pets of them: I have to buy a new one every year. Any title is a cheat, but a title is only a name and need say no more about what it entitles than 'John' says about a man or 'Desirée' about a woman (though I must admit that such provocative christenings have a way of turning sour: I once knew a very plain and undesired Desirée). The present title is a mere reminder that these essays are pieces of journalism. *Urgent Copy*, written large on the envelope, is a talisman meant to ensure speedy and safe delivery, but it usually has the effect of slowing delivery down. Now these articles have been put to bed between hard covers, and there is no urgency at all.

London   A.B.

1

The Greene and the Red:
Politics in the Novels of Graham Greene

I HAD better begin by making my own position clear. I come of an old though not particularly distinguished Lancashire Catholic family, one that held to the faith through the Reformation and had its quota of undistinguished martyrs, was Royalist during the Civil War and hid its quota of undistinguished Royalist leaders in huts in Lancashire cloughs, and supported the Pretenders after 1688. There are several such families in England, particularly in the north-west, and they have made less mark in modern Catholic literature than have the converts. There is a tendency in old Catholic families to record a number of apostasies with the coming of the days of toleration, though—as Evelyn Waugh demonstrates romantically in *Brideshead Revisited*—deathbed reconciliations are very common; with the intellectual scions of the old Catholic families the faith rarely fires the imagination as it does with new converts, even where the faith burns at all. The English Catholic novel in our own age is almost entirely a product of conversion.

Of the English Catholic novelists, Graham Greene is by far the most interesting, since he is probably the least orthodox. The implied doctrines of his novels approach Jansenism, which has been repeatedly condemned by Rome. Cornelius Jansen, founder of the theological school whose most famous and brilliant adherent was Pascal, came too near to Calvinism to be orthodox: he found too much semi-Pelagianism in the 'laxist' Jesuits; he affirmed and re-affirmed the more 'rigorist' doctrines of St Augustine. In Jansen, original sin was not mere 'imputation': it expressed itself in the depravity of nature (whose order was, contrary to official teaching, distinct from the supernatural order), in appetite and in concupiscence. The horror of the natural world is one of the most fascinating aspects of Greene's fiction. Sin is not cool and intellectual matter for theological dissertations: sin is expressed in the joyless sex of *Brighton Rock*, with its broken toenails in the bed; the carious landscape of *The Power and the Glory*; the hell of Haiti in *The Comedians*.

A religious faith should beget its own politics. To adhere to a political system that denies God is not possible to the Christian, though some Christians have used doublethink to reconcile the contradictions. Thus, both Italy and France have their communist Catholics, and England had a distinguished Anglican dean who clung to Marxism against all official remonstrances. In such instances one does not have to look beyond the expediency of the nominal: one cannot hold opposed beliefs and maintain total orthodoxy in both. The political positions of most English Catholics have been dictated as much by the instinct for survival as by matters of doctrinal compatibility. They were Royalist almost to a man in the Great Rebellion and, with the Parliamentary victory, they suffered for two kinds of faith. They naturally supported the Jacobite cause, and they had no economic stake in Whiggism, though they had good grounds for being favourable to nineteenth-century Liberalism. Many Catholics today find it possible to be socialists, since British socialism—with its slogan 'pragmatism'—does not insist, as does pure Marxist doctrine, on a materialistic interpretation of history. And yet any political ideology that rejects original sin and believes in moral progress ought strictly to be viewed with suspicion by Catholics.

Deeper than party politics lies the whole question of national allegiance. The British State tolerates the Catholic Church, but the Catholic Church, being a supranational body, has no representation in the establishment: there are no Catholic bishops in the House of Lords, though it was found possible to put Donald Soper there. To honour the monarch is to acknowledge the hegemony of the Church of England. Catholic patriotism must necessarily be of a qualified kind, since not only is the present involved but also the past, the

remembered wrongs of history. These latter are, to the really em-
bittered, incarnated or lapidified in the cathedrals and churches
which, once Catholic, are now Protestant. No Catholic novelist is
able to resist the temptation of underlining the architectural squalor
of the churches where his heroes or heroines hear mass. But the real
historical wrongs are not easily forgotten. There is a significant
passage in Greene's *The Heart of the Matter*. When the Colonial
Secretary of the West African colony says, 'The Roman Catholic
Syrians are claiming they are a persecuted minority and that the
police are in the pay of the Moslem Syrians', the Catholic convert
Scobie replies: 'The same thing would have happened the other way
round—only it would have been worse. Parliament has more
affection for Moslems than Catholics.'

Graham Greene's self-expatriation—once intermittent but now,
it seems, permanent—could never be interpreted as a failure of
devotion to England. The Jansenist in him is led to the places where
the squalor of sin is exposed in its rawest forms. But, unlike Evelyn
Waugh, who fictionally identified himself with the fortunes of
English Catholics tied, by land or family bonds, to England, Greene
is concerned with the Catholic soul working out its salvation or
damnation in isolation: the furniture of England is a distraction and
an irrelevance. Admittedly, two of his finest novels—*Brighton Rock*
and *The End of the Affair*—have English settings, but they are not the
English settings of the ordinary bourgeois English novel: we have
the jungle of gang warfare in the first and the jungle of the Blitz in
the second. A parochial England, one in which party politics can be
an important concern, hardly seems to Greene a suitable stage for the
enactment of spiritual drama. Moreover, his Catholicism reveals,
with every new book, its international character. The enemies of the
true belief walk the great world, not the parish. The politics of
Greene are world politics.

In *The Power and the Glory* we observe a local revolution in a
small and remote state, but the lineaments of the new dispensation
are familiar and international: the cult of the spiritual holds back the
people, whose true enemies are the priests; the great goal is material
prosperity; the leader knows best. The progressive slogans are, as

always, accompanied by retrogressive enactments, best symbolized in prohibition. The imperfect priest on the run from the state police searches desperately for a bottle of wine with which to say mass. He procures one, only to have it drained by corrupt and hypocritical representatives of the new order, who toast human progress in it. It is 'human progress' that is the shibboleth of the antichrist, and it does not matter which political ideology is committed to it. American democracy and Russian communism alike profess the same goal, but at least one knows where one stands with a materialistic philosophy that openly avows its materialism. In *Our Man in Havana* the American Consul-General speaks at the Traders' luncheon:

> He spoke of the spiritual links between the democracies—he seemed to number Cuba among the democracies. Trade was important because without trade there would be no spiritual links, or perhaps it was the other way round. He spoke of American aid to distressed countries which would enable them to buy more goods and by buying more goods strengthen the spiritual links ... It had been a great pleasure for the American Consul-General to be invited to this lunch today and to meet the leading representatives of European trade and so strengthen still further the spiritual links ...

This is harmless enough. Greene's reputation for anti-Americanism did not begin here. It started with that still very topical novel set in Saigon.

The Quiet American is a work of fiction told in first-person narrative, and it was wrong of some commentators to identify the narrator with the author—a most implausible identification, anyway. With a first-person narrative there is no obligation on the author's part to be fair, just, dispassionate; and the anti-Americanism of the book springs from the natural jealousy and vindictiveness of the narrator. On the other hand, there is no doubt that the image of the American campaign in Vietnam accords pretty well with Greene's own American philosophy: the Americans may mean well, but they are naive, and in any case benevolence is dangerous if it is an expression of a twisted view of the desirable life. Greene, being a writer, hates semantic tyrannies, and he considers that too many Americans respond adversely to the term 'communism' without giving themselves a chance to examine the referent of the term. Evidently, some aspects of communism cannot rationally be rejected, but it is the very irrationality of official American policy that earns Greene's scorn. Dubbed anti-American, he is assumed by pro-Americans to be anti-democratic and pro-communist, but the issue is not as simple as that. The issue essentially involves religion and, in the endless cold war, matters of spiritual faith seem to have no role.

But to a Catholic there can be no real taking of sides. Americanism is bad in that it is fundamentally hypocritical. Talk of the 'free world' often means an obsession with American security, American trade, the augmentation of an American-led community dedicated to more and more feverish material consumption; it does not necessarily mean the spread of democratic rights. Greene finds this hypocrisy best, or worst, manifested in the Haiti of *The Comedians*. The tyranny of 'Papa Doc' and the terrorism of the *Tonton Macoute* are more hideous than anything that Soviet Russia can provide, but, since Haiti does not invoke the forbidden name of communism, America will be friendly. It is hard to find worse evil than that represented in Haiti, but America—though she may wrap her materialistic doctrines in the language of spiritual aspiration—is not in the least concerned with evil. Remembering the Jansenist dichotomy, we can regard all politics as belonging to the natural order which never touches the supernatural. But America, transmitting her power through the world, pretends that she is crusading; this is the unforgivable hypocrisy.

Communism is hypocritical with its claims to free the enslaved, and its own aims are as materialistic as those of Americanism. But the fact that spiritual values are actively resisted under communism saves its adherents from the bigger hypocrisy. Moreover, a political doctrine that is committed to improvement of the material lot of the people, yet signally fails to do so, seems to have been visited by an ironical paraclete: it is not yet clogged with butter and drowning in Coca-Cola vats; it is nearer the angels than it wishes to be. The sordid *mise-en-scène* that best expresses the sinfulness of the natural order is probably easier to find on the other side of the Iron Curtain than on the other side of the Atlantic. A place that seems to breathe sin is, paradoxically, spiritually healthier than an aseptic garden city.

Almost the closing passage of *The Comedians* sums up the relationship between the Greene and the Red so admirably that it asks to be quoted at length. The martyr Doctor Magiot, who has had the courage to resist the evil which that other doctor represents, leaves a letter to the narrator in which he attempts to reconcile the anomalies of his own position:

> ... I have grown to dislike the word 'Marxist'. It is used so often to describe only a particular economic plan—in certain cases and in certain times, here in Haiti, in Cuba, in Vietnam, in India. But Communism, my friend, is more than Marxism, just as Catholicism—remember I was born a Catholic too—is more than the Roman Curia. There is a *mystique* as well as a *politique*. We are humanists, you and I ... Communists have committed great crimes, but at least they have not stood aside, like an established society, and been indifferent. I would rather have blood on my hands than water like Pilate ... I implore you—a knock on the door may not allow me to finish this sentence, so take it as the last request of a dying man—if you have abandoned one faith, do not abandon all faith. There is always an alternative to the faith we lose. Or is it the same faith under another mask?

Doctor Magiot is 'committed'; the other main characters are not: they are the 'comedians' of the title, confusers of acting with action. But, in an evil world, it behoves a man to defend or promote the good, even at the risk of making a mistake: 'I would rather have blood on my hands than water like Pilate.' It is the 'established society' that is most likely to talk about ideals and yet act as though the consumption of materials were the end of life. The communist state is still in the process of 'becoming', as is the kingdom of heaven, and—since in an evil community good can be brought about only through revolution—its techniques are apter for killing evil than are those of an affluent and settled democracy. 'Communism is more than Marxism.' In Vietnam, communism can mean an agrarian reform sorely needed by a backward and ignorant people; Americanism—the doctrine of the towns—means teaching that same people to develop the urban appetites of the consumer.

Whether one accepts these notions or not, they seem implied in the later fiction of Graham Greene. A Catholic must accept that any kind of political commitment is dangerous, since no *politique* can coincide exactly with the Christian *mystique* (though a Jansenist will not worry too much about that kind of dichotomy). Yet if Christianity can no longer provide appropriate modes of political action, where can the committed Catholic look? Only to a system with a faith, even if that faith is heretical. If some Catholic novelists have been able to resist the big troubling theme of commitment, that is because they have remained the products of English parochialism. Evelyn Waugh's broken reed of a Catholic, Guy Crouchback (broken, I mean, as a man, not as a believer), meets the postwar world in Yugoslavia and does not like it. Scott-King, who is not a Catholic but may be taken as speaking for his creator, thinks it a bad thing that schoolboys should be made to learn about Modern Europe. All of Greene's later heroes enter, of their own free will, a bigger and more terrible world than Modern Europe.

British politics are too small for Greene, and, in *A Burnt-Out Case*, one has the feeling that British people are also becoming too small for anything but satirical treatment. The journalist Parkinson, the one representative of both his races in the colonial Congo, is a bloated joke whose opportunist and materialistic philosophy—a sort of parodic Americanism—is qualified by an inability to do anything with the truth except manipulate it in the service of 'news' and, through this habit, instinctively get the truth wrong. And yet the mere presence of an Englishman sweating in the tropics, wounded eyes looking out over his pink gin, is enough to remind us that the British colonist is a more acceptable figure to Greene than the comfortable bourgeois stay-at-home. One is impressed by Greene's own nostalgia for the Rider Haggard, Conan Doyle, John Buchan hero, pursuing the cause of British decency in some fever-ridden outpost. His most sympathetic character remains Scobie, the colonial government officer who, like Aristides the Just, is traduced by the petty minds of men and women who have brought lending-library gossipy suburban England with them into the African darkness.

English Catholics, even converts, are tempted by more heresies than are the children of Mediterranean baroque Christianity. The greatest temptation is provided by the British heresiarch Pelagius, a monk who denied original sin, doubted the need of divine grace to achieve salvation, and thought that man could attain some sort of perfection by his own efforts. His doctrines, which flourish in our mild air, are at the root of both the major political ideologies of this country, though they are at their more conspicuous in socialism. If an English Catholic does not wish to be tainted by Pelagianism, he had better seek the exile either of Evelyn Waugh's 'idiosyncratic Toryism', which can properly flourish only in a small manor cut off from the traffic, or of one of the barbarous places of the world. Surprisingly enough, such barbarous places take kindly to the heresies that have come out of France, a most civilized place: it is easy to be Albigensian or (which is not so bad) Jansenist in Cuba, Haiti, or the Heart of Darkness. But once a Catholic lays open his soul to the corruptions of the great world of commitment, he must accept a kind of empiricism if he is not to be damned, drawing from the natural order what may conceivably further the terrestrial ends of the supernatural order. In Greene's fiction, however, there is little flavour of empiricism (which, after all, has something of Pelagianism about it). There are instead paradoxes and anomalies—the sinner who is really a saint, the philanthropist who is really a destroyer. And there are dangerous epigrams like 'There is always an alternative to the faith we lose'. No significance need be attached to the fact that Graham Greene is now living not too many kilometres away from Port-Royal. His beliefs are his own affair; we are merely concerned with his fiction. And fiction, as we know, has to be stranger than truth.

Waugh Begins

WE NEED no cybernetic word-count to demonstrate how frequently the verb 'repine', in its negative conjugation, occurs in the works of Mr Evelyn Waugh. None of his later heroes—Scott-King, Gilbert Pinfold, Guy Crouchback, the author himself—ever repines, in spite of the march of barbarism, the failure of the vintage, and the decay of classical syntax. The pose is robed and stoic. In the last imperial outpost the doomed values of language and chivalry are upheld, though always with a certain discreet self-mockery. Indeed, Scott-King takes a definite masochistic pleasure (not uncommon here, we are told, though unknown to the New World) in the rise of horrible Modern Europe. The red-eyed scavenger is creeping in. Mr Waugh goes so far as to open the gates of Hampstead to him, cooing about its peace:

> Oh, but I have done an unselfish thing in telling him this! For I know he will yearn to be about the business of Balbus, and, as likely as not, he will plant himself upon the meadow with the willows, that looks so spring-like from my book-room door today. Nevertheless one must not repine. My work in this line is done. Balbus has built his wall.

The style, and the slippered epoch it so well expresses, will tell the reader which Mr Waugh this is—not the comic-stoic mock-Augustan novelist but the whimsical man-of-letters, managing director of Chapman & Hall, friend of the great fraud Gosse. But the 'one must not repine' is a significant link, a shared nose or villainous trick of the eye. The father, despite all the differences in the world, prepares us for the son.

And, of course, in reading this first volume of Mr Waugh's autobiography,* we are most interested in the genesis of a vocation, a temperament, and a style. We can ignore the remoter heredity,

* *A Little Learning: The first volume of an Autobiography* (Chapman & Hall, 1964).

though Mr Waugh makes it very entertaining; what we cannot ignore is the father, with his continual 'flamboyant declamation to imaginary audiences', his despondent waltz-song ('*Nobody cares for me in the least. Everyone thinks I'm a horrible beast*'), his mercuriality and his dramatic asthma, but, most of all, the limitations of his literary taste. 'Mr Rupert Brooke,' he wrote, 'has the itch to say a thing in such an arresting fashion as to shock the literary purist into attention even against his will.' The art of D. H. Lawrence needs 'a shower bath of vital ideas'. T. S. Eliot is the drunken slave who, in the classic custom, was exhibited at the height of a feast to the sons of the household, 'to the end that they, being ashamed at the ignominious folly of his gesticulations, might determine never to be tempted into such a pitiable condition themselves.' Well, the son's best novel takes its title from *The Waste Land*, but, with some inevitable advancing of the frontier of taste, the limitations have been passed on. Does not Mr Pinfold abhor jazz and Picasso? Did not his creator affirm on television that James Joyce went mad to please the Americans?

The Gibbonian classicism of *A Little Learning* is a great joy, but it is an act, a posture, and it derives from the father's more Dickensian histrionics as much as the fictional gift itself. It is no more a 'natural' style than the Elianism of Mr Waugh's father's bookish contemporaries, though it evokes an England of firmer tastes and more powerful convictions than were known to E. V. Lucas (whom Mr Waugh cites as his father's peer), Jack Squire, or W. W. Jacobs. The perfect mastery of the exact conceptual locution, often implying —as in Gibbon's own *Autobiography*—a moral judgment that is not really there, is the source of all of Mr Waugh's humour and irony, as well as his carefully outmoded elegance. But when he falls from his own high standards—as when he uses the ghastly neologism 'undergraduette' in the Oxford part of the book—we are shocked as we are shocked by no other author. In Mr Waugh style is a kind of morality, and a solecism strikes with the force of an act of delinquency. But such lapses are very rare. Stylistically this is a consummate achievement, yet (and this is no paradox) the beauty of the writing draws away our concern with the subject-matter as recorded *fact*. Was Mr Waugh's Oxford, for instance, really as he describes it?

It reads, with the Arcadia of *Brideshead Revisited*, like some world of idyll far older than anything Mr Waugh could have known. Still, we do not care much, and though Mr Waugh's three delightful maiden aunts undoubtedly have historical referents, he is as welcome as is Apthorpe to invent them so long as we continue to be beguiled by the wonder of form and language. The professional fiction writer seeks the suspension of our disbelief when he writes a novel; it is hard to break the habit of credulity when we read his autobiography. Credulity, though, is a different condition from the ineluctable need to accept fact as fact.

The youth who emerges from this book is neither forward nor, as Mr Waugh himself is only too ready to admit, particularly likeable. At Lancing he and his cronies christened a boy, for no good reason, 'Dungy.' 'Once this large, desperate youth approached me in the cloisters and said: "If you'll stop calling me 'Dungy' I'll do anything you like. I'll publicly kick *any one* in another House." I replied:"Oh, go and kick yourself, Dungy." ' Along with the 'malice and calculation' went a gulosity that was to reappear in *Brideshead Revisited*, though later (and I believe wrongly) expunged:

> [We] began with crumpets, eight or more a head, dripping with butter. From there we swiftly passed to cake, pastry and, in season, strawberries and cream, until at six we tottered into chapel taut and stupefied with eating ... Little pots of *foie gras* and caviar occasionally came from London and we were as nice in the brewing of tea as a circle of maiden ladies.

And so on. Lust is the only deadly sin not to appear, and Mr Waugh's youth, after a phase of mutual exhibition with a little girl, is innocent of sexuality. Indeed, the only sexual revelation in the entire book comes at the end, and the prototype of Captain Grimes— Mr Waugh's colleague at a school not much like Llanabba—makes it. There had been a vast outing in honour of the headmaster's birthday:

> When it was all over and the boys in bed we sat in the common-room deploring the miseries of the day. Grimes alone

23

sat with the complacent smile of an Etruscan funerary effigy.

'I confess *I* enjoyed myself greatly,' he said as we groused.

We regarded him incredulously. '*Enjoyed* yourself, Grimes? What did you find to enjoy?'

'Knox minor,' he said with radiant simplicity. 'I felt the games a little too boisterous, so I took Knox minor away behind some rocks. I removed his boots and stockings, opened my trousers, put his dear little foot there and experienced a most satisfying emission.'

There are pederasts of more distinction in the book, but no other podorasts.

As for the young artist, we are reminded that Mr Waugh, though he bloomed as a novelist early, started with the ambition to be a calligrapher and illustrator—an ambition as modest as that of the father in the field destined for the son. We have met Mr Waugh's illustrations to his own novels and, with the indulgence appropriate to the *violon d'Ingres*, admired. There are other examples of his first and secondary art here and the technique is, I should think, faultless. The aim is cognate with that of the prose stylist—to achieve ironic effects (I am thinking particularly of 'The Tragical Death of Mr Will. Huskisson') through a severely classical, almost sculptural, line, but the flavour is of a mere hobby—like the flavour of the essays of Lucas and the senior Waugh. And, even in the author's attitude to the art that became his profession, there is something amateur and hobbyish: we need the discipline of Latin and Greek in order to write good English prose: 'the old-fashioned test of an English sentence—will it translate?—still stands after we have lost the trick of translation.' That excludes a great deal of modern English literature, much of it valuable, and it fixes the writer at an immovable frontier, administering the laws of a dead empire. But Mr Waugh is probably disingenuous here, as he is in his very opening sentence: 'Only when one has lost all curiosity about the future has one reached the age to write an autobiography.' It is that charming television act again—the old man in a dry month. Mr Waugh is writing for the future.

The reader will be surprised at the lack of any literary passion in this first phase of Mr Waugh's development—no books set him on fire, unless they are about the pre-Raphaelites. The young man who reads History and leaves Oxford with a bad third betrays no concern with scholarship. Mr Waugh, an ironic statue in a toga, practitioner of perfect prose, has always tended to frighten us as Gibbon or Johnson or Junius frightens us—with the hint of a formidable library, much of it in his brain. We need not be frightened any more, nor need we cringe, with an underdog whine, in the presence of the accents of aristocracy. Mr Waugh's father worked in an office, worried about money, and went to Lord's or the cinema before going home to Hampstead. At Oxford the contacts with the ruling class begin, and there is a sufficiency of name-dropping. The *Brideshead Revisited* postures are a legitimate indulgence for a novelist unrid of his father's romanticism, but the dream of a great Catholic aristocracy has a faint whiff of the sentimental about it. That there is no sentimentality in the harking back to Augustan solidity—temperamentally, if not historically, cognate—is a tribute to Mr Waugh's perfect artistry, though artistry itself is all poses.

Mr Waugh's conversion to Catholicism will appear, one presumes, in the next volume. A cradle-Catholic myself, and hence one of a long line of underdogs, I tend both to despise (always unjustly) and envy (sometimes justly) a man like Mr Waugh who, with calm eighteenth-century logic, can sail into the Church after the sort of *echt* English upbringing presented in *A Little Learning*. It is the best of both worlds. Mr Waugh gives us what he calls 'A Brief History of My Religious Opinions', and the cradle-Catholic is aware of the great social, as well as theological, gulf fixed. In an earlier chapter we look in wonder on St Jude's, Hampstead Garden Suburb, and its eccentric incumbent:

> Mr Bourchier was a totally preposterous parson. When he felt festal he declared a feast, whatever the season or occasion marked on the calendar. He dressed up, he paraded about, lights and incense were carried before him. When the mood took him he improvised his own peculiar ceremonies. Once he

25

presented himself on the chancel steps, vested in a cope and bearing from his own breakfast table a large silver salt-cellar. 'My people,' he announced, 'you are the salt of the earth,' and scattered a spoonful on the carpet before us ... Despite all Mr Bourchier's extravagant display I had some glimpse of higher mysteries.

Well, this was the England of Mr Waugh's boyhood and it is perhaps no more difficult for the Old Catholic to understand than the world of the minor public school with its 'good Church traditions'. The curious reader will take delight in pincering out from the brew the gobbets and slivers of genuine influence—the medieval illuminations, the comedy of bourgeois life, the individualists of Oxford and, above all, the paternal devotion to tradition.

This first volume, like Mr Waugh's first novel, records a decline and fall. An academic failure, indecisive in his choice of vocation, inclined, like St Augustine himself, to debauchery, in need of a greater solidity than Anglican Hampstead could provide, young Evelyn Waugh looked at the successes of his friends and tried to escape from his loneliness and dejection. Less resilient than Paul Pennyfeather, his wounds unpalliated by the large confidence of 'Grimes', he sought a sempiternal quietus in the waters of the North Wales coast. The jellyfish stung him and sent him back to the future; the sea proved lustral, not lethal. Naturally, we rejoice. We look forward to reading about the larger learning, a lifetime's lessons on how not to repine.

Postscript, 1966. We *would* have looked forward ...

The Comedy of Ultimate Truths

THE late Pope John said that any day was a good day to die. He might, nevertheless, have conceded that some days are better than others, and that no Christian could ask more than to die on Easter morning—suddenly, without fuss, having just celebrated the truth of Christ's, and hence man's, resurrection. That is how Evelyn Waugh died. Those of us who loved the books without knowing the man must set a decent limit to our mourning. We regret that there will be no more books; at the same time, we are grateful for the *œuvre* we have—one of the richest in all modern literature.

Evelyn Waugh had intimated to the world, off and on during the last ten years, that he was not merely resigned to the propinquity of death but actively ready to embrace it. The first words of *A Little Learning* are: 'Only when one has lost all curiosity about the future has one reached the age to write an autobiography.' For Gilbert Pinfold it was never later than he thought. Waugh knew that the barbarism of the age could not be redeemed. His great war chronicle, *Sword of Honour*, records the passing not merely of the religion of his youth but of the secular values that once sustained Western civilization. Waugh had, like his hero Guy Crouchback, fought in what at first looked like a crusade, only to see it develop into a sweaty tug-of-war between teams of indistinguishable louts (that is how Scott-King saw it), its outcome the establishment of a Modern Europe animated by cynicism, hypocrisy, the devices of most un-jesuitical equivocation. Unconditional surrender had to be made to the facts of history, but the new anti-values must be passively resisted.

The good man retires from the world, cherishing fragments from an incorrupt past, cultivating style, assuming stoical poses that are not without a certain discreet self-mockery. The final capitulation to barbarism seemed to Waugh to be preparing itself in his own Church; the truth remained the same, but the garments of the truth were becoming flashy and vulgar. In the canon of the gentleman and austere artist, vulgarity was a kind of sin. Avoiding it, Waugh seemed sometimes to err on the side of a kind of Augustan superbity.

He was a self-taught aristocrat whose background was decently bourgeois. Critics who condemned alleged evidences of snobbery in his writings (usually with the underdog whine that Mr Pinfold's ear was sharp to detect) missed something deeper even than the

27

patrician pose that was inseparable from his comic technique: they missed the Shakespearian hunger for order and stability. 'Take but degree away, untune that string, / And, hark, what discord follows.' Waugh's humour is never flippant. *Decline and Fall* would not have maintained its freshness for nearly forty years if it had not been based on one of the big themes of our Western literature—the right of the decent man to find decency in the world.

Comic heroes like Paul Pennyfeather and William Boot are too innocent to engage a decadent civilization, but there is an order above the human (perhaps the comic and the miraculous are cognate) which brings them through safely; the dangerous worlds they enter are purgatorial, not infernal. Hell is reserved for one novel only, perhaps Waugh's best. Tony Last, in *A Handful of Dust*, acquiesces in the breakdown of order and ends his days up the Amazon, reading Dickens to an illiterate half-caste: his innocence has been appropriate to a younger son, but not to a small aristocrat with large responsibilities; hence his punishment. It is in this novel that, despite the fine comic flashes, we come closest to a vision of spiritual emptiness unredeemable by any god of laughter. Brenda Last competes with Ford Madox Ford's Sylvia Tietjens for the title of worst woman in the world.

Brideshead Revisited fulfils the quest for certainty, though the image of a Catholic aristocracy, with its penumbra of a remote besieged chivalry, a secular hierarchy threatened by the dirty world but proudly falling back on a prepared eschatological position, has seemed over-romantic, even sentimental, to non-Catholic readers. It remains a soldier's dream, a consolation of drab days and a deprived palate, disturbingly sensuous, even slavering with gulosity, as though God were somehow made manifest in the *haute cuisine*. The Puritan that lurks in every English Catholic was responsible for the later redaction of the book, the pruning of the poetry of self-indulgence. It was the revising itch, the scrupulosity of the artist rather than the moralist, which led Waugh to make changes (perhaps less justifiable) in *Sword of Honour*, which now stands as a single great novel, no longer a trilogy, and the final monument to his many gifts— those of the exact historian (military, social, religious), the superb recorder of swift action, the creator of larger-than-life comic characters, the Augustan stylist.

If Waugh is to be remembered as a comic novelist, that implies no relegation to a secondary status, as though it were a meaner achievement to make people laugh than to make them cry. He recognized his kinship with P. G. Wodehouse, but comedy with him was not merely entertainment, summer-holiday stuff: it was a medium for the expression of ultimate truths, some of them very bitter. Apthorpe, like young Lord Tangent, has to die. The appalling 'nonsense' which Cedric Line makes of the embarkation in *Put Out More Flags* is desperately funny, but it also encapsulates the real nonsense of the pre-Churchillian days, when England had still not learned what war was about. And even at its most light-hearted, the comedy finds an exact gravity of locution: Waugh's comic underworld—smugglers, deserters, burglars, night-club courtesans—are accorded the dignity of language appropriate to personages who have, in their various bizarre ways, arrived at acceptable modes of order. The humour is, in the best sense, aristocratic.

Critics may now go to work on Waugh's place in the hierarchy of British writers (equal to Greene? to Forster?) and list his literary creditors (Firband? Ford Madox Ford?), but mere authors will continue to despair of their ability to approach that prose perfection, though the mere existence of the challenge must make them better writers. Readers will regret that the *Autobiography*, which promised so brilliantly, can now never take the shelf as an expository masterpiece, and that the crass patterns of modern life—on both sides of the Atlantic—will never again find so detached and elegant and devastating a castigator. But, to use Evelyn Waugh's favourite phrase, we must not repine. We have what we have, which is a great deal, and—as the author would wish, if he could have brought himself to accept that we should be thankful at all—we thank God for it.

Dark Disease: A European Tradition

IT's difficult for the British critic to decide what makes a European novel different from an American one, and this is in spite of the fact that he has all the assessive advantages—the neutrality of his offshore island, the knowledge that the British novel has (through language and history) powerful affinities with the American and (through history and geography) points of contact with the European. Perhaps the British novel is, to the British critic, a high wall with a low door and no ladder, preventing a view of both America and Europe at the same time.

But, looking at Berto's remarkable novel,* I seem to see in it elements which, though they have touched British fiction, have never seemed to play any part at all in the novels of America. These elements are not technical; indeed, Berto's style, with its avantgarde whiff, its monologuising, its typewriterese, comes very close to what we so often expect from the 'big' contemporary American novel, candid, amorphous, sex-troped, poring over pores in a magnifying mirror. It is the subject-matter that seems alien to the American way of fictional life. *Incubus* is about hatred of the father; this hatred is expressed as an incurable physical disease. The fusion belongs to the author himself; the elements of the fusion belong to Europe. They do not belong to America.

Of course, I have to qualify right away, chiefly for the benefit of those who will say 'What about Hawthorne?' Let's keep it modern: Hawthorne is too close to a tradition that America had to outwear. 'Oedipus schmeedipus', as the Jewish lady said, and that is pretty well the attitude of American fiction to one of the great tortured themes of Europe.

The big American novels thrust out into the Atlantic or else into the West; when they're tempted to set their comfortable *mise en scène* in an inward-looking, self-satisfied township, then they become

---

* *Incubus* by Giuseppe Berto (Alfred A. Knopf and Hodder & Stoughton, 1966).

European and can admit the ghastly luxuries of incest and family guilt. Nothing better testifies the stability of ancient Athens than their playwrights' concentration on *hubris*: pioneer societies have no time for that. The pioneer American father had to be a god; the matriarchies that followed were a natural reaction, but they can't admit the true Oedipus motif—a luxury of settled patriarchies. If the American novelist wants guilt, he'll have to seek it in the Electra motif or in homosexuality.

As for disease—chronic, obsessive, indulged—that too has had a very small part to play in American literature. Perhaps the fear of real, physical, disease that animates American life and leads to a morbid (so it seems to a European) preoccupation with wrapped food, pills, and clean water, has its origins in a metaphor: Europe was the charnel, full of mortified systems and carious intolerances; America was to be the sun-swept loggia of political and social health. Again, how could a land full of fish, flesh and fowl, two harvests a year and (on the margin) the useful sassafras fail to promote a large glowing muscularity, admitting death only in old age or in the swift clean accidents of the hard life?

There have recently been American novels—nearly all set in New York (which can sometimes be seen as an annex of filthy Europe)—in which wealthy women slowly and elegantly die of cancer, but they are a mere sport. And slow death may be ennobled by that very American institution, the psychopomp, the specialist who shows the best way to the land beyond, the black California.

It is right for the European novel to be interested in disease, since Europe itself is a disease—exquisitely but treacherously mined with fistulas. *Don Quixote, Madame Bovary, Crime and Punishment, Doktor Faustus* all concentrate at great length on a long illness of one kind or another. When an American hero doesn't feel well he wanders the great plains and rivers, or else he turns himself into Henderson the Rain King. In Europe we take to our beds and cosset the malaise or the agony, waiting—like Giuseppe Berto's hero—till 'it will be time to say *Nunc dimittis servum tuum Domine*'.

Male Oscuro—that is Berto's Italian title, and it's a hard title to translate. Call it 'dark ailment' or 'obscure abomination', and it will carry few connotations for the American reader (and not perhaps the right ones for the British). *Incubus* oversimplifies into safe metaphor or the world of dream, which the bright morning will soon dissolve. Translators had the same difficulty with Moravia's *La Noia* (and, while we're at it, we might as well admit the total untranslatability of *accidie*, *ennui*, and *Angst*).

Now, Berto meets the West half-way by offering the experiences of his hero as 'further support for the doctrine of psychoanalysis' (whatever that precisely means) and admitting the viability of curative processes. But if the narrator of *Incubus* thinks he wants to be rid of his disease he's being dishonest with himself, and indeed the whole manner of the setting-forth of his case-history is disingenuous. To the European, analysis is a means of making spiritual disease more interesting—not a necessary catharsis but a luxurious self-indulgence.

Here it is, then—an unstanched flow, rarely paragraphed, unbroken by dialogue, a single long chapter of illness somehow rejoiced in, since it can end only in *Nunc dimittis*. 'Sometimes it also came through common stomach-aches or simple movements of intestinal gas things which for me are connected with the concept of cancer, or else with little pains in the left side of the thorax and a tingling sensation also in the left arm which obviously can be connected with the idea of myocardial infraction . . .' But really it is 'the malefic influence coming from the tomb where rested so to speak that father with whom I had it seemed an ethical debt beyond all paying'. And, of course, the 'ethical debt' and the father-hatred resolve themselves into good old guilt, and sex comes into it as well:

' ... I had fornicated while less than ten minutes' walk away with my father proceeding towards his horrible cancerous death, and therefore, in an attempt to feel a little less miserable, I began to think that maybe it wasn't cancer, and in any case I could hope that the fairly optimistic doctor was right, and in the long run an artificial anus might even be preferable to death, you could never judge these things until it's your own skin you have to decide about ... '

And once we're on to guilt we're on to religion. Berto's hero can't palliate his guilt in the normal ways open to Catholics, since he can't admit of channels of either purgation or of grace. After the long processes of freeing himself from the occasions of sin (meaning women), the guilt and the burden grow no less. The conclusion he has come to about the incubus is orthodox enough from the viewpoint of depth-psychology, but from the Catholic angle it is heretical. He will rid himself of his father only by becoming his father, 'and since I have confused this father of mine now dead for so many years with God in the final analysis I am tending to unite myself with God which unless I am mistaken is the chief end of all religion.'

Naturally, the priest to whom he presents this argument is not at all convinced; he 'starts talking to me about the sacraments and the Communion of the Faith which is the Holy Roman Catholic Apostolic Church with all her laws and symbols and institutions.' The time for these, says Berto's sufferer, is not yet; first there has to be the sojourn in the desert and the ultimate, physical, identification which the normal processes of time and age will bring (' ... meanwhile I have become bald at least half-way back on my head and especially on my neck I have many wrinkles and one day if I feel like opening the envelope with the photographs of my dead father I'll see how far I've come with the physical resemblance, whereas I believe the spiritual resemblance or identification is just about achieved ... ').

I observe that an inescapable conclusion is coming upon me as regards the un-American nature of this remarkable novel (remarkably—let me say this now—translated by William Weaver). The conclusion is that the materials of the book are only available to a European Catholic novelist, and that the American fictional tradition will not admit any analogue to the self-torture of writers like Mauriac, Greene and (now) Giuseppe Berto. The contemporary American religious novel, complete with roads to damnation and sainthood, is the monopoly of Jews like Bernard Malamud, nor has it been possible to turn Kennedy into a specifically Catholic martyr. In Agee, Catholic guilt and Christ-identification are available to a boy who will, one is sure, grow out of all that.

Now, the view of life as a long disease runs counter to the American philosophy which produces the great American novels, but it is a natural enough view to the Romance mind. The Jew and the Catholic will meet, if they are heretical enough, on identifying God and the father: Kafka, claimed alike by Jews and Christians as a religious allegorist, though he is more than that, externalizes the father but still makes him a sort of God-incubus, Jacob's wrestler by day as well as night.

There is nothing in the American tradition which allows of filial guilt-hate-fear; and one will be surprised if the American Catholic novel ever produces anything darker than the brilliant comedy of a book like *Morte d'Urban*. Should Signor Berto ever become a naturalized American, it is doubtful if he could naturalize the imaginative processes which produce his fiction. His kind of novel will always be merely a very welcome though highly explosive import.

2

The First Madame Bovary

GUSTAVE FLAUBERT was the protomartyr of fiction but, the world being what it is, there have been plenty of people ready to regard his self-sacrifice to artistic perfection as a kind of beastly self-indulgence. There is something inhuman (and hence beastly — like the college rooms of Sir Anthony Gloster's son) about such devotion to art. Flaubert, the sedentary bachelor, rejecting even love for literature, agonizing in unnatural seclusion over the *mot juste*, blueprinting his books like complex pieces of machinery — is it not right that life should take revenge on such a man and refuse to lodge in his works? And so, while Emma Bovary is admired, it is with the admiration proper to a wonderfully made automaton: she is not, we are told (by Mr Priestley, for one), comparable with Anna Karenina. The big bouncing Balzac took less care, but how instinct with life (presumably precisely because he took less care) all his characters are! Henry James never sold out an edition, but Hugh Walpole was knighted for services to the best-seller. Art is bunk. Flaubert may have been a martyr, but the lost cause is the damned cause. It is sinful to take the novel too seriously.

Another reprehensible attribute of Flaubert is his unwillingness to preach, but that naturally follows out of his primal fault: art ceases to be art once it becomes didactic. In any case, Flaubert had nothing to preach about, except the badness of the Second Empire bourgeoisie. Born into that coarse and hypocritical society, he saw it was unredeemable: there was only one thing to do and that was get out. This was not the way of Dickens or Hugo or Balzac or Dostoievsky or Tolstoy, and there is a hint of justice about the accusations levelled at Flaubert: one does not mind disengagement, but isn't it likely to lead to failure of love, and can one possibly write well without love? Isn't there also something very nastily bourgeois about a writer who rejects his class and yet portrays it and expects it to buy his books? Flaubert, after all, wasn't just writing for himself or for the Goncourts.

The careful objectivity of Flaubert's novels is one of their great virtues, but it often strikes as a limitation—or, rather, something made perforce out of a limitation. He was scared of being too involved in his characters. He was scared of committing himself to enthusiasms, scared even of the romantic element in his own make-up. He looks forward to Mr Prufrock. The Shelleyan aspirations and golden dreams of his youth were tacitly mocked by bourgeois society, but it was essential that he also should mock them. Jean-Paul said something about 'warm baths of sentiment followed by cold showers of irony', and that was precisely Flaubert's recipe for artistic cleanliness.

'*Madame Bovary, c'est moi*,' he tells us, and we can see why. The hopeless appetite of his heroine symbolizes Flaubert's own desperate romanticism, in which longing subsisted in a void, grossly exceeding any possible object. In *Madame Bovary* this has to be punished, though in terms of art, not of morality. Irony is art's vengeance, and so is death. If we want the genesis of the whole process, we had better read Flaubert's first novel—published posthumously and, in English, only just back in print.* I have not read it in French, and so I have to take the word of Francis Steegmuller, who has edited Frank Jellinek's translation and written a preface, that Flaubert's prose (at the age of nineteen) is full of Chateaubriand-like beauties. The English is decent enough, and one can trust its rhythms. The content is pure sensibility, and *The Sorrows of Werther* is positively restrained in comparison with this exophthalmic exhibition of self-pity, ardour, narcissism.

November has very little story. The young narrator recounts his 'ardent aspirations towards a wild and turbulent existence'; the torments and ecstasies of pubescence find most florid expression for the

---

* *November*. Translated by Frank Jellinek. Edited, with an introduction, by Francis Steegmuller (Michael Joseph, 1966).

first half of the book. Then comes action. The boy visits a prostitute. Marie, and she displays a passion for him too great for professional simulation: 'How beautiful you are, my angel! You are as beautiful as the day! Kiss me, ah, love me! A kiss, quick, a kiss!' And then: 'Where did you come from, oh angel of love, of desire, of delight? Who was your mother? What were her thoughts when she conceived you? Did she dream of the strength of African lions?'—and so on. This is good boy's dream stuff, but it is something more. After a page-shaking orgasm or so, we come to Marie's life-story—highly literary and sturdily erotic—and her Bovaryesque search for supreme love. It is the boy's own search. And yet she is not there when he next calls; he never sees her again; the two have confronted each other as in a mirror, no more. The boy is ruined: 'In the beginning, before Marie, my melancholy had some fire, some grand quality: now it is stupid, the melancholy of a man soaked in cheap brandy, the sleep of a dead drunk.' He longs for Malabar, the Ganges, Andalusia; he wishes to die of cholera in Calcutta or plague in Constantinople; he cries out finally for love. But who (in Rilkean phrase) will hear him among the angelic orders?

We now discover that we have been reading a manuscript preserved by a man who knew its author. The great romantic cantilenas are over, and we are given a rigorous analysis of the defects of character of that young narrator and a cold account of his end: 'At length, last December, he died; but slowly, little by little, solely by the force of thought, without any organic malady, as one dies of sorrow—which may seem incredible to those who have greatly suffered, but must be tolerated in a novel, for the sake of our love of the marvellous.' And then a single paragraph which breathes pure mature Flaubert: 'He asked that his body be opened, for fear of being buried alive, but he absolutely refused to be embalmed.' We end on a cold douche, as in *Hérodias* and *Madame Bovary* itself.

We can regard *November* as filleted Flaubert—segments of what is to be complex and organic laid out for inspection on a pathologist's slab. A young Madame Bovary is presented, but she is androgynous: we are in a dream region, easier for the immature artist to function in than an exactly rendered provincial town. The irony needed to

37

chill the exaggerated ardour is still to be generated; in the meantime we must make do with a whole separate compartment devoted to the case for the prosecution. The technique is one of juxtaposition— more legalistic than aesthetic—and we are reminded that Flaubert, the son of a doctor, was himself to become a lawyer. He never lost the cold clinical attitude, but he learned an objectivity more dramatic than any judicial summing-up. *November* is not really a novel at all, but Flaubert has, through writing it, learned how a novel can be made.

A man may learn tricks and skills, but he cannot learn to change his true nature. The real Flaubert is present, in *November*, in all his facets. There is the observant eye which seems too exact to be true, as though the author were fabricating reality rather than describing it: 'The cows slipped in the mud as they went down the slope, crushing a few apples left in the grass.' There is an embryonic fascination with the distasteful, later to be worked into the great horrible art of *Salammbô*: 'Old men fouled me with their decrepit enjoyments, and I would awake to find them wheezing and rheumy-eyed beside me.' Also there is the phantasmagoric: 'On Christmas Eve, I saw a great naked woman standing there with rolling eyes; she was quite a hundred feet tall, but she moved, growing longer and thinner as she went, and finally dissolved, each limb remaining there apart; the head flew off first while the rest still moved.'

One could argue that the quintessential Flaubert is a fantasist more than a realist, and that the details of the world are observed only that they may be manipulated into a highly subjective music. The man in *Madame Bovary* who loses his leg does so in order that his wooden stump may orchestrate Emma's dying consciousness with a '*son sec*'. Félicité, in *Un Cœur Simple*, sees a '*perroquet gigantesque*' hovering over her own deathbed, the apocalyptic end of her sailor brother's very ordinary parrot. *La Tentation de Saint Antoine* is a super-Goethean *Walpurgisnacht*, crammed with learned visions but also dishes of solidifying gravy. The story of *St Julien L'Hospitalier* is a miraculous fable with a leprous embrace in it. At the end of *Hérodias*, the carriers of John the Baptist's head have to take it in turns because it is so heavy. The notation of reality gives weight, and hence horror, to dreams. The naturalistic novel does not really derive from Flaubert, unless by naturalism we mean the gratuitous poring over gangrene and caries. He remained a romantic but had to qualify his romanticism with exact notation of the exterior world. He was very like Shelley, who had a yearning spirit and a clinical mind.

Flaubert's obsession with the problems of his art may be regarded as morbid: '*Quelle lourde machine à construire qu'un livre, et compliquée surtout.*' But he remains the great example of devotion, the true witness or martyr by whose tears of blood a less exacting world of literary endeavour is sustained. He had nothing to say, and his art illuminates only his own temperament. But, as this piece of juvenilia shows, that temperament was a very solid *donnée*.

Dickens Loud and Clear

I WRITE this in England, on Christmas Eve. I should really be out drinking. But in the age of Lévi-Strauss and the British Humanists, Christmas becomes an increasing embarrassment. Indifference to the feast is impossible, and so the only two available postures are Scrooge-like—bah-humbug or whoops-how-I-love-the-whole-world. Both are 'camp', though unreformed Scrooge is closer to the decent human norm and less likely to feel shame or crapula. How we curse Dickens for bringing Christ and Dionysus together. And yet the eupepsia, mistletoe kisses and loud protestations of universal charity represent neither naivety nor hypocrisy. Christmas is a play to be acted. We remove our make-up and forget our lines the day after Boxing Day, but the performance was worth while. It demonstrated in the dark an approach to life that might—had history gone differently—have been as viable as the one to which we're committed. Every year the great showman bangs his drum and reminds us. And so, after this sad seasonal flourish, to our theme.

Professor William H. Pritchard, of Amherst College, Massachusetts, in his perceptive study *The Novels of Anthony Burgess*, has drawn my attention (and whose attention could he, in the context, better expect to draw?) to a book by Mr Robert Garis called *The Dickens Theatre*. The art of entertainment as exemplified by Dickens (so says Mr Garis) is 'loud and distinct'; it eschews complex characterization on Tolstoyan or Jamesian lines; the reader must apprehend everything at once as a highly coloured simplicity, just as he would when attending a Victorian playhouse. See a Dickens novel as a prolonged display of showmanship—the barker's spiel or the music-hall chairman's comic sesquipedalian *tour de force* introducing or dismissing turn after turn—and you will not start grumbling about a lack of Lamb House delicacy. The comic catch-phrases and the deliberate jerking of tears or indignation are devices proper to popular theatre, and that is what Dickens was trying to produce.

This is, as we know, not true purely in a figurative sense. Dickens was a full-blooded actor in the limited style of his time; he was mad about the putting on of melodramas; he achieved his final lionization (and incidentally broke his health) by the public reading of his own works. T. S. Eliot saw the dramatic tradition which began with Marlowe and continued with Ben Jonson and Massinger as reaching a late end with the 'decadent genius' of Dickens. Undoubtedly Dickens and Jonson come closest in creating an art of some depth out of the monoscopic interplay, or mere juxtaposition, of what the earlier master called 'humours'. Face, Mosca, Zeal-of-the-land Busy and Sir Epicure Mammon are close relatives of Bumble, Uriah Heep, Squeers and Mrs Gamp. But if Dickens represents a decadence, a falling-off from the classical purity of taste which prevents Jonson from ever becoming coarse, sentimental or mechanical, this must be accounted to the appalling dramatic, as opposed to fictional, tradition that Dickens inherited. The Regulating Acts had limited the presentation of 'legitimate' drama to the theatres under royal patronage—chiefly Drury Lane and Covent Garden. Acting techniques, in such huge auditoria, where subtlety would be lost on the galleries, had to be based on crude gesture and cruder rhetoric. In the smaller playhouses of London, where only musical entertainment was officially allowed, drama crept back in over the music—literally melodrama. Whatever was to be seen on the stage in Dickens's lifetime, it never rose above the level of pop theatre.

Dickens's achievement was to create serious literary art out of pop material. This must seem to us very modern, though we will have difficulty in finding any piece of fiction today that is bold enough to fulfil in words what is pretty regularly done in the visual media. I was recently sent from San Francisco a highly philosophical, not to say theological, novel whose chief characters were borrowed from the Popeye cartoons. The courage of this is exceptional; there seems to be nobody here who will transmute the elements of 'Garth' into a legitimate vision of life. Of course, Dickens worked in a rhetorical tradition that had not really been broken since Shakespeare—one that permitted the exploitation of language in even the most popular medium; he also worked in a climate of Christian evangelism that allowed big unqualified moral gestures. Language and morality add dimensions to his cartoons and turn them into literature. We lack enthusiasm and are embarrassed by moral fervour and grandiloquence alike. That is why our attitude to Dickens is ambivalent—nostalgia mixed with distaste, *nausée* in the presence of the spreading chestnut tree. We would really prefer not to be embarrassed, which is much to our credit.

Looking through *Oliver Twist*, which is the first volume in the new Clarendon Dickens,* I am struck anew by the *composite* nature of the entertainment offered. We are given a novel, but we are also given the 'score' of a dramatic recitation. The punctuation of *Oliver Twist* in its 1838–41 serial form follows normal printing-house conventions. But in the 1846 book edition Dickens is working out an eccentric but consistent system of 'rhetorical' punctuation, designed to show how the voice is to be used rather than what the logical relationship is between the limbs of the syntax:

> He had scarcely washed himself: and made everything tidy,
> by emptying the basin out of the window, agreeably to the
> Jew's directions: when the Dodger returned; accompanied by a

---

* *Oliver Twist.* Edited by Kathleen Tillotson. The Clarendon Dickens. General editors: John Butt and Kathleen Tillotson (O.U.P., 1966).

very sprightly young friend, whom Oliver had seen smoking on the previous night; and who was now formally introduced to him as Charley Bates.

And again:

I wish some well-fed philosopher, whose meat and drink turn to gall within him; whose blood is ice, whose heart is iron; could have seen Oliver Twist ...

Kathleen Tillotson tells us that certain early critics were not happy about the 'fantastic style' of Dickens's usage and applauded his return (assisted by the silent correction of the printers) to orthodox punctuation. But, rightly, she says: 'One has only to read passages aloud to be convinced that Dickens knew what he was doing.'

Indeed, what might be termed Dickens's colonization (full and semi) is an aspect of style. He is encouraged in the building of complex sentences by the knowledge that he can clarify their structure with exact breathing signals. That first sentence quoted above strikes with no awkwardness when read aloud according to Dickens's own directions; give it orthodox punctuation and take it in solely with the eye, and it becomes a very clumsy construction. Dickens is working in an auditory tradition, and if he cannot himself deliver his work to us in his own voice, he can at least show the paterfamilias, reading aloud in the parlour after dinner, how the job is done. The tyranny of orthodox rules, as exerted in most modern Dickens editions, hammers the words flat and blows out the stage candles.

Another aspect of the composite entertainment is the Cruikshank illustrations. In only two writers do we find a genuine integration of literature and visual art, and both are Victorians. Clever young Dr Jonathan Miller's television production of *Alice in Wonderland* ignored Tenniel; and yet Tenniel is complementary to Carroll. Similarly, in Dickens the drawings have an authority which could not attach to a mere superadded set of decorations or points of relief for the reading eye. Dickens seems to have proposed to Cruikshank the subjects for illustration ('the place which I think will make a good Illustration is at p. 17' or 'you will find a very good subject at page 10'); he was evidently only too willing to fix his characters externally, as visual entities on a kind of stage. His own task, in his auditory medium, is to characterize in auditory terms. Thus, our introduction to Fagin in the text is very general: 'a very old shrivelled Jew' with a 'villainous-looking and repulsive face.' It is up to Cruikshank to show us what his particular lineaments are; Dickens gives us his voice: 'Ah, you're a-staring at the pocket-handkerchiefs! eh, my dear? There are a good many of 'em, ain't there? We've just looked 'em out, ready for the wash; that's all, Oliver; that's all. Ha! ha! ha!'

Dickens's lovers are, if I am right in suggesting that the general approach to him to him is ambivalent, also his detractors. We accept his greatness with reserve, perhaps finding nothing of his that can compare with *Madame Bovary* or *Le Rouge et le Noir* or *Crime and Punishment*. Eliot's term 'decadent' sticks, along with 'flawed', 'grotesque', 'sentimental' and the rest of the qualifiers. It is possible that we are judging him by the wrong standards and fitting him into a tradition to which he does not properly belong. Ben Jonson cannot be adjudged inferior to Shakespeare, since their dramaturgical aims were totally opposed: there is no ground for comparison and hence none for judgment. But if we accept that *Volpone* and *The Alchemist* are superb works of art and, in their genre, could not be bettered, then we shall be able to say that they stand on the same tread of artistic value as *Hamlet* or *King Lear*. There is nothing better than the best. Dickens was practising in a tradition distinct from the current of France—a tradition closer to the stage than to the study. His real predecessors are the Jacobean 'humour' satirists; he has, of course, no successors, except in Russia. If we could go back to the family reading aloud of Dickens, we should understand better what he was trying to do. The way to satisfaction is, in the words of Professor Pritchard, to delight 'in the showman's ability energetically to command a large and various number of acts by an inexhaustibly creative language.' The satisfaction, needless to say, is very large.

The Brotherhood

WHEN the time came round in our suburb for repapering the front room, when I was a child, it was customary to send out for new second-hand pictures, since everybody was supposed to be sick of looking at the old ones. The new ones were bought with rather less selectivity than if they had been cabbages. If they were better than the old ones, it was because they were less flyblown and the hooks were firmer. Nobody liked them, but you had to have pictures on the walls. The pictures were all the same—scrupulously exact transcriptions of the external world, a scene from a costume melo-drama, a literary anecdote or a trite moral point.

In other words, they were all in the tradition of Millais—debased Pre-Raphaelitism. A young man's revolution had at last yielded to the Academicians, which meant to the sabbatarian piety and mech-anistic mysticism of the bourgeoisie. The true horror of the Victorian age lies in the yoking of the well-made machine with the sick soul, the breeding of the chimera of an engine animated by stock moral responses. The Pre-Raphaelites began by revolting against the mech-anical postures of an artistic establishment that misunderstood Reynolds and misread Raphael. Like Rousseau and Wordsworth, they wished to get back to live nature, not to nature withered and turned brown by poetic diction. But fidelity to nature meant, even-tually, turning into a copying machine, and the need to hold nature on the canvas meant the imposition of the extrinsic—postures derived from literature first, later from moral tracts.

For the exact transcription of nature, with not a leaf out of place, involves the rejection of contrived visual patterns, and it is by these that the artist justifies his existence. In the very brief phase of the Pre-Raphaelite Brotherhood, before the Brothers went their own ways, it seemed possible to achieve such patterns—so long as the literary theme was regarded as a mere pretext for continuing to paint. Millais's *Isabella*, a remarkable and altogether satisfying picture, does not need to be referred back to Keats's poem about the pot of basil: indeed, we are less interested in Lorenzo's sheep's eyes as he offers a lith of orange to Isabella than in purely pictorial elements which seem, from the point of view of the literary subject, to be quite centripetal. In the foreground, a brother of Isabella thrusts out a leg to kick her dog, presumably in protest against the budding affair. But the meaning is lost in the purely aesthetic pleasure we derive from the way in which this leg seems to hold up a whole table-load of curiously flattened eaters. The canvas is a small formal miracle, full of conflict, distortion and ironic humour. If this is Pre-Raphaelitism, one thanks God for it.

But it is not altogether Pre-Raphaelitism: it is close to Rossetti-anism, which is not quite the same thing. Rossetti, one of the founder-members of the Brotherhood and, since he was also a poet, its most articulate propagandist, could not—like Ford Madox Brown and Holman Hunt and Millais—go back all that easily to the nature that prevailed before, allegedly, Raphael browned everything up. He was fired by a vision and somewhat weak on perspective, drawn more to the ardour of art than the arduousness of craft. There is nothing amateur about his Brothers' works, but his own—especially the early Marian ones—look like a literary man's hobby.

Yet, because Rossetti had the poet's intensity of vision, *The Girlhood of Mary Virgin* and *Ecce Ancilla Domini* are superior in art, though inferior in craftsmanship, to Holman Hunt's *Early Britons Sheltering a Missionary from the Druids* and Millais's *Christ in the House of His Parents*. The Hunt and Millais are not really more than the sum of their parts. Hunt has to *tell* us that the Britons are Christian converts; untitled, his picture could just as well be of a divinity student in drag who has had a heart attack on a paper chase. In the Millais, the infant Christ has hurt his hand on a nail, but how imposed and slick the prolepsis is. The Rossettis, however, breathe a devotional quality which is no mere formality, despite the symbolic props, the archaic quaintness.

Rossetti is, of course, literally a Pre-Raphaelite in that he looks back (his weakness in perspective was an asset here) to Giotto, but the movement was not intended to jettison everything painters had learned since thirteenth-century Florence. Yet when we think of Pre-Raphaelitism we are assailed by Blessed Damozel visions, the non-odour of heraldic lilies, the daring return to modality in Berlioz's *L'Enfance du Christ*, Rossetti the poet looking up 'stunning words' in glossaries of medieval literature. Men like Ford Madox Brown and Charles Collins succumbed in odd pictures to the allure of archaism—Brown's *Wickliffe Reading His Translation of the Bible*, for instance (very Florentine), and Collins's *Convent Thoughts*, in which the enlilied nun (with, lest we miss the message, SICUT LILIUM in ornamental script above) is on the verge of Victorian sickliness as well as a lily-pond. But this was not what Millaisian Pre-Raphaelitism was really about. The lilies are not heraldic; they are real. Ruskin said of the Collins picture (referring to the *alisma plantago* as well as the lilies): 'as a mere botanical study ... this picture would be invaluable to me, and I heartily wish it were mine.'

That comes from the defence of the Brotherhood that, urged by Coventry Patmore lest the whole movement be sneered out of the galleries, Ruskin wrote to *The Times*, replying to an attack so virulent that only an established critical reputation could counter it. It alleged that the Pre-Raphaelites had 'an aversion to beauty in every shape, and a singular devotion to the minute accidents of their subjects, including, or rather seeking out, every excess of sharpness and deformity'. This meant that St Joseph's feet should look fresh as from the chiropodist, not dirty as from a morning in a workshop. Ruskin praised the PRB on the ground 'that, as far as in them lies, they will draw either what they see, or what they suppose might have been the actual facts of the scene they desire to represent, irrespective of any conventional rules of picture-making'. It was not what we would call an aesthetic defence, merely a defence against the attack perennially levelled at all new art: 'This is a distortion: life is not like that.' So the road to respectability, which meant academic acceptance, was opened up for these painters, and Christina Rossetti was able to write:

> ... he at last the champion great Millais
> Attaining Academic opulence

Winds up his signature with ARA.
So rivers merge in the perpetual sea:
So luscious fruit must fall when over-ripe;
And so the consummated PRB.

G. H. Fleming's book* is a good plain study of Rossetti's relationship with the movement. Mary Lutyens† is concerned with the
more painful personal themes that underlie Millais's progress to
baronetcy, wealth and uxoriousness. He 'sold out', we know; he
painted *Bubbles* and *The Boyhood of Raleigh*. How much did marriage
to Effie, who had been Ruskin's wife, have to do with it? Did she,
plump mother of his many children, coax him to the retailing of
highly saleable prettiness? It seems to me that, cut off from the sane
and visionary Rossetti, Millais was destined, without external influ-
ences, to go the way he went. The non-artistic life of Millais is not
interesting; that of Ruskin is—excruciatingly so. It is all here in the
letters which, with Mary Lutyens's links, tell the sequel to the story
of her *Effie in Venice*. The Ruskin marriage was never consummated,
and eventually Effie got an annulment. Ruskin was prepared to prove
he was not impotent (one wonders how); presumably proof would
entail the engaging of female pubic hair, and it was apparently the
sight of this on Effie that shocked his innocent soul. We talk of art
as the mirror of life, but here was one aspect of life that—thanks to a
taboo still unbroken—art was unable to teach John Ruskin.

The whole business is acutely embarrassing. Ruskin had admired
classical statues and closely examined the paintwork on nudes, but
gross human reality horrified him. Little girls—who were innocent,
made no sexual demands, and had no pubic hair—were later to help
reconcile him to the female form worshipped by painters, but ultimately Ruskin stands, on his own admission, as a man unmovable by
anything except copies of life and abstract stone artefacts. Reading
James S. Dearden's edition of Arthur Severn's memoir,‡ one tries

* *Rossetti and the Pre-Raphaelite Brotherhood* by G. H. Fleming (Hart-Davis, 1967).
† *Millais and the Ruskins* by Mary Lutyens (Murray, 1967).
‡ *The Professor*. Arthur Severn's Memoir of John Ruskin. Edited by James S. Dearden
  (Allen & Unwin, 1967).

again to call up some gobbets of affection for a man who loved animals, idolized art and hated Utilitarianism, but it is all very difficult. He wants to regenerate English life and spiritualize the lot of the artisan; to do this, he writes the letters of *Fors Clavigera* from the Baedeker spots of Europe. One tries to imagine the artisan, slurping tea from his saucer, sympathizing with Ruskin, who 'can't write this morning, because of the accursed whistling of the dirty steam engine of the omnibus for the Lido, waiting at the quay of the Ducal Palace for the dirty population of Venice ... ' Poor man, poor mother's boy.

It's not just that Ruskin is Victorian. Rossetti is Victorian, too, and very attractive—a man unshockable by pubic hair. And there's something very compelling about all that brief Brotherhood—setting up their gear in a real carpenter's shop, painting a flock of sheep from a butcher's sheep's head, daring (as Holman Hunt did for *The Light of the World*) pneumonia on winter's nights in order to make an accurate copy of lunar shadows. Ruskin may have been a lordly critic, but these men were professional craftsmen. One goes back to them with love whenever one of our art students starts whining that nobody will buy the canvases he's ridden over with a wet bicycle.

The Answerer

BRITISH musicians have been better Whitman publicists than British men of letters. Whitman, a hard poet to quote (as Uncle Ponderevo admits in *Tono-Bungay*), was learned by heart by thousands of provincial choral singers—those who tackled Delius's *Sea Drift*, Vaughan Williams's *A Sea Symphony*, Holst's *Dirge for Two Veterans*, eventually Bliss's *Morning Heroes*. Because Whitman, like the Bible, seemed to stand on the margin of art, composers saw that they could add some art to him. More than that, he was democratic, even sweaty, and the right librettists for a musical renaissance that turned against the Mendelssohnian salons and went to the sempiternal soil. Whitman's free verse (not *vers libre*, a very salony thing) was a corrective to the four-square folkiness that bedevilled so many rural rhapsodies and even *The Planets*, but his rhythms were lyrical or declamatory, not—like Eliot and Pound (who eventually made a pact with Whitman, having 'detested him long enough') —muffled, arhetorical, conversational.

Whitman's verse-technique is still of interest to the prosodist. His basic rhythm is an epic one—the Virgilian dactyl-spondee—and his line often hexametric:

> I perceive that the ghastly glimmer is noonday sunbeams
>   reflected,
> And debouch to the steady and central from the offspring
>   great and small.

He sometimes sounds like Clough's *Amours de Voyage*, though it would be hard to imagine a greater disparity of tone and attitude than that which subsists between these two Victorians. Nevertheless, both Clough and Whitman saw that the loose hexameter could admit the contemporary and sometimes the colloquial:

> I too am not a bit tamed, I too am untranslatable,
> I sound my barbaric yawp over the roofs of the world.
> I bequeath myself to the dirt to grow from the grass I love.
> If you want me again look for me under your boot-soles.

When Whitman becomes 'free', it is as though he justifies truncation or extension of the basic hexameter by some unspoken theory of a line-statement or line-image. Flouting classical procedure in refusing to allow any spill-over from line to line, he invokes a tradition older than Virgil—that of Hebrew poetry. British composers, their noses well-trained, sniffed the Bible in Whitman:

> If you would understand me go to the heights or water-
>   shore,
> The nearest gnat is an explanation, and a drop or motion of
>   waves a key.

There are passages of Whitman, as of Blake, which have a ring of something from the Apocrypha. This is appropriate for the age of the American Vision which produced him, or which he—and President Lincoln and Mrs Beecher Stowe—helped to produce.

Whitman's verse-style is so consistent (he only very rarely tried strophic forms and was not happy in them) that any volume of his can encompass single-line 'inscriptions' as well as poems as long as 'Song of Myself': chippings and totem-poles attest the one tree. There is never any sense of the fragmentary, since—as his overall title indicates—if he is to present the American plain he must do so through its constituent blades, leaves and clumps. He has only one subject—acceptance of the life-death cycle and reverence for it—and, since he uses an invariable technique, *Leaves of Grass* has a unity to be found in few other poets' collected volumes. The consistency of subject-matter and rhythm is also in the language. This is an idiosyncratic compound of the colloquial, the technical (but to admit the colloquial has always been to admit the technical) and the traditionally 'poetic'. The latter sometimes comes out in otiose eye-contractions like 'ebb'd' and 'walk'd' and 'seiz'd'; sometimes in inversions that deliberately point the dactylic rhythm ('I sing the body electric'), most often in the drawing on the common stockpot of the nineteenth century (' ... for well dear brother I know, / If thou wast not granted to sing thou would'st surely die'). Some of his loan-words— 'allons', 'eleve', 'eidolons', 'camerado'—are there to internationalize his material. In 'To Foreign Lands' he says:

> I heard that you ask'd for something to prove this puzzle
>   the New World,
> And to define America, her athletic Democracy,
> Therefore I send you my poems that you behold in them
>   what you wanted.

But Whitman's aim is rather to present a universal democratic vista in terms of the American myth. The America of his poems sometimes seems as symbolic as that of Blake, and the bearded figure that strides across it with a big hello—the Answerer, all things to all men—is as much a home-made archetype as the Giant Albion.

What makes Whitman antipathetic to many Europeans is his quality of uncompromising acceptance. We take it for granted that the poet should be sick, and it is the convention to sneer at the eupeptic and wince at the possessor of the loud voice, blessing his friend in the morning. 'The disease of modern life' that Matthew Arnold tried to diagnose turned into health when it crossed the Atlantic. Whitman seems to advocate anarchy, telling the States: '*Resist much, obey little,* / Once unquestioning obedience, once fully enslaved'; like Blake, he accepts an antinomian universe: 'I am not the poet of goodness only, I do not decline to be the poet of wickedness also ... Evil propels me and reform of evil propels me, I stand indifferent'; he welcomes Darwinianism, science, technology. More than anything, he is a flesh-glorifier—pagan rather than on the muscular-Christian pattern of Charles Kingsley:

> Walt Whitman, a kosmos, of Manhattan the son,
> Turbulent, fleshy, sensual, eating, drinking and breeding ...
> I believe in the flesh and the appetites,
> Seeing, hearing, feeling, are miracles, and each part and
>   tag of me is a miracle.

Browning, too, glorified the flesh but only by first making it remote, pushing it back into an Italian painting or an imagined song of David. Whitman's carnality is here-and-now stuff, taking place under the sun in Kansas or Wisconsin or on fish-shaped Paumanok.

It is a sensuality omnifutuant rather than (what John Addington Symonds thought it might be) 'homo-erotic'. Whitman was always quick to assert his heterosexuality and boast of his illegitimate offspring: one has no reason to disbelieve him. But the mythical Answerer he makes of himself has to be androgynous. The volume of poems called *Calamus* rejoices in male love, but it is not a collection of love poems in the conventional sense. It is as if Whitman were looking for erotic symbols of an asexual union. After celebrating

> two simple men I saw today on the pier in the midst of the
>   crowd, parting the parting of dear friends,

The one to remain hung on the other's neck and passionately
kiss'd him,
While the one to depart tightly prest the one to remain in
his arms,

Whitman gives us a poem saying:

I believe the main purport of these States is to found a superb
friendship, exalté, previously unknown,
Because I perceive it waits, and has been always waiting,
latent in all men.

The juxtaposition is not accidental.

As one of the nineteenth-century innovators, Whitman can be
ranked with Hopkins; Hopkins himself was aware of an affinity,
though he did not relish it (he asked Bridges if Whitman had
written anything like 'Harry Ploughman' and said that he would
be sorry if he had). Whitman's vocabulary is very wide (though not
from delving into the recherché so much as admitting a new—much
wider than Tennysonian—subject-matter) and his rhetorical sweep
is symphonic. One of the most important of his innovations—
reviled in his day as a barbarism—is the rhetorical catalogue, the
enumeration in line after long line of visual phenomena, either taken
from the natural world or the man-made. It required courage to
list at enormous length rather than to take the conventional path
of generalization, but the courage has been posthumously rewarded.
The catalogues of 'Song of Myself' are magnificent; the unremitting
detail of 'Drum Taps' makes it probably the finest long war-poem
of all time. Perhaps only an American poet could see the rhetorical
possibilities of this enumerative technique; the immense plurality of
the United States is made for this kind of celebration, and even a
plain roll-call ('Mississippi with bends and chutes, / And my Illinois
fields, and my Kansas fields, and my fields of Missouri ... ') can lift
the heart without much help from a poet. America herself dictated
the technique to a man passionately in love with America. It is, of
course, a technique that looked forward to the epic cinema of
Griffiths, poetry derived from the juxtaposition of visual images.

The America that Whitman presented in his poems was a visionary country, built in an epic fantasia on the theme 'E Pluribus Unum'. Such an America, roamed by the linker, the joiner-of-hands, the Answerer, who says 'indifferently and alike *How are you friend?* to the President at his levee, and ... *Good-day my brother*, to Cudge that hoes in the sugar-field', never existed and never could. Men are meaner and less forgivable than Whitman was willing to see, and perhaps his democratic vistas fill too many modern Americans with discomfort, making them shut their eyes to his greatness. It is different for scholars, of course: this new edition of *Leaves of Grass*★ is one of the most beautiful books to have come recently out of America, and Harold W. Blodgett and Sculley Bradley have lavished great industry on its preparation. Also, which is right for this poet, much love.

Gash Gold-Vermilion

MY FIRST copy of Gerard Manley Hopkins's poems was the second edition of 1930—a slim blue volume about the same size as the newly published selection† with which Hopkins joins Dryden, Keats, Spenser and other poets in the 'New Oxford English Series'.

The new, fourth, edition of the *Complete Poems*,‡ published at the same time, is twice as big, but not, unfortunately, with newly discovered 'terrible' sonnets or odes of the scope of the two shipwreck poems. There are just more fragments than before, and more fugitive verse, and the tale is completed—until the fifth edition—with poems in Latin, Greek and Welsh. Some of the verse written between 1862 and 1868 is to be prized—particularly 'The Summer Malison' ('No rains shall fresh the flats of sea, / Nor close the clayfield's sharded sores, / And every heart think loathingly / Its dearest changed to bores'—that last line is frightening), and one fragment

★ *Leaves of Grass* by Walt Whitman. Edited by Harold W. Blodgett and Sculley Bradley (University of London Press, 1966).
† Chosen and edited by Graham Storey (O.U.P., 1967).
‡ Edited by W. H. Gardner and N. H. Mackenzie (O.U.P., 1967).

seems to show that Hopkins might once have taken a Meredithian way: 'She schools the flighty pupils of her eyes, / With levelled lashes stilling their disquiet; / She puts in leash her paired lips lest surprise / Bare the condition of a realm at riot.' But the real *œuvre* is unchanged – except that the sonnet beginning 'The shepherd's brow, fronting forked lightning' is now, rightly, removed from the appendix to the main body. And some of the emendations of Hopkins's friend and first editor, Robert Bridges, have been boldly thrown out and the readings of the original manuscripts restored.

Bridges could be incredibly wanting in ear. In that final sonnet addressed to himself, he made one line read: 'Within her wears, bears, cares and moulds the same,' thus killing a sequence based on mingled end-rime and head-rime. Hopkins-lovers always penned in the original 'combs' for 'moulds', and now they have 'combs' in print. In 'The Soldier' Bridges had 'He of all can handle a rope best' where Hopkins wrote 'reeve a rope best' – an exact technical word as well as a necessary head-rime. Re-reading 'The Brothers', I am shocked to find 'Eh, how all rung! / Young dog, he did give tongue!' changed by the present editors to 'There! The hall rung! / Dog, he did give tongue!' – justified by another manuscript reading but inferior to the version I've known by heart for thirty-five years.

At least, I *think* it's inferior. But once I had an edition of a Chopin nocturne with a misprinted note that made an uncharacteristic dissonance. I got to accept and like this and was disappointed when told eventually that Chopin never wrote it. I think, though, that Hopkins, when revising his work, was over-influenced by a man who was very small beer as a poet; his verse had that small audience for too long, even posthumously. And I think that Bridges erred in holding back publication till 1918 (Hopkins died in 1889): he was too timid, though not too timid to steal – though even there timidly – some of his friend's rhythms. There were poets killed before 1918 who might at least have been granted the pleasure and inspiration of a poetry they were well qualified to understand.

Discussing such inspiration, W. H. Gardner says: ' ... it is likely that James Joyce, E. E. Cummings, and Dylan Thomas were decisively affected by a reading of Hopkins.' Thomas less than you'd

think (no sprung rhythm, anyway), Cummings minimally, Joyce
not at all. There is, admittedly, a passage in *Finnegans Wake* that
seems deliberately to evoke Hopkins (the description of the sleeping
Isobel towards the end), but Joyce's mature style was formed before
Hopkins was published. And yet the two men pursued the same end
out of the same temperament, and it is an irony that it was only
chronology that prevented their meeting. Hopkins was a professor
at University College, Dublin, where Joyce was eventually a student,
but Joyce was only seven when Hopkins died. Hopkins became a
Jesuit, and Joyce was Jesuit-trained. Both made aesthetic philosophies
out of the schoolmen—Joyce from Aquinas, Hopkins from Duns
Scotus. Joyce saw 'epiphanies' flashing out of the current of everyday
life; Hopkins observed nature and felt the 'instress' of 'inscapes'.

Both were obsessed with language and knowledgeable about
music (Hopkins's song 'Falling Rain' uses quarter-tones long before
the experimental Central Europeans). Make a context question out
of mixed fragments, and you will sometimes find it hard to tell one
author from the other. 'Forwardlike, but however, and like favourable heaven heard these' might do for a Stephen Dedalus interior
monologue; actually it comes from 'The Bugler's First Communion'; 'Muddy swinesnouts, hands, root and root, gripe and
wrest them' is from *Ulysses* but would do for a Hopkins poem
about martyrs. The eschewal of hyphens helps the resemblance:
'fallowbootfellow' will do for both. But the kinship goes deeper
than compressed syntax, a love of compound words, and a devotion
to Anglo-Saxonisms. Musicians both, they were both concerned
with bringing literature closer to music.

I don't, of course, mean that they pursued conventional 'melodi-
ousness', like unmusical Swinburne who, hearing 'Three Blind Mice'
for the first time in his maturity, said that it evoked 'the cruel beauty
of the Borgias'. It was rather that they envied music its power of
expression through rhythmic patterns, and also the complexity of
meaning granted by that multilinear technique which is the glory
of the music of the West. All that sprung rhythm does is to give the
prosodic foot the same rights as a beat in music. A musical bar can
have four crotchets or eight quavers or sixteen semi-quavers, but

there are still only four beats. A line in a Hopkins sonnet always has its statutory five beats (or six, if it is an Alexandrine sonnet), and there can be any number of syllables from five to twenty—sometimes more, if we get *senza misura* 'outriders'. 'Who fired France for Mary without spot' has nine syllables; 'Cuckoo-echoing, bell-swarmèd, lake-charmèd, rook-racked, river-rounded' has sixteen: both lines come from the same sonnet. Music always had the freedom of prose with the intensity of verse; since Hopkins, English poetry has been able to enjoy liberty without laxity, on the analogy of music. This is why Hopkins is sometimes called 'the liberator'.

But there's more to it than just rhythm. There have to be the *sforzandi* of music—heavy head-rimes, like 'part, pen, pack' (which means 'separate the sheep from the goats; pen the sheep and send the goats packing') and there have to be internal rhymes, like 'each tucked string tells, each hung bell's / Bow swung finds tongue to fling out broad its name', so that we seem to be listening to the effects of repetition-with-a-difference that are the essence of melodic phrases. But, most important of all, every line must have the solidity of content of a sequence of chords, or else the sense of multiple significance we find in a passage of counterpoint. There's no space for the purely functional, since in music nothing is purely functional.

Hence that compression in Hopkins that sometimes causes difficulty: 'the uttermost mark / Our passion-plunged giant risen' or 'rare gold, bold steel, bare / In both; care but share care ... ' or 'that treads through, prickproof, thick / Thousands of thorns, thoughts'. In striving to catch a single meaning, we catch more than one; sometimes—as with 'thorns, thoughts'—two words seem to merge into each other, becoming a new word, and what one might call an auditory iridescence gives a powerful contrapuntal effect.

Joyce lived later and was able to go further. Words like 'cropse' (which means 'a body interred and, through its fertilization of the earth, able to produce vegetation which may stand as a figure of the possibility of human resurrection') are the logical conclusion of the Hopkinsian method: contrapuntal simultaneity is achieved without the tricks of speed or syntactical ambiguity. But Joyce's aim was comic, while Hopkins brought what he glumly knew would be called 'oddity' to the inscaping of ecstasy or spiritual agony. 'I am gall, I am heartburn' to express the bitterness of the taste of damnation, which is the taste of oneself, is a dangerous phrase, and my old professor, H. B. Charlton (who spoke of Hopkins as though he were a young upstart), could always get an easy seminar laugh by talking about metaphorical stomach trouble. There are plenty of more sophisticated sniggers available nowadays for those who find Hopkins's response to male beauty—physical or spiritual—classically queer: 'When limber liquid youth, that to all I teach / Yields tender as a pushed peach' or the close catalogue of the strength and beauty of Harry Ploughman. And sometimes the colloquial ('black, ever so black on it') or the stuttering ('Behind where, where was a, where was a place?') carries connotations of affectedness guaranteed, with the right camp reciter, to bring the house down. Hopkins took frightful risks, but they are all justified by the sudden blaze of success, when the odd strikes as the right and inevitable.

'Success' is an inadequate word for a poet who never aimed at the rhetorical or technical *tour de force* for its own sake. He is, as we have to be reminded, not one of those little priests whom Joyce remarked at UCD—writers of devotional verse; he is a religious poet of the highest rank—perhaps greater than Donne, certainly greater than Herbert and Crashaw. The devotional writer deals in conventional images of piety; the religious poet shocks, even outrages, by wresting the truths of his faith from their safe dull sanctuaries and placing them in the physical world. Herbert does it: ' "You must sit down," says Love, "and taste my meat." / So I did sit and eat.'

Hopkins does it more often. The natural world is notated with such freshness that we tend to think that he is merely a superb nature poet, a Wordsworth with genius. And then we're suddenly hit by the 'instress' of revelation: theological properties are as real as the kestrel or the fresh-firecoal chestnut-falls. Reading him, even the agnostic may regret that the 'Marvellous Milk' is no longer 'Walsingham way' and join in calling 'Our King back, Oh, upon English souls!'—'Pride, rose, prince, hero of us, high-priest, / Our hearts' charity's hearth's fire, our thoughts' chivalry's throng's Lord.' This is big magic, which no good Jesuit ought to be able to use.

3

Enemy of Twilight

'AND the mist on the Wicklow hills,' said Louis MacNeice, 'is close, as close as the peasantry were to the landlord, as the Irish to the Anglo-Irish ... ' Well, not all the Anglo-Irish were close to the Irish, and those that thought themselves most close were often least. In the Irish literary renaissance (which was chiefly Anglo-Irish), a good test of closeness was provided by a sort of scale of popular vilification. No Irishman ever got mad with an Anglo-Irish writer who presented the Irish as holy, ethereal, sober, and sexless; let any Anglo-Irish writer get close enough to see the Irish as hypocritical, materialistic, drunken and salacious, and the quicklime would be got ready. *The Countess Cathleen* caused anger at the Abbey Theatre, because it showed an Irishwoman selling her soul that the people might have bread; Yeats, then, must have been pretty close to the Irish. The greatest anger of all was reserved for John Millington Synge, so he must have been very close.

The Playboy of the Western World was first presented at the Abbey in 1905. William Fay considered that the first two acts were pretty safe, but foresaw that there was going to be a row over the third. He begged Synge to turn Pegeen Mike into a decent colleen, not one who puts a rope round her lover and burns his leg with a white-hot bit of peat. But Synge had already rewritten the third act thirteen times, and that was enough. Fay was right, though. The first two acts flowed through without a murmur. In the third act, Christy said: 'And to think I'm long years hearing women talking that talk, to all bloody fools'; the catcalls began. Then came 'A drift of chosen females standing in their shifts itself'; all hell broke loose, fighting started, the call-boy grabbed an axe to kill the first man who crossed the footlights. This was only the first night. By the last night there were 500 police keeping order.

'A vile and inhuman story told in the foulest language we have ever listened to from a public platform' (Arthur Griffith). 'The hideous caricature would be slanderous of a Kaffir kraal' (*Freeman's Journal*). But it was the word 'shifts' that really caused the trouble, making the pit call: 'Lower the bloody curtain, and give us something we bloody well want.' Lady Gregory asked the theatre charwoman whether she considered the use of the word indecent, and was told that she did: even when talking to herself she would refer to the garment as a chemise. And she added: 'Isn't Mr Synge a bloody old snot to write such a play'—though, out of deference to her ladyship, she said that to the stage carpenter.

It wasn't Synge's naturalism that offended so much as his fusion of naturalism and heightened folk-poetry. He made the mistake of choosing Irish earth rather than Irish mist—Red Dan, Sally and Tubber Fair instead of Angus, Maeve and the Garden of Fand. The early Yeats and the changeless AE tried to feed the Irish on fairy candyfloss and lead them to the Land of Heart's Desire; Synge smelled stirabout and felt the palpable rock of Aran on his bottom. If he had contrived an urban instead of a folk realism it wouldn't have been too hard to place him—a dirty Zola or Anatole France type man corrupted by Paris, one who could be dismissed without a hearing. His crime was to find murder condoned in County Mayo and as much poetry in the real country libido as in the fancied country soul. Once his hypnotic rhythms started playing, his audience sat back for a gorge of decent blarney and blarneyed decency, like *The Colleen Bawn*; what they got instead was Ireland as seen by the Western World—fine talk covering drunkenness ('there were five men, aye, and six men, stretched out retching speechless on the holy stones'), vindictiveness, amorality, connivance at crime, the lechery of the timid. It was stronger meat than would be served at a high tea in Rathfarnham.

But Synge, for all his intermittent wild-goosery, loved Ireland, knew Ireland, even spoke Irish (which was more than a lot of the Fenians did), and was dedicated as much as Joyce to bringing real

Ireland into European literature. Like so many Irish writers, he didn't at first know what he wanted. A failed musician in Germany, a Racinean and minor poet in Paris, he had to be told by Yeats (in Paris, naturally: no Irish writer has ever been able to leave Paris alone) to get out there to Aran and live with the peasants and try to express their soul. Yeats himself had just been to Aran, where almost the first words spoken to him were: 'If the gentleman has done a crime, we'll hide him. There was a gentleman that killed his father, and I had him in my own home six months till he got away to America.'

Synge, when he got there, was to hear the same sort of story again and again and store it up for *The Playboy*. Aran was the making of him as a writer. It gave him plots for his plays, as well as an uncorrupted vernacular that was very rich. It also gave him an entrée into the true Celtic madness, which is not psychotic but merely a poetic confusion of the real and the imagined. His uncle had been there before him as a failed Protestant missionary, his only monument to this day a ruined church on Inishmore. Synge went not to convert but to listen. He listened hard.

The second volume of his collected works* contains his two major prose books, *The Aran Islands* and *In Wicklow and West Kerry*. If you can call them travel-books, they are among the best travel-books ever written. There is nothing of the self-conscious stylist showing off (as there is, alas, in *Arabia Deserta*, *Eöthen* and even *Sea and Sardinia*). The people themselves provide the style and the colour; Synge records with a self-denying plainness. 'Priests is queer people,' says a girl, 'and I don't know who isn't.' There is nothing to say after that, unless it is something said by another islander: 'A man who is not afraid of the sea will soon be drownded, for he will be going out on a day he shouldn't. But we do be afraid of the sea, and we do only be drownded now and again.' The English spoken by Gaelic speakers has a terrible fascination; one can see the necessity in Synge for pushing to the limit, drunk with the possibilities of indigenous syntax, preposterous imagery, logic that looks madder than it is, form that takes off from sense.

* *Collected Works*. Vol. II. Prose. Edited by Alan Price (O.U.P., 1966).

Pegeen Mike says to the Widow Quin: 'Doesn't the world know you reared a black ram at your own breast, so that the Lord Bishop of Connaught felt the elements of a Christian, and he after eating it in a kidney stew?' And Christy Mahon says to Pegeen: 'If the mitred bishops seen you that time, they'd be the like of the holy prophets, I'm thinking, do be straining the bars of Paradise to lay eyes on the Lady Helen of Troy, and she abroad, pacing back and forward, with a nosegay in her golden shawl.' The wild cadences of the West are caught in something artful enough, but Synge never stops sounding authentic: nothing is too exaggerated to be true rural Irish, and nothing in that vernacular is unmelodious enough to strike with a force harsher than that of mere phatic communication. When, as a student, I came home drunk, my stepmother from Galway, rebuked me with 'We thought you going to the university would be a blessing and a salvation, but 'tis turned out to be a curse and a ruin'. I did not feel rebuked. Perhaps, then, 'shift' and 'bloody' struck with such force in *The Playboy* because of that lordly cocoon of delirious word-play: to meet them was like being jolted out of a dream. And yet Synge's language is no dream-fabric: it is a natural product of colonialism, a Saxon-Celtic hybrid for philologists to pick at, not (like the crepuscular homespun of the Dublin fairies) the mere fanciful coin of a minor poet.

Minor poet Synge was: this is confirmed by a re-reading of the first volume of the collected works, in which all the verse, translations, drafts and fragments were brought together by Robin Skelton. Like Joyce, Synge was a lion that had no skill in dandling the kid; both were too big for the dainty lyric and not big enough for the ultimate Yeatsian rhetoric, which was a kind of stripped Protestant Anglo-Irish not at all close to the never-stripped (read *The Ginger Man* on this) Catholic Irish. The next two volumes will be very exciting, since, under Dr Ann Saddlemyer's editorship, they will give us the plays. Here, in the meantime, is the raw material of those plays and a riveting expository skill which has one echoing *At Swim-Two-Birds*: 'A pint of plain is your only man.' There is a fair amount of prose not published before, including some literary notes which reveal equally Irish boldness ('Every healthy mind is more interested in *Tit-Bits* than in *Idylls of the King*'—very Bloom-cloacal) and Irish timidity: 'A book ... that one feels ashamed to read in a cottage of Dingle Bay one may fairly call a book that is not healthy—or universal.'

The evidence of wide reading in European literature should serve to remind a new generation that Synge was not closing in to parochial art when, in 1902, he sat down to write *Riders to the Sea*. While Joyce was an Ibsen-worshipping undergraduate, Synge was producing a kind of European tragedy that Europe had forgotten how to produce:

> It's a great rest I'll have now, and great sleeping in the long nights after Samhain, if it's only a bit of wet flour we do have to eat, and maybe a fish that would be stinking ... Michael has a clean burial in the far north, by the grace of the Almighty God. Bartley will have a fine coffin out of the white boards, and a deep grave surely. What more can we want than that? No man at all can be living for ever, and we must be satisfied.

Satisfied? Our stoicism is not that of either Synge or the Aran Islands. That Synge should die at thirty-eight of Hodgkin's disease is another grudge we have to carry against the Destroyer.

Cast a Cold Eye: the Yeats Centenary

THREE days before the year's Joyce junketings at Sandycove, ritual Steinach operations ought to be performed in Sligo, Howth, Bedford Park and Byzantium. On June 13th, 1865, William Butler Yeats was born. Perhaps none of the books I have been reading* may be called celebratory, but they seem to presuppose the public statue,

* *The Vast Design —Patterns in W. B. Yeats's Æsthetic* by Edward Engelberg (University of Toronto and O.U.P., 1964).
W. B. Yeats —Selected Criticism. Edited with introduction and notes by A. Norman Jeffares (Macmillan, 1965).
Yeats by Peter Ure (Oliver & Boyd, 1965).

the plaque, and the corporation drinking-fountain. With the general acceptance of Yeats's greatness a lot of life has gone out of Yeats criticism: the last really stimulating book about him was, I think, Professor Kermode's *Romantic Image*. Professor Engelberg has turned Yeats into a Goethe and, with a thoroughness appropriately Teutonic, picks away at a poet's untrustworthy aesthetic philosophy. Professor Jeffares gives us a selection of Yeats's criticism, so that we can read about the 'coarse' language of *Lady Chatterley's Lover* being 'ancient, humble and terrible' and renew our referred shame at the Introduction to the *Oxford Book of Modern Verse*. Professor Ure's little handbook is merely useful and sensible, which is saying a lot, and, after the Engelbergian tortuosities, it is rather reassuring. Talking about the 'Byzantium' poems, he says: 'The Yeatsian aesthetic, like the Yeatsian eschatology, resolves into a final metaphor that reconciles all metaphors:

> I hail the superhuman;
> I call it death-in-life and life-in-death.'

This, I think, absolves us from worrying too much about Yeats's system of thought. His doctrines, when expressed in metaphysical or theosophical terms, look profound enough, especially when they end up, as they always do, in mystical paradoxes. Professor Ure is, rightly I think, more concerned with an *œuvre* than a system. If, like his, our interest is in the poems and the plays, we shall find that Yeats's content resolves into the common stock of all poets—the opposition of the moving river to the static stone, the agony of transience, the need to build something on which to rejoice.

Joyce was luckier than Yeats. He had been taught Aquinas and Aristotle (two allomorphs of the rock in the 'Scylla and Charybdis' of *Ulysses*) and was able to forge a sufficient aesthetic out of them. Yeats, like AE, though not so fatuously, stood for the whirlpool, Madame Blavatsky and the yogibogeybox. The misty mysticism was not Yeats's fault. An Anglo-Irish agnostic, he was aware of Ireland's destiny and the poet's part in persuading the poor old woman to see herself as a radiant young bride. But he had been caught up in English *fin de siècle* romanticism, which was more about

63

death than re-birth. The language of the Cheshire Cheese poets was apt for the expression of vague desires and vaguer regrets, and it was, at first, the only language that Yeats had. Myth and image were another matter. The English poets had no myths, except those of Pre-Raphaelite tapestry, and their imagery was more decorative than functional. Ireland had plenty of myths, so that was all right. But to create a positive life-enhancing poetry out of the materials of romanticism, Yeats had to make his imagery mean something. This meant going in for symbolism, a symbol being a meaningful image, but—as with William Blake—symbols ought to derive from a philosophical system, psychological archetypes not yet being in fashion. Yeats joined the Order of the Golden Dawn in the Nineties, and he found his symbols in Theosophy and Rosicrucianism (Maud Gonne as mystical rose; Mrs Yeats being dictated to by the 'Unknown Instructors').

Yeats was not long in founding his own system, in which history and human personality conform to the twenty-eight phases of the moon, and gyres or spirals represent the self-destroying and self-renewing processes of civilization. The Unknown Instructors said: 'We have come to give you metaphors for poetry'—the true object of the astral exercise. What makes Yeats a greater poet than Blake is the fact that his metaphors, though derived from a system, make powerful poetic sense even when we know nothing about that system. Last-night Prom audiences aspire to building Jerusalem in England's green and pleasant land, but they miss the Blakian intention if they don't know that Jerusalem means the liberation of the senses and the imagination or that the dark Satanic mills are not factories but churches. But do we really need educating about 'turning and turning in the widening gyre' or 'Come from the holy fire, perne in a gyre' or 'a vast image out of *Anima Mundi*' before we can get the authentic poetic shudder? Yeats's achievement was not a system but an astonishing rhetoric or grandiloquence. To try to work out the secrets of his verbal magic (impossible, of course) should be the true task of the Yeats scholars.

One Yeats strength seems to derive, by a suitably poetic paradox. from that very preoccupation with symbols. The symbols would shoot away from the poem back to their extra-poetic references if they were not hammered into the verse with powerful muscles. This meant working away at syntax, something on which the *fin de siècle* men were weak. Eventually the muffling of rhymes was to indicate the true provenance of the poetic structure—in the syntax, not in an imposed verse-form. This, of course, is only a part of it. Professor Engelberg reminds us of the 'resolution of antinomies', the attempt to achieve a moment of equipoise between opposing forces —the expansive epic and the lyric contraction, the stony solidity of art and the river-flux of life itself. Yeats's highly personal rhetoric can move, without a single bar of modulation, from ordinary flux-stuff like 'fish, flesh and fowl' or 'lock, stock and barrel' or what the nuns teach the schoolchildren to the big Byzantine sublimities.

I suppose ultimately the authority derives from the rhythm, which means the syntax—not the accumulation of lines to fill a stanza, but the sense of a thought-out statement. There is no reasoned rhetoric left in England, neither sermons nor anything political that is not demagogic, but the tone of Yeats in his greatest period fits well into the oratorical needs of a word-conscious emergent nation. One may add that the range of Yeats's imagery and vocabulary alike is appropriate to a society not yet fully industrialized. The flux of life has little to do with the damp souls of housemaids or the smell of steaks in passageways, but it has everything to do with the pastoral, with pigs and scarecrows and fiddlers—symbols of vague nostalgia only in the English poets of the same period, soon entirely inadmissible in 'serious' verse.

Yeats schooled himself out of books, but he is not a 'literary' poet like T. S. Eliot. When Swift and Burke and Goldsmith are mentioned, it is as great Irish figures to be remembered and revered. Yeats may translate Swift's epitaph into English or write a fine play about invoking the spirit of Swift, but his work owes nothing to Swift, or to anyone else. When Yeats's images are 'literary' they draw, conventionally but wonderfully, on such classical props as Leda and the Seven Sleepers; they do not, like those of Eliot, invoke other writers whom the poet has made part of himself. Eliot is a great critic, but his achievement in criticism is not merely parallel

65

to his achievement in verse—one is an aspect of the other. Eliot thus belongs to a literary tradition, while Yeats is just himself. Despite his propaganda on behalf of the Irish novelists and playwrights, Yeats does not really encourage the world to read any work but his own.

Lonely, idiosyncratic, fantastically eclectic, any aesthetic he propounds makes sense only in relation to his own practice. He cannot be trusted when he delivers judgment on other writers, and one of the most horrible mistakes of the age was to place the compilation of the *Oxford Book of Modern Verse* in his hands. 'I have rejected these poems for the same reason that made Arnold withdraw his *Empedocles on Etna* from circulation; passive suffering is not a theme for poetry. In all the great tragedies, tragedy is a joy to the man who dies; in Greece the tragic chorus danced.' Thus Yeats justifies his omission of the poets of the Great War, including Wilfred Owen. Eliot is 'a satirist rather than poet'. Among the really big names are W. J. Turner and Dorothy Wellesley. Robert Bridges is capable of magnificence. William Watson is, at his best, nobly eloquent. It is only fair to state that Yeats did his anthologizing two years after undergoing the Steinach rejuvenation operation. It was at this time that I first heard him, almost every week, it seemed, on the radio, harsh and enthusiastic about the reciting of poetry to music, music being—to him who had no ear—a fife and a drum. In those last years he seemed to have all his own way.

We ought not to let him have all his own way now, even in this year of his centenary. The greatest poet since Hopkins, a very considerable playwright, he is dangerous when he writes prose and even more dangerous when scholars start to take his prose too seriously. But, in 1965, we would do well to take his verse very seriously indeed, which means not poring over it in the study, but declaiming it to the waves and over pints of draught Guinness:

> When Pearse summoned Cuchulain to his side,
> What stalked through the Post Office? What intellect,
> What calculation, number, measurement, replied?
> We Irish, born into that ancient sect
> But thrown upon the filthy modern tide

And by its formless spawning fury wrecked,
Climb to our proper dark, that we may trace
The lineaments of a plummet-measured face.

The Two Shaws

WHEN I was in the sixth form in the late 1930s, it was considered smart to say that Shaw's prefaces were better than his plays. Young intellectuals are very austere people, and they prefer a straight draught of didacticism to a tract disguised as entertainment. Shaw, in our view, was a teacher, not a playwright, and as a teacher he seemed, even as an old man, revolutionary. The revolutionary spirit had, to us young men, little to do with time: it was a sharp rational knife that appeared at intervals throughout history to cut into cant. *Ecrasez l'infâme.* We had already met Shaw as Voltaire. The only differences were the beard and the language, but, after the bombast of Hugo, *Candide* was as easy to read as *The Black Girl in Search of God.* Indeed, it was very nearly the same book. And, for that matter, as far as I can remember, Shaw told us that he was really Voltaire.

When schoolboys are fighting their way out of the irrationalities of childhood and pubescence, to order life on a basis of reason seems the most desirable thing in the world. Also, in the heady sixth-form climate of privilege—hands in pockets, cigarettes between lessons— it seems capable of fulfilment. It takes a long time to realize that the rational is only a small segment of the human complex, that the spirit of reason is difficult to invoke, and that there are as many dangers in the rational as in the irrational. God help us all if everything we did had to be justified syllogistically. But the adolescent, though given to aggression and lust, is emotionally cold, and ratiocination can be a substitute for feeling. In my day, adolescents homed to Shaw as to an understanding liberal adult. In fact, of course, he was only an adolescent like themselves, ourselves. Shaw had to wait nearly forty years to make the sixth form, but when he got there he stayed there.

This is not a disparagement; it is an expression of envy that Shaw should be able to maintain all his life the virtues of adolescence with so few of its vices. Moreover, he himself could hardly take this predication as a sneer, since he yearned for the world's adulthood and, in *Back to Methuselah*, wrote a long allegory of growing up. But to be an adolescent was imposed upon him by history. The great science masters of the nineteenth century made decent religious boys doubt and even lose their faith. Something had to be erected in the place of religion, and this turned out to be a brand of liberalism which, inevitably, had something of the aspirational flavour of religion about it. Wells dreamed adolescent Utopias, but grew disillusioned and, at the end, cried to the world: 'You *damned* fools!' Shaw never grew disillusioned; he merely wondered at the stick-in-the-mud torpor of 'our supposedly progressive civilization'. He thinks that new readers of his Prefaces 'will conclude that I am a daring young innovator of eighteen instead of what I am in fact: a sage of seventy-eight who, having long ago given up his contemporaries as hopeless, looks to future generations, brought up quite differently, to make a better job of life than our present respectables and right honourables and reverends can.' Wells despaired of *homo sapiens*; Shaw merely of his own time.

The tone of that introduction to the collected Prefaces is the tone of Samuel Butler, Shaw's master. Why many of us approach the Prefaces dubiously in adulthood is because Shaw shows evidence of having learnt from too many masters. Express Darwinianism or Bergsonianism or Sweetism or Webbism in that prose which Pitman taught to flow, a prose variously reminiscent (Defoe, Tom Paine, the King James Bible, the garrulous tinker who has belonged to a Corresponding Society), and you seem to get the quintessence of a new thing called Shavianism. But Shavianism is not a philosophy; it is a bundle of disparate manifestoes unified by a personality. Shavianisms are things said by an unforgettable voice, associated with the look of a 'milk-fed satyr' (Eric Linklater's phrase) and a persona recognizable chiefly by idiosyncrasies like left-foot and right-foot socks, vegetarianism, 'rational' clothes, and the postcard-sending habit. If you want an intellectual unifier you will find it only in the dim word 'rationalism', which stands for a skeleton. Finally the personality itself disappears. Shaw was not egotistic, but he was egoistic. The comic assertion of self often looks like an attempt to convince himself that he exists, that 'GBS' is not just the string that ties up a parcel, but a genuine identity.

The last play in the collected volume is a moderately amusing libretto for puppets called *Shakes and Shav*. Shav browbeats Shakes, crying his own superiority as a playwright. This is a joke that went on all Shaw's life, and he perhaps so wearisomely cracked it because he recognized that he was too like Shakespeare for his own comfort. Not, of course, like in the poetic and tragic gifts, but like enough in a dramaturgical instinct so powerful that it swamped the dramaturgist and threatened to rob him of his identity. Shakespeare has no personality, only a mask; Shaw, anxious to be the known, feared and respected teacher, had to construct an animated statue, finger-pointing, beard-wagging, called GBS. He was forced to be both Pygmalion and Galatea. But none of this could prevent his being a great dramatist, perhaps second only to Shakespeare. As in our sixth-form days, we are still compelled to choose between the plays and the prefaces. It is the plays, of course, that win.

And yet, clearly, both are constructed by the same man, if we can talk of construction with a playwright so willing to let the *vis dramatica* exert its plastic power, unchecked by formal exigencies. The typical Shaw hero is a great believer in reason, and Shaw will impose reason where—as with his historical characters, for instance— we are least disposed to find reason reasonable. His Caesar and Charles II are eminently cool and tolerant, philosopher kings, and we feel that Shaw would be compelled to present, say, Tamburlaine as fundamentally very decent and open to any public-spirited St Pancras argument. Yet, as Ophelia says, 'we know what we are but know not what we may be,' and what makes Shaw great is the sudden thrust of the prophetic or a sense of the numinous. Shaw will not admit this in himself, only in his characters. If there is a shaping force beyond our knowledge or volition, this is probably the *élan vital*, which knows very well what it is doing and is perhaps informed by the best Fabian principles. But the life force doesn't cause Caesar's shaft of rage at a needless death and his brief vision of the Christ, nor does it speak to Saint Joan in bells or heavenly voices. Shaw has to rationalize his interest in Joan by calling her the first Protestant, a manifestation of the life force in history, but, when he is dramatizing and not rationalizing, he accepts the religious temperament and is fascinated by it. The smooth and amusing dialectic of *In Good King Charles's Golden Days* is broken tellingly, almost frighteningly, by George Fox's fanatical madness at the noise of the church bells. And when Lilith speaks at the end of *Back to Methuselah*, we hear the rhythms and tones of Biblical prophecy and experience the authentic shudder of those who know they are in the presence of a mystery.

I am not trying to make out that Shaw was a crypto-Christian, though one has the impression that he is a crypto-Anglican like Samuel Butler. But the artist dealing with imponderables fights against the WEA lecturer reasoning from self-evident premises. Yet ultimately both playwright and preface-maker meet in a tradition of dissent whose prose is inspired by the Bible. Once we have either of these two fat volumes* on our knees we can almost hear Shaw encouraging us to go on with our self-education. They sit there, a pair of interchangeable cats, immovable but not asleep. The great craft of readability holds them there, and, with the plays, one is tempted to think that readability may last longer than actability. We don't need actors when we have such satisfying word-portraits, nor a décor when the settings are so firmly described (in time as well as space). Shaw the failed novelist writes fine novels when he pretends to be writing plays, and *Pygmalion*—his most popular—gets fed up with being a play and ends up as a novel. Shaw was closer to Ben Jonson than to Shakespeare in liking to publish 'works', not just write scripts for actors. Prefaces helped to fill out a published play to book-size, as well as, by a kind of con-trick, to seem to transfer a mere entertainment to a zone of puritanical respectability. An age more permissive than his own is happy to take the plays neat. They,

* *The Complete Plays of Bernard Shaw. The Complete Prefaces of Bernard Shaw* (Paul Hamlyn, 1965).

in this new, fine, strong, cheap edition, can stand on a permanent lectern; the Prefaces will serve as a door-stopper.

The Perfect Shavian

THERE are various reasons for wanting to read the letters of men of letters, and we had better decide on our reasons for wanting to read those of Bernard Shaw, since we are going to get a lot of them. This first volume, covering the period 1874–97, has 877 pages in it;* there are three more volumes to come; the total number of letters to be published will amount to over 2,500. Let me say at once that Dan H. Laurence has made a superb job of the editing. He places every letter in its context with notes—sometimes extensive—in square brackets; he gives us potted biographies not only of Shaw's correspondents but of personages, real or fictional, mentioned in the letters; not even the flimsiest allusion goes untraced. This whole corpus will, if we are to judge by its first instalment, be in the finest tradition of American scholarship. It is the sort of work that the British, lashed to their sense of social purpose, seem to be past doing.

It must be confessed, however, that one approaches Shaw the correspondent with something less than curiosity. We know Shaw; Shaw made sure that we should know him. There are probably few homes in the English-speaking world that do not have a Shaw post-card tucked away in a drawer somewhere. And what Shaw said in his letters he said also in the writings for which he was paid. One might except here what he wrote to Ellen Terry and Charlotte Payne-Townshend, who became his wife. But as he spoke of love to Ellen and Charlotte contemporaneously, and as the avowals seem to have been unrelated to any breathier, less articulate, confessions, we may take them as *Epipsychidion* stuff or dramaturgical rehearsals. This is unfair, and it is meant to be. 'Fair play to Shaw' would be a

* *Collected Letters.* Vol. I. Edited by Dan H. Laurence (Max Reinhardt, 1965).

preposterous slogan, one to be ripped to tatters by the Fabian Life-Force.

Two things come through in this volume, from 1874 to the end: one is the consistent devotion to work, the other is the consistent egoism. The first owes nothing to nervous compulsion, but a great deal to the drive of the free-lance, guilty when there is nothing to do; the second derives from too many factors for easy analysis. A shiftless father has, of course, a great deal to do with both, as has the shiftlessness of the whole Irish nation—twin horrible examples. It is as well to be convinced of worth before worth appears, especially if one is going to make a business out of writing. Perhaps one of the least attractive aspects of the earlier letters is the hard-bargain-driving behind a mask of suavity. Shaw, first as last, was his own literary agent, eventually his own publisher. One has to be able to think of one's work as a commodity, not as heart's blood, before one can set oneself to tough negotiating about it. The English are not used to the self-selling artist, nor to the puritanical scrupulosity that sends back money it thinks it hasn't earned. The Shavian monster leapt into London, fully armed, and didn't abate its monstrosity one jot in nearly eighty years.

In 1885 the monster takes to the Sanitary Woollen System of Dr Gustav Jaeger and needs only Socialism and a bicycle and a beard to hide smallpox scars, as well as some stewed fruit, Hovis, and walnuts, for it to become the sempiternal bandersnatch. The correspondence becomes voluminous—a leprechaun voice nagging away at everybody, men, women, friends, strangers alike. Even kindness (to a tyro woman novelist; to Golding-Bright, who wanted to be a drama critic) takes on nagging lineaments: ask for help, and you will be given it in the form of a lesson—complete with introduction, main body under headings (seasoned with copious illustrations from the instructor's own experience) and, as the writer's lids droop in the three-in-the-morning lamplight, recapitulation and peroration. When the plays begin (with *Widowers' Houses*), the obsession with dramatic mechanics begins too, along with lengthy self-justification or (as with *The Philanderer*) total and embarrassing self-condemnation. Then there is the vestryman's work in St Pancras, the harangues by the East India Dock gates, the incessant scribbling on train journeys to meetings in the Midlands, convalescence with the Webbs and animated discussion about public sewers. The letters never for one instant touch on ennui, self-doubt, depression. If it is all an act, it is an act well-sustained; if only it would let up and be human, crapulous, dyspeptic, sexually repressed.

When humanity comes, it comes with a shock, and from other people (in square brackets)—like Richard Mansfield's astonishing judgment on *Candida* or Ellen Terry's own little outburst about the same play. Even Shaw's dog-tiredness finds heroic expression, though it is only the running-down of an engine that sleep will recharge, followed by a platter of rational foods. It is conceivable, of course, that one's frequent revulsion is a sinner's response to sanctity: we don't have to take the concern about bodily odourlessness and a pure stomach in the plays, which are about adulterers and meat-eaters and hence close to our own lives. But the letters give us Shaw the pure-oiled busy sewing-machine. The machine admits sex, but it is a sex one mistrusts. He adores Ellen Terry physically, he says, and the last letter of the volume ends 'Ellen-hungry', but the two are not to meet till the next instalment (at the Stage Society in 1900). The gallantry, the wooing poses, the show of appetite—these are wonderfully maintained, but behind Jaeger and apples and milk.

There are very many letters here which have not been published before (particularly to Charlotte), but one approaches nothing very avidly. This is Shaw's own fault: one has no mystery if one sticks to woollens. It is, in fact, one's foreknowledge that there will be no new revelations of personality, of working methods, of public or private experience, that blunts the taste. The truest motive for reading the letters of a man of letters—the disclosures on the margin—has little pertinence here. For all that, we must have them and we're going to get them; nor is it likely that, having got them, we would willingly be without them. Every hair of the beard of a saint must, however sour-facedly, be cherished, every scale of the bandersnatch.

Dear Mr Shame's Voice

THE patron saint of the post-Jamesian American novel is also the patron saint of the contemporary American Joyce-cult. When Sylvia Beach invited Joyce and Scott Fitzgerald to dinner, Fitzgerald offered to jump out of the window as a tribute to the master's greatness. 'That young man must be mad,' said Joyce later. 'I'm afraid he'll do himself some injury.' Joyce's posthumous admirers are not mad, nor will they do themselves any injury: their extravagance is more calculated. Instead of leaping out of windows, they creep into the Haunted Inkbottle by any available hole in the wall, in galoshes and with a fingerprint-outfit. They pay homage to the dead by dragging him into the pathology lab. The four books I have in front of me* are all American and all recent. They confirm my belief that American English departments have two main activities that amount to industries: one is the plucking of the Joyce-bird, now down to the more microscopic feathers; the other is the amassing of European literary holographs, drafts, toilet-paper jottings against the coming of Cisatlantic Doomsday. These preoccupations are, of course, cognate: they both need time and money, of which (and American business has told us they are the same thing) American universities must possess a great deal.

Let me not seem sour and ungrateful. British students of *Finnegans Wake*, all six of us, owe much to Mrs Glasheen and to Messrs Campbell, Robinson and Ellmann. The unpicking of that great tapestry of sleep asks for all the resources of waking scholarship. What worries me is the sort of gratuitous scholarship which transfers

---

* *Joyce's 'Portrait': Criticisms and Critiques.* Edited by Thomas Connolly (Peter Owen, 1964).

A New Approach to Joyce by Robert S. Ryf (University of California Press and C.U.P., 1964).

The Art of James Joyce by A. Walton Litz (Galaxy Books, O.U.P., 1964).

Joyce's Benefictions by Helmut Bonheim (University of California Press and C.U.P., 1964).

the probing techniques of the *Wake*-men to the symbol-flavoured naturalism of *A Portrait of the Artist as a Young Man*. Even minor novelists like myself have known the clumsy jabs of the American exegetists. I wrote a light-hearted book called *A Clockwork Orange* to which a certain amount of misguided semantic speculation has been applied. 'Why does Mr Burgess use this particular image at this particular point in the narrative? Can it possibly be because ... ?' I am here; I am only too ready to be asked, though I may not know the answer. But some scholars don't like going to authoritative sources. 'To hell with your theory,' said one Harvard man to another; 'I've got data.' 'Data shmata,' was the reply; 'I *like* my theory.' Just so. All the Joyce scholars of America must thank God that Joyce is dead.

As for *A Portrait*, Thomas Connolly, of the University of Buffalo, has brought together a number of learned essays by many hands, with titles ranging from 'The Sacrificial Butter' to 'Augustine's Theodicy and Joyce's Æsthetics' ('Oh, rocks,' Molly Bloom might say. 'Tell us in plain words'). There is an appendix of examination questions like, 'How does the disposition of the prize money prophesy Stephen's spiritual dryness at the beginning of Chapter 4?' and 'In what way does the pandying contribute massively to Stephen's understanding of his environment?' My mouth goes dry, as in the witness- or confession-box, and a nightmare illusion of never having read the book (even though I've known it for thirty-odd years) comes upon me. One accepts the symbolism of *A Portrait* as the universalizing poet's cunning (the wet-dry and hot-cold oppositions, the motif of flight and so on), but the professors seem intent on reducing a great work of naturalism to a mere collocation of symbols. 'Why is Stephen's father called Simon?' I am almost driven into the no-nonsense arms of Bradley and the woman who wrote *The Girlhood of Shakespeare's Heroines*. 'Because,' I want to reply, 'that's what he was christened.' Stephen Dedalus, you will remember, goes to his lectures after a breakfast of fried bread, passing a house for mad nuns on the way. A mad nun cries: 'Jesus, Jesus!' You will be glad to know that the fried bread is eucharistic and that Stephen is addressed, in a transport of Sibyl's insight, as the Christ. But Ellmann's biography shows this to be a mere transcription of actuality, not

75

symbolistic cunning. And if Stephen is the Christ, how can he also be Icarus-Lucifer? One of Joyce's masters, Bruno the Nolan, taught that opposites are reconciled in heaven. Surely here is an opposition too massive for even that consummation?

Robert S. Ryf suggests that we use *A Portrait* as a guide to Joyce's other works, but he himself might be a more reliable guide if he betrayed a more intimate knowledge of his key-book. Mrs Riordan, whom the Dedalus children call 'Dante', is *not* an aunt, nor (consult common sense, as well as Ellmann) does that nickname carry any literary connotation. Ingenuity can often go so far as to miss the whole point. Stephen talks to one of the priests at the university, an English convert. Bitterly he thinks: 'The language in which we are speaking is his before it is mine. How different are the words *home, Christ, ale, master,* on his lips and on mine.' Professor Ryf comments: 'The words selected here are of course highly functional, around which images of usurpation, displacement, and betrayal hover.' But surely the difference the sound-conscious Stephen has in mind is a phonetic one: the English priest has a set of *echt* English vowels and Stephen has not. And what have 'usurpation, displacement, and betrayal' to do with ale?

The American scholars are, inevitably, less assailable when it comes to *Finnegans Wake*. Professor Litz plays first and second drafts like trump-cards and has great fun teasing out the strands of the whole gigantic palimpsest. There the Americans, with their proud *caches* of manuscripts, must beat the whole world, but a study of emergent artistry tends to prove as barren as symbol-juggling. The impression we get (and get also in Professor Ryf's book) is of a tide of symbolism rising steadily from *Dubliners* on, eventually—in *Finnegans Wake*—drowning the naturalistic. But Joyce saw this final work as near-scientific, a sober attempt to find a verbal equivalent for each phase of a hard night's dreaming. There's more to it than that, of course, but we lose everything if we forget that a middle-aged publican in Chapelizod is snoring in bed on a Saturday night, his middle-aged wife beside him, and that his guilty desire for his nubile daughter Isobel unleashes a sinful thunderclap which sets the whole cycle of history rumbling round. *Finnegans Wake* is a costume-ball whose motif is Guilty Love—Swift and Stella, Parnell and Kitty O'Shea, Ibsen's Master Builder, Tristram. The incest-theme is no mere intellectual *donnée* but the stuff of true fiction.

Edmund Wilson saw all this in 1939, and his essay in *The Wound and the Bow* needs little emendation from more recent, and more scholarly, studies. Mr Helmut Bonheim seeks now to confute Mr Wilson's claim that '*Finnegans Wake* is most obscure where it makes the most embarrassing revelations'. There is a passage towards the end of *Finnegans Wake* which Mr Bonheim cites. The publican-hero Earwicker has wakened from his dream and has attempted intercourse with his wife. This innocent and legitimate ceremony at once provokes a fantasy of sexual perversion that would be revolting did it not topple over the edge into farce. It is written in good plain prose—no dream-distortion here—and Mr Bonheim exhibits it with a 'Your witness' to Mr Wilson. What Mr Bonheim, and many of the clever scholars, ignore is that Earwicker is not now dreaming, that there is no incestuous guilt to bundle up in the obscurity of sleep-language. Another person is dreaming, however, and this dreamer dreams (a sort of automatic dream-pilot) when Earwicker is not dreaming. This dreamer is free of guilt, for he is the artist, Joyce himself. Where would a common Dublin publican gain his knowledge of history, of the Kabbala, of 'Triv and Quad', of the Pigott forgeries which incriminated Parnell, of all the languages of the world, if a greater dreamer were not enclosing his own dream? The scholars often cannot see the wood for the trees.

I hope I do not seem to be disparaging scholarship. I reiterate my gratitude for the sweat and poring and ingenuity of the American professors, but I feel the time has come for Joyce—a demotic writer if ever there was one—to be released from the Babylonish captivity of the professors and presented to the people as one of the great comic writers of all time. The trouble is that he is an insuperable temptation to scholars who, finding Stephen's father's hairy face at the beginning of *A Portrait*, and remembering this when they meet God ('With his broad and hairy face, to Ireland a disgrace') in *Finnegans Wake*, drool in synthetiser's bliss. Any great writer's *œuvre* is a totality, a cumulative revelation of a personal vision, but this is the time for (as with the dead Finnegan) crumbling the bread of this great writer's body and throwing the fragments to the people. He is being crowned by the scholars and shut up in the throne-room without being given the chance to rule (with a near-Shakespearian authority) in the hearts of ordinary decent people who love books.

Shem the Penman

'BUT THIS prying into the family life of a great man,' protests George Russell in *Ulysses*. 'I mean, when we read the poetry of *King Lear* what is it to us how the poet lived? Peeping and prying into green-room gossip of the day, the poet's drinking, the poet's debts. We have *King Lear*: and it is immortal.' Stephen Dedalus, on the other hand, urges the relevance of the *biographia* to the *literaria*. And when John Eglinton says of Anne Hathway, 'She died, for literature at least, before she was born,' Stephen replies, 'She died sixty-seven years after she was born. She bore his children and she laid pennies on his eyes to keep his eyelids closed when he lay on his deathbed.'

Nora Joyce died sixty-five years after she was born. Otherwise, Stephen's statement about Anne will serve prophetically, since Stephen is James Joyce, for his own widow. We ourselves observe the parallel, and it is no blasphemy. Shakespeare and Joyce, in all world literature, come closest in aim, technique and achievement. And what, for lack of matter, we cannot do for the one we are implicitly enjoined to do for the other. Hence the piety of collecting Joyce's letters, the detailed unveiling not only of drinks and debts but of marital intimacy. Stuart Gilbert's selection showed mostly Mr Joyce, a public man in tennis shoes carrying a walking-stick. In one phase of the correspondence collected by Richard Ellmann,* Joyce is totally undressed; indeed, the nakedness is almost an excoriation. Stephen might approve for Shakespeare; would he approve for

* *Letters of James Joyce*. Vols. 2 and 3. Edited by Richard Ellmann (Faber, 1966).

himself? Some of us will take on the burden of vicarious disapproval — perhaps solely out of outmoded pudeur that Joyce, in the shades, might laugh at.

After all, he went further than any writer in depicting boldly what the world has preferred to regard as secret and shameful — Bloom's masturbation, Earwicker's incestuous fantasies and voyeurism, the menses of Nausicaa and Penelope. But, after the image of grave formality that emerges from the Gilbert letters, an image corroborated in Ellmann's biography, we are not prepared for the satyr that leaps out in the newly published letters to Nora Barnacle. The God of creation has ceased to stand indifferent above his work, paring his finger-nails; he has entered the flesh of Leopold Bloom.

Yet if we want to relate man and creator, which is the true purpose of reading an artist's letters, we ought to wade in shamelessly and take all the intimacy we can get. The bulk of the 'public' letters in these two big volumes is far from riveting. Joyce asserts his rights as man and artist to publishers, Pinker, Sir Horace Rumbold (for whom the hangman in *Ulysses* is named), the world at large, even His Majesty the King. He nags his brother Stanislaus for money, enabling Stanislaus to strengthen his claim to be one of the great saints of the age. He is courteous to Harriet Shaw Weaver, his quixotic benefactress. He is generous to Shaw, friendly to Budgen, a thaumaturgic granter of new life to Svevo and Dujardin. In other words, we are given more of what, in Gilbert's volume and Ellmann's biography, we already have in plenty. We range from blunt (though never rude) unliterary language to cunning jesuitical courtliness, not only in English but in French, German, and two kinds of Italian. Undoubtedly, more of such letters will be unearthed in time (there is already a sizeable appendix of late deliveries in Volume 3): we have not yet heard the last of Joyce the beggar, pleader of rights, propagandist. These, though, have little to do with the portrayal of the artist.

Take Joyce away from men and put him among women, and we catch a glimpse of the provenance of the art. The letters in these volumes are not all Joyce's, but it is perhaps the biggest tribute to Joyce that we are happier to read what mother and wife write to him than what he writes to them: it is as though his own creations step out of books into life. 'What useful discovery did Socrates learn from Xanthippe?' asks Eglinton, sneering. Stephen replies: 'Dialectic, and from his mother how to bring thoughts into the world.' Ask what Joyce learned from Nora, and here is one answer:

> Well I feel very knocked up to day you don't know what a thunderstorm is but if you went through one here you would not be worth much it was something dreadful it began last night about half past nine we were in the dining room with a few people and as it had been raining all day the people did not expect it and all of a sudden it came on lightening thunderbolts I thought it was our last I was almost stiff with fright for about twenty minutes then it poured and we went to bed about half past ten but I did not sleep then a hurricane began and lightening which lasted till halfpast five this morning ...

And so on, a couple of pages of authentic Molly Bloom. As for the sweet doomed mother of Stephen Dedalus, we hear what Ellmann calls her 'faultless simplicity' in a reply to her arrogant son, self-pityingly starving in Paris:

> My dear Jim if you are disappointed in my letter and if as usual I fail to understand what you would wish to explain, believe me it is not from any want of a longing desire to do so and speak the words you want but as you often said I am stupid and cannot grasp the great thoughts much as I desire to do so. Do not wear your soul out with tears but be as usually brave and look hopefully to the future.

Joyce doesn't attempt to make the Stephen of *Ulysses* very likeable, but at least that swollen-headed young poetaster is visited by attacks of 'agenbite of inwit' and wonders if *amor matris* may not be the most important thing in the world. The Catholic Church and the farrow-eating sow that is Ireland are incarnated in a patient, sorrowing, ignorant mother, and we have to accept the exorcising of her wraith with a cry of 'Shite' and an ashplant-striking of the gas-lamp.

But in the letters everything is different. The young Joyce is a monster of a son; the mother is a heroine.

Joyce was not, apparently, looking for a mother-substitute in Nora Barnacle, chambermaid at Finn's Hotel. But the sexual yearnings expressed in some of his letters to her are very curious: he wants to creep into her womb and become a foetus again; he wishes to be whipped and humiliated by her. These letters were all written in 1909, when Nora was in Trieste and Joyce back in Ireland. Their function was patently to induce teleorgasms in both, and I leave it to sexologists to relate the anal fixations, the masochism and fetichism to filial guilt. But we are confirmed in our suspicion that a great deal of the Bloom in the Nighttown scene is pure Joyce.

And there is another petal of Bloom in that strange affair (really an unaffair) with Martha Fleischmann. Professor Straumann of Zurich University takes over from Ellmann to annotate this chapter of the Joyce odyssey. In the autumn of 1918 Joyce saw Martha, stared, started, apologized. She reminded him, he said, of a girl he had once seen on the beach in Ireland. We think less of the Nausicaa episode in *Ulysses* than of the moment of wonder at the end of Chapter IV in *A Portrait*. Somewhat adolescent letters followed (Joyce was then thirty-six, though he pretended to her to be *nel mezzo del cammin*, like Dante), and Joyce made an attempt at disguising his handwriting by using the 'Greek e'. Well, the residue of that queer *Schwärmerei* is to be found in *Ulysses*. Bloom corresponds with a Martha (using the 'Greek e'), and the operatic Martha ('Come, thou lost one, come, thou dear one') provides a recurring motif. Everything that happened to Joyce was for artistic use.

Mr Ellmann is not merely an admirable editor. He continues to be an admirable biographer, prefacing each group of letters with a succinct account of what was happening to Joyce while they were being written, and showing that same affectionate irreverence which marks every page of the biography. Thus: 'His letters to his son Giorgio and his daughter Lucia demonstrate his talent, when they were in the dumps, for finding miseries of his own equivalent to theirs, with which he proposed to cheer them up.' And again: 'To live in Pola had been embarrassing for Joyce, to live in Rome irritating, to live in Trieste quaint but inconvenient. After those cities Zurich had been at least safe and unavoidable. To live in Paris came for a time suspiciously close to being pleasant.' And Ellmann's summaries of what Joyce was attempting in *Ulysses* and *Finnegans Wake* strike with an icy freshness: it is though our youth is restored, and we are about to meet those great works for the first time.

But the letters themselves, called together from the academic corners of the free world, tell their own story. It is not a story which could be repeated in our own age. Though, as Ellmann says in his biography, we are slowly learning to become Joyce's contemporaries, that is only in respect of his books. This tale of exile is a tale that had to end in 1941. Exiled from his homeland, the last of the fanatic artists, Joyce was buffeted over Europe by two wars, knew private patronage (perhaps its last great beneficiary) and—rare today—the generous community of fellow-artists. Today an American academic community would cosset him, look forward to his death, and indulge in no carping at even his most fantastic experiments. Ireland, old faithful, would still reject him. England would be, as before, indifferent. And yet he is one of the glories of our language.

Ulysses: How Well Has It Worn?

IT WAS not a book that burst suddenly on the world. When, on his fortieth birthday, February 2nd, 1922, Joyce was handed the first copy of *Ulysses*, bound in the colours of the Greek flag and full of misprints, his mood was more apt for Ithaca than for engaging Polyphemus or the Laestrygonians. *Ulysses* was almost the last of the great serialized novels, and its scandal was old hat. The typescript of the 'Sirens' chapter had been intercepted during the war, on the suspicion of its being in code. The husband of the typist of the 'Circe' episode had thrown all that patient work into the fire. There had been obscenity charges in America. The appearance of the first edition (printed in Dijon, published in Paris) merely extended the scandal to a wider public. Five hundred copies of the second edition (Egoist Press, London) were seized by the New York Post Office; 499 copies of the same firm's third edition of 500 were grabbed by the British Customs at Folkestone. The days of the smuggling and pirating of *Ulysses* began: it was accepted as the dirtiest book in the world.

Too many reputable critics saw the dirt and nothing else. Now, thanks to the tradition of fictional candour that *Ulysses* initiated, the Dublin of June 16th, 1904, seems bathed in reticence, continence, and Catholic decency. American books like *Last Exit to Brooklyn* and the sodomistic *Totempole* go about as far as fiction may be expected to go. In *Ulysses* there is one act of adultery, one auto-erotic ecstasy (symbolically presented), one outburst of soldier's obscenity, and one—admittedly prolonged—visit to the lavatory. There is neither sexual inversion nor perversion (transvestism is reserved to comic fantasy) and absolutely no nose-rubbing in the dirt. What is proclaimed in the book is the glory of family relationships reflected in the stability of larger communities.

Early readers of *Ulysses*, though they found no difficulty in understanding the dirt, complained about the unintelligibility of what they took to be clean. I believe that the complaint is as widespread as ever it was, and it has not been diminished by stage-adaptations like *Ulysses in Nighttown* and *Bloomsday*. Playgoers and television-viewers, seeing Stephen Dedalus and Leopold and Molly Bloom in Edwardian dress (undress for Molly), functioning in an Edwardian Dublin, have been satisfied that *Ulysses* has real characters, just like *Clayhanger* and *The Forsyte Saga*, but have been disappointed that these characters do not seem to do anything interesting or significant. They are baffled and frustrated by the absence of plot. The point about *Ulysses* is still being missed: time cannot turn it into an ordinary novel, even one that pushes naturalism to the limit. If Joyce belongs to the line of Dickens, it is only in a Pickwickian sense.

For Joyce's aim was to exploit myth, symbol and language and to eschew the contrivances of plot. By the time each chapter has celebrated a book of the Odyssey, an organ of the human body, an art or a science, and a colour, and has revelled in a special and appropriate literary technique, we become aware that Joyce has been conducting a ritual rather than telling a story. The purpose of all fiction is to make life seem more interesting than it really is, and this is generally achieved through artful manipulation of events. Joyce's method is to admit the drabness, even to show more of it than previous novelists had dared, but then to make it a pretext for the celebration (sometimes ironic, but not always) of the whole of human culture. A visit to a Dublin newspaper office sets free all Aeolus's winds, summarizes the history of the press, and exhibits the art of rhetoric. An hour in a lying-in hospital is both a treatise on embryology and a parodic history of English prose, as well as a secret rite in honour of the Oxen of the Sun, symbols of fertility. All this is too much for the plain reader, who wants to know only what Bloom and Stephen are doing.

Ulysses has not worn at all, since it has never been used—except by an inner circle of devotees that has not grown much. If it had shown the way to a new kind of fiction it might have developed a sort of pioneer shabbiness, but very few novelists have learnt anything from it. The device of interior monologue, in which the three main characters probe to the nerve, without anaesthetic, was not Joyce's invention: Jane Austen had used it, and Samuel Butler; Virginia Woolf elaborated the technique independently of Joyce. The symbolism served the end of one book and one only; it could not fertilize others. *Ulysses* evokes no historical literary movement; it is horribly unique, and no generation can build on the experience of previous ones in learning to approach it. From the average reader it demands an exorbitant interest in language, one that the reading of most other fiction does nothing to promote. But perhaps, very slowly, that interest is coming. Outside a pub in Wales, one night last summer, a pork butcher looked up at the sky and turned to me to remark: 'The heaventree of stars hung with humid nightblue fruit.'

Enduring Saturday

EVERYBODY'S starting-point for a Samuel Beckett anabasis is *Waiting for Godot*; many, alas, get no further than that terribly lucid charade, bogged down in it as though it were itself the *merde universelle* and not a mere restrained whiff. The real full rich rank Beckett, the murmurous mud, is to be found in the novels, and these are still not well enough known. They are difficult, true, but they are short; their message, though hard to take, is easy; their deplorable monstrous heroes resolve into the same figure, once smelt, never forgotten—the *quidam* of *How It Is*, reduced by Josephine Jacobsen and William R. Mueller* to 'Q'. Senior bookmen may find this an ambiguous bit of algebra, remembering that most unbeckettian yea-sayer Sir Arthur Quiller-Couch. Oh, one doesn't know, though. We're all in it really, strapped to a porcupine sofa, waiting for God and water, becalmed in our filth on Beckett's enduring Saturday.

Readers of this perceptive study could do worse than start with the appendix, an article reprinted from *Man in the Modern Theatre*, which, with *Godot* at its centre, takes up this Saturday notion and develops it very helpfully. First, let us consider Beckett as a dramatist of the absurd. Camus, in *The Myth of Sisyphus*, delimited the concept of absurdity for us. Establish that 'divorce between the mind that desires and the world that disappoints' and the sense of absurdity comes flooding in, leading the modern mind to despair or to rebellion or, in extreme cases, to a kind of religious rehabilitation. Now the work of art that is born out of a conviction of the absurdity of the human condition may not get so far as the full philosophical statement of *The Myth of Sisyphus*. It may merely show men (not so often women) face to face with the absurd, stuck in a void which cannot breed the choice so necessary to the existentialist. It may, if it is an ambitious work of art, try to convey to the reader or auditor

* *The Testament of Samuel Beckett* by Josephine Jacobsen and William R. Mueller (Faber, 1966).

the whole *quidditas* of absurdity. This will entail a non-naturalistic approach to the subject-matter, the use of impressionistic or symbolic devices, the creation of a crepuscular time-space continuum. Once history throws up the concept, we are already waiting for Beckett. What makes *Waiting for Godot* a popular play (and it is that, despite the ritual of the lowbrow sneer) is that in it the Camusian and the demotic denotations of absurdity conjoin. In Beckett we see the absurdity of absurdity.

Vladimir and Estragon wait, no more. They pass through the forms of despair and rebellion, but, not being Camus heroes, they do not act; they only wait. If in Camus we catch echoes of the stoicism of Seneca, in Beckett we smell the leavings of Christian hope. This is not to say that *Waiting for Godot*, with its allusions to the thieves who were crucified with Christ, with its property tree by which the tramps have been told to wait, is to be regarded as a Christian morality: very far from it. But the symbols of Christianity are drenched with suggestive richness, and any Western artist who rejects them is a fool: the rite is the poet's rest. And so Beckett's enduring Saturday is the one that comes between Good Friday and Easter Day, except that time has a stop after Christ's crucifixion. Saturday refuses to become Sunday, and we are stuck with 'a large measure of despair and a small measure of hope'. The thing to do is to wait, even though we can be quite sure that the waiting will not be rewarded. Life is a wretched grey Saturday, but it has to be lived through.

Josephine Jacobsen and William Mueller pursue the basic Beckett theme, with its manifold seedy refinements, through all his works. But, with that admirable Germano–American concern for fundamentals, they are not content merely to finger the outer shell of Beckett's philosophy: there is a theory of knowledge, an epistemology to be considered. This, rightly, they first find stated in Beckett's book on Proust. The later French master sees in the earlier a revolt against the traditional modes of observing the phenomenal world, extolling a 'non-logical statement of phenomena in the order and exactitude of their perception, before they have been distorted into intelligibility in order to be forced into a chain of cause and effect'.

This is Proust's 'impressionism'; it is also Beckett's. Things are inexplicable; the scientific mirror lies; we know nothing. His aesthetic is dedicated to the stripping off of illusion, showing what is left after the dissolution of shape, colour, habit, logic.

The stripping of old wallpaper is a long job. There are many rooms in a house; layer after layer is disclosed to the conscientious peeler. Beckett has already stated his thesis; the task of incarnating it in art is not done yet—hence the novel after novel and (public simplifications) play after play. Moreover, the writer has to use language, and language is full of phenomenal traps. Beckett's control of language is as great as Joyce's, but—and here many are misled by biographical association, thinking it must also be literary—his aim is totally different. Joyce willed language into becoming reality—the Real Presence in the purely symbolic bread. Beckett puns and plays, but words resound with false echoes. It is best to end up with 'dish and pot, dish and pot', the verifiable realities of eating and excreting, though—as Malone dies—even these recede. Mrs Jacobsen and Mr Mueller might have pointed out that the stripped verbal medium of Beckett derives from an initial total mastery of traditional 'literary' English which now reads embarrassingly. The following is from *Murphy*:

> The leaves began to lift and scatter, the higher branches to complain, the sky broke and curdled over flecks of skim blue, the pine of smoke toppled into the east and vanished, the pond was suddenly a little panic of grey and white, of water and gulls and sails.

That is the end of the line. After that, French; ultimately, silence. But before the silence the human reductions go on waiting—Watt, Molloy, Malone and the others—on the Saturday that will not set. 'My characters have nothing,' said Beckett once. 'I'm working with impotence, ignorance ... My little exploration is that whole zone of being that has always been set aside by artists as something unusable —as something by definition incompatible with art.' Artists have had to revise their views about art since this artist appeared.

The Writer as Drunk

LITERATURE of the better sort makes little impact on the British people, unless it can be factitiously associated with scandal. The three best-known names of the modern period are, to the man in and woman on the street, Oscar Wilde, Dylan Thomas and Brendan Behan. All three behaved badly, and all three were Celts. The bad behaviour culminated in social or physical ruin which had a ritualistic quality about it, as though time had ordained that Anglo-Saxon guilt should be purged vicariously by Celts of great talent. Perhaps this same guilt has something to do with the inability to behave naturally and sin like a decent, or indecent, human being. Anglo-Saxon sin has generally been collective and historical, hence somewhat abstract; the notorious Celtic writer-sinners have served to demonstrate that the Fall is a perennial and palpable and personal catastrophe, to be punished in the individual flesh. Oscar Wilde's sin remains, admittedly, one reserved to a comparatively small segment of Anglo-Saxon society; the sins of those two more recent hero-victims are available to the least cultivated of men, though most lack the courage, stamina and (yes) money to push them to the limit. And, of course, there's also the question of talent. Much can be forgiven a poet that is totally culpable in a dustman or journalist.

All three of these men are remembered by their Christian names:

Here lies Oscar (rest him, God)
Not earth to earth but sod to sod.
It was because of men like this
That hell was fashioned bottomless.

In America, visiting British writers are greeted at cocktail parties by faculty wives with 'Can you screw as good as Dylan?' Men in Shepherd's Bush pubs keen over dead Brendan. Legends of the varied prowess of both Brendan and Dylan are eagerly turned into fantastic folk-myth. Both swore greatly and drank very heavily; Dylan, additionally, had the reputation—unjustified by biographical fact—of being a satyromaniac. Both (and this seems to me a large injustice to Dylan) are evaluated on about the same level by the British public; indeed—because Brendan was the more spectacularly drunken of the two—the Irish genius has been lauded above the Welsh. I personally don't think there can be any comparison. Dylan was the greatest lyric poet of the twentieth century; Brendan was a man with a lot of talk in him but a very limited creative gift. Dylan was incapable of shoddy work; Brendan's later writings were perfunctory and done for money. The drink never got into Dylan's poems; Brendan sometimes reads like a man eager to get his five hundred words done before the pubs open.

Drunkenness is said to be a substitute for art; why, then, should artists get drunk? Not, presumably, because of a block, a desire to create and a sudden baffling inability to do so; both Dylan and Brendan were creating, after a fashion, to the last, and the drinking bouts were going on all the time. There was no question of alcohol being a stimulus to creation, however: it is very difficult to write well with a bottle beside one. Neither Dylan nor Brendan ever kept much drink in the house; they were essentially pub-men. I know little of the terminology of pathological drinking, but I should regard the true dipsomaniac as the quiet home-drinker—sipping all day, my dear, like a dowager, as Anthony Blanche puts it. Talk of Dylan's mixed-up insides and Brendan's diabetes and despair at being excommunicated for his IRA activities—I don't think this gets us far. I would say that both men drank because pub-drinking remains the last of our creative social acts: for a man desperate to communicate in words, only the rising tide of alcohol in a cosy, stuffy atmosphere, the delirious prospect of the seventh veil dropping from the mind, can provide the right *bardic* satisfaction. Communication on paper is never enough; one needs a flesh-and-blood audience. But a theatre audience is not enough, either—too impersonal and remote. I'm speaking, of course, of a particular kind of artist—the rhetorical writer with an ancestral memory of the word-man's social function, the bardic job. Primed with wine in the kitchen, the bard confronted

the tipsy warriors at the feast's end. The Welsh and the Irish rhetorician sang and rhapsodized in debased London's so-called literary
pubs. They could find nothing better.

But the drink took hold. We have all seen glassy-eyed Dylan and
heard obstreperous Brendan. Fired at the first with what the drink
imparts, the inflamed rhetorician is deaf to voices that niggle about
diminishing returns. Only those with no true capacity for drinking
really know when to stop. And, of course, there were the other
factors: Brendan's genuine diabetic thirst; Dylan's medicine; the
bardic misery at being on any level lower than the euphoric.
Brinnin's book on Dylan in America tells one whole story; now
Mrs Jeffs complements it with her own tale of Brendan.* Her work
is, if anything, a more solid job than Brinnin's—more matter with
less art—but, since Brendan's downfall follows no very original
pattern, it inevitably seems full of déjà vu, and it cannot avoid a
Brinnin-type nothing-for-tears peroration.

If sociability led Brendan on the road to excess (missing the
Palace of Wisdom on the way), as well as guilt and despair and what
else could be dissolved only in alcohol, that same sociability found
sober expression in a less assertive need for people—the lineaments of
helplessness and innocence. Both Brendan and Dylan were totally
without guilt or malice, prelapsarian prodigies who acted out the
Fall but were not really involved in it. The weakness of both (and
Mrs Jeffs doesn't try to mitigate Brendan's weakness) called for help
from the strong and responsible to an almost destructive extent.
Brinnin and Liz and Sarah, and the rest of the saints of the Dylaniad,
recognized this demoniac cannibalism of the poet, but it only showed
its teeth in his private life; the dangerous and damning thing about
Brendan was that he cried for help in his art. Mrs Jeffs gave this help,
justifying it on the ground that she worked for Hutchinson, Brendan's publisher, whose legitimate commercial aim was to get books
out of him and make money out of them. When Brendan, in
drunken euphoria, had committed himself to an American publisher
other than the one to whom he was contractually bound, he wanted
that help to continue, and Mrs Jeffs wavered. She was approaching

* *Brendan Behan, Man and Showman* by Rae Jeffs (Hutchinson, 1966).

the ultimate in devotion. As personal devotion it was altogether laudable; as devotion to art it was less justifiable.

As a poet, Dylan was proud and alone, needing no help from anyone. The rigour of his approach to his art, the drafts piling high to reach a peak of impossible perfection, remains an example to all poets, drunk or sober. There is nothing like that in Brendan. He wrote a fine autobiographical book called *Borstal Boy* and two plays of little shape but immense vigour. Then all that was left was talk. Books had somehow to be made out of this talk, so along came Mrs Jeffs with the tape-recorder. The later works—all very slight affairs, though engaging—are edited tape, untouched by hand. Can we call them literature?

There's no reason why not. To speak into a microphone is not very different from dictating to an amanuensis: *Paradise Lost* and the later novels of Henry James are undoubtedly literature, and they were dictated. But with Brendan we always tremble on the frontier of what is merely excellent Irish talk, and the tape-recorder is revealed as more his instrument than the typewriter. But can talk be literature? Only as musical improvisation can be musical composition. With talk we get rhythm, the pulse of immediacy, the breath of sincerity, but we don't get those other properties of art—shape, precision, economy. We get half-art, art indubitably minor.

Dylan's art was not minor: it was shaped, cut, polished, intensified to the limit. Look for a parallel to him in the literature of the past, and you won't go far wrong if you adduce Virgil. But who does Brendan compare with? Probably one of the hack Elizabethans with the gift of the gab (but all the Elizabethans, like all the Irish, had that), an easy sardonicism, an ability (ready pen or ready amanuensis) to get it down on paper. Brendan reminds me of Greene, a man with rotting kidneys, an insatiable thirst, a need to keep going with the writing craft even when there was nothing to say. Leaving his mistress and his brat Fortunatus at home in sordid lodgings, Greene would swagger in the taverns with his henchman, Cutting Ball the pickpocket, and then, drunk and doomed, go back to write desperately. Like Brendan, he is remembered as a personality as much as a quasi-literary man. He became mawkish and tearful at the end, repenting his dissoluteness. Brendan never did, but he got a Catholic funeral.

Let me commend Mrs Jeffs's book as a shocking, worrying, enlightening portrait of one of those Falstaffian figures that, as Mr Priestley reminds us, have to be destroyed in this pursed, prissy age and society, either from within or without. Brendan may have been a nuisance, but he was alive, and he proclaimed to a large public that the art of letters, however minor its practice, belonged to life and not just to libraries. And soon, after a decent interval, let time send in the next Celtic sacrifice.

Man and Artist: Homage to Dylan

I WAS going to begin by saying that, on the evidence of these three books,* it looked as if a new Dylan Thomas season was beginning. Stupid. He's no cyclical god of fertility and waste (the link is prodigality), but a poet studied, if not read, all the year round. The unscholarly would be astonished to know how many post-graduate man-hours are devoted to him in the United States, and how many doctoral theses emerge from safaris through his polysemic forests. Dylan himself would be bewildered and, despite this deification, still short of money.

The poet goes on all the time; the man is accorded celebration of an intermittent sort, as when Mr FitzGibbon produced his fine biography and, now, gives us a selection of his letters. Those who were in his circle, or on its fringe, are prompted once more to reminisce, pondering the great mystery of the divide between man and artist, though a bridge is to be found in that all-too-human innocence which was so much exploited, and a personal allure that

* *Selected Letters of Dylan Thomas.* Edited by Constantine FitzGibbon (Dent, 1966).
The Craft and Art of Dylan Thomas by William T. Moynihan (O.U.P., 1966).
A Garland for Dylan Thomas by George J. Firmage and Oscar Williams (Vision Press, 1966).

can only be termed bardic. I have no new items to add to the legend, except that he once played me a few bars of Scriabin in G flat and that he would cow his stomach with lime juice for breakfast in the Richmond station bar.

The universal impression of irresponsibility to everything except his art is not necessarily modified after a reading of his letters. For, to Dylan, an artistic purpose—on one level or another—always attached to the use of words, spoken or written. His devotion to language was absolute, and there is hardly one letter in this volume that does not stand up well to a purely literary examination. Such an examination, of course, must always be gratuitous in the case of letters, but the writing is so fresh, the imagery so original, the tone so attractive, that we start thinking again of the letter as an art-form. Often Dylan's impulse was expository—the need to define his poetic aims—and some of his expositions (like those to Henry Treece and Vernon Watkins) have already assumed the status of public aesthetic manifestos: they could not have been better done if they had been commissioned at a high fee.

Others, like those to Princess Caetani of *Botteghe Oscure*, are not only art but artful—a conscious display of charm and talent, with the chime of two ha'pennies unable to rub themselves together. Such letters were drafted and redrafted, and they are fine pieces of imaginative prose. We know that Dylan laboured 'by singing light / Not for ambition or bread', but he needed to earn with his pen. One must consider ruefully now how much these letters have earned and are going to earn, both as books and as manuscripts snapped up by American universities. He was no niggard of words; he always gave more away (and this is true of everything he had) than he got.

Charm and likeability are here all the time, as richly edible as Welsh-cakes. Faults are transmuted to outrageous virtues: the lies— and there are many, patent ones—are an aspect of innocence and that imaginative inability to distinguish between truth and fiction. What, to those who know nothing about poetic alchemy, must be most disturbing is the brutal conflict between the fictive emotions of his art and his real-life attitudes to the subject-matter of that art. 'After the Funeral' is one of the great elegiac poems of all time; his declared reaction to the news of the death of Ann Jones (in a letter to Pamela Hansford Johnson) is one of mild regret. His case is that of any major literary artist. The universal amiability of the man was a badge of comparative indifference to human relationships; the attachments of lesser men were converted into the passionate intensities of his verse.

Professor Moynihan's close study of Dylan's poetry makes much use of the letters, and it points the dichotomy between the poet and the man. It also demonstrates, valuably, how little we must rely on the poet when he is talking about his own poems. Dylan propounded a powerful general aesthetic; he was usually sound on other men's work. But when he attempted an exegesis of such a difficult poem as, say, the first 'Altarwise' sonnet, he could make it 'even more baffling than it was before'. Exegesis is not the artist's job but the critic's. When men reared in old schools complained of Dylan's obscurity, they were really demanding from poetry a separable or paraphrasable 'meaning'. Dylan's aim was to pack many semantic layers into a single phrase or even word (it was, of course, also Joyce's later aim), and it is the deliberate exploitation of ambiguity that makes his poems as densely rich as they are. The extraction of a single toothpaste gout of 'meaning' no more applies to them than it does to music.

Professor Moynihan knows all about this, and his approach to the poems is in terms of their elements, though he admits the big generalities—'developing concepts of love and faith', Creation, Fall, Regeneration and so on. He has no stars in his eyes. He sees that Hopkins managed complexity without fracturing syntax, whereas some of Dylan's most idiosyncratic obscurities spring from syntactical weakness (though one could argue that his 'spatialization' of language, his looking at events simultaneously, had to be impatient of normal time-based structures). This is a thoughtful and helpful book, though it is not quite indispensable.

Finally, *A Garland for Dylan Thomas* is one of the most touching memorials we have. Fellow-poets, not biographers and critics, pay their sad proud tributes, and it would be invidious, in this flood of talent, to say whose tribute is the best. Louis MacNiece's 'Canto' in

MAN AND ARTIST: HOMAGE TO DYLAN

terza rima is the best-shaped; Emanuel Litvinoff's five lines ('All of us aged in that instant') has the most immediate, lachrymal, quality; Norman Cameron's 'The Dirty Little Accuser' sums up the personal exasperation of knowing Dylan which turned out to be a facet of guilt:

> Yet there's this check on our righteous jubilation:
> Now that the little accuser is gone, of course,
> We shall never be able to answer his accusation.

Dylan, as these poets testify, was all things—'Saint Binge' and 'our angel of defeat', 'Dai Barleycorn', 'Prince of Singers'. In death, as Fred Cogswell says, he has become carrion for the pedants, who

> ... damning with a Judas kiss, pull down
> Your reputation just to make their own.

He will survive them all—cadgers, succubae, professors. He grows in life and stature every year.

4

Lewis as Spaceman

THOSE of us who have accumulated big unsystematic libraries find Wyndham Lewis a curiously unlosable writer. My signed first edition of *The Apes of God* always gets in the way when I'm looking for something else: like a big unwanted dog, it interposes its bulk and demands at least to be distractedly patted. But I rarely take it out. I have a copy of the July 1915 issue of *Blast*, with its Pound and Eliot poems and its stop-press obituary on (*mort pour la patrie*) Gaudier-Brzeska. I occasionally re-read many of the contributions, but I never want to go through Lewis's exhortations or manifestos. Nothing dates so quickly as the gnomic didactic or reads so boringly. Lewis the painter remains alive and fresh; Lewis the author was always somehow stillborn. His works are huge monsters frozen in the act of snarling or clawing, the children of manifesto rather than real impulse. Had Lewis not been so good a pictorial artist, he would not have formulated the literary theory he did. The theory came first and the books after. That's where the trouble starts.

Pictorial art is, of course, spatial: emptiness is filled with solid objects that the observer instantaneously views. The art of the novel is temporal, like the art of music, though most great novelists have been uneasy about time: three contemporaries of Lewis—Proust, Joyce and Virginia Woolf—were obsessed with dredging the lastingly significant out of an endless flux they knew to be oppressive. Concentrate, said Proust, on the events that seem to ride on time, and they will become real things, not mere occurrences; *le temps retrouvé* is a kind of eternity and the flux is no more. Virginia Woolf encapsulated history in *Orlando* and *Between the Acts*, so that time became a solidity to hold in the hand. The year of *Finnegans Wake*—AD 1132

—is strictly symbolic: 11 for the renewal in digital counting (the resurrection), 32 for the velocity of falling bodies (the fall). But to Lewis all these authors were slaves of the flux: the eye, that non-temporal all-down-in-one-swallow organ, would provide the best release from its thraldom. Fiction should be a kind of painting.

Lewis's own words were these: 'Dogmatically ... I am for the Great Without, for the method of *external* approach.' The external approach relied 'on the evidence of the eye rather than of the more emotional organs of sense'. Fill up your novel with solid bodies and you have put time in its place. Certain limitations will ensue, but these can be made into virtues. To a painter like Lewis human beings are bodies as chairs and apples and buildings are bodies; Bergson (whom Lewis and his contemporaries read) taught that when human bodies and inanimate bodies meet and collide in a common zone, then laughter must follow. Lewis was committed to the comic, but the manifesto-maker in him preferred to call it satire. Of his kind of satire, *The Apes of God* is as good an example as any.

In my view it is not good satire. Satire should (pardon the pun) be swift, and *The Apes of God*—all 650 pages of it in the recently published Penguin edition*—merely shambles along. The impression of extreme slowness derives from the careful brushwork, but we should be looking at the results of this, not be asked to admire the process. It is the time and the paint that Lewis gives us, not the instantaneous image dredged out of time; we're borne along—by a dreadful irony—in a flux that's near-frozen:

> ... Dick flung his body into a sofa (which gasped in its wheezy bowels) and then slightly eructated, with a heavy zigzag move-ment up his body, the back of his flat occiput becoming for a moment as stiff as a poker—from hair *en brosse*, flourishing straight up into the air in the same plane as his neck, and so in a sheer undeviating drop to his coccyx, against the high-backed squatting apparatus to which he had brutally committed his person. Once more a ball of wind made its way irresistibly up his neck. His trunk shook, contracted and relaxed, to assist the slight explosion.

* Penguin Modern Classics, 1966.

These are the ingredients of a picture, but the taste of a cake is not to be found in its recipe. It is the writers without painting talent who have produced the best word-pictures; knowing that time cannot be conquered with the waving of a manifesto, they learn the trick of taking a quick photograph while time is off its guard. Lewis's method not only breeds ponderous rhythms, but encourages time-consuming verbosity for its own sake.

The external approach turns human beings into objects of immense solidity powered by creaking clockwork. Introspection being out, we have to learn about these human beings by the behaviourist method, and this takes a long time. When we evaluate them it is usually in mechanistic terms, and, after a lengthy sentence that freezes a Charleston step on to canvas, we admire their ability to make human movements with the indulgence proper for a robot at a schoolboys' exhibition of the 'thirties. It is not well done, but one is surprised to see it done at all.

The object of Lewis's satire is insufficient for the massive apparatus that (does anyone remember Heath Robinson?) Lewis sets into motion for its devastation. It is nothing more than the little London art-world of the late 'twenties—the dabblers, dilettantes and racketeers. A youth so innocent as to be mindless—winds of inanity whistling through a huge sculpted body—is set by his mentor to learn the ways of the Apes, and this he does, with immense slowness and eye-aching detail. Some things that shocked in 1930, when the book first appeared, will not shock now—the Lesbian Apes, for instance. Indeed, Lewis's own capacity to be shocked (that artist's solidity often has the puddingy heaviness of *Jean Bull philosophe*) militates against the satire, but not so much as the way in which, after thirty-five years, the life has gone out of the satirized.

For all these strictures, *The Apes of God* ought to be read, if not all through (life being short). The big indigestible prose draws on a vast vocabulary and can be precise if not concise; it is also the idiosyncratic garment of a great, if pig- and wrong-headed, British personality. The visual concentration is a fine corrective in an age of careless and perfunctory description. It is no bad thing to send young novelists to art-class or to set them to the reading of exhibition catalogues—a useful part of their training, though it should not be the whole of their life. But, as a satirical novel, *The Apes of God* is an awe-inspiring failure. In *Finnegans Wake*, Joyce put a good deal of Lewis into the Ondt, collector of solid objects. Time was not to be conquered in that way; time had to be converted into form, story, melody. That's why the Gracehoper (Joyce himself) sang:

Your feats end enormous, your volumes immense.
(May the Graces I hoped for sing your Ondtship song sense!),
Your genus is worldwide, your spacest sublime!
But, Holy Saltmartin, why can't you beat time?

Lament for a Maker

IT IS strangely unnerving to reflect that we shall never, without committing the solecism that only delayed shock can excuse, be able to talk about 'Mr Eliot' again. The handleless 'Eliot' placed him among the great dead while he was still alive. 'T. S. Eliot' suggested a kind of literary tycoonery and a no-nonsense anti-romanticism (we'd never dream of talking about 'R. Brooke' or 'D. Thomas'). But 'Mr Eliot' carried connotations of gratitude that one of the immortals was still our contemporary, also the affection—qualified by the gentlest of mockery, learnt from the man himself, also a certain fear, which he never taught—that is due to a respected teacher. The days of his great pronouncements are long over, but we were always ready to be freshly directed on some point of faith or art or morals. Mr Eliot (the habit will persist for a while) was always right, or rather he had so modified our modes of thinking and evaluation that we could never find him wrong. Whatever is valuable in contemporary Western civilization, so we like to believe, can be referred ultimately to Eliot's plain if fragmentary statements about the nature of the good society. As for literature, the tastes of all of us have been Eliotian for the past forty-five years. He was a maker in a double sense: he made not only his poetry but also the minds that read it. With great patience he schooled us away from shock or bewilderment towards acceptance, eventually love, of his work. Love became a habit. In time, the Eliotian cadences, whether verse or prose, turned into our instinctive music; young poets and critics had to teach themselves to resist the quiet but insistent voice. But there could never be any thoroughgoing reaction. To reject Eliot was to welcome anarchy.

A great poet and critic will never work solely on a coterie, or even on the merely cultivated. When the news of Eliot's death came through, commercial television had just presented an abridgement of Middleton's *The Changeling*. Watching it, I thought that this could never have happened if Eliot hadn't opened our eyes to the greatness of the Jacobeans. Spike Milligan, on a comic TV show, could say, 'Not with a banger but a wimpy', and most of his audience caught the reference. Weather forecasters would joke about April being the cruellest month. Demagogues would quote John Donne and novelists make titles out of Donne's poems or religious meditations. The metaphysical poets, still quaint and unreadable in my schooldays, became A-level set-books. And, though not everybody could follow Eliot to the final austerities of Anglicanism, Royalism and Classicism, his affirmation of the importance of tradition was accepted even by the *avant-garde*. For, with Eliot, the past was not a dull and venerable ancestor but a living force which modified the present and was in turn modified by it. Time was not an army of unalterable law; time was a kind of ectoplasm. One of the shocks of *The Waste Land* was to find past and present co-existing, even fusing. It was an analogous shock to the opening one of *Prufrock*, in which the evening is a patient etherized upon a table. Eliot broke down the old divisions, and he insisted on revolutionary syntheses which proved, on examination, to be as old as the hills, part of disregarded tradition. He was most radical when he was most conservative.

Eliot's claim to greatness as a poet is based on a very small body of work. Such a claim is more easily substantiated when a poet writes much: it would be surprising if the prolific Longfellow did not produce at least a few good poems. But it is doubtful if posterity will want to discard more than a handful of Eliot's poems—perhaps the

Rock choruses, perhaps some of the last of his occasional verses. *The Waste Land* and *Four Quartets* are alike great commentaries on eras of crisis and change, but the permanence of their greatness resides in their concentration on the permanent in human experience. Three of the plays will, I think, remain in the repertory, and this in spite of flaws which the author was the first to recognize. His right to be called the greatest of modern verse-innovators may perhaps yield in time to that of Ezra Pound, *il miglior fabbro*. But Eliot is sane where Pound is cranky, though it has taken the world a long time to recognize the sanity. His magical achievement is to make out of the sane, the reasonable, the scholarly, even the flat and prosaic, a poetry which induces the authentic tingling down the spine and even moves to tears (who can remain dry-eyed during Thomas's sermon or in the last scene of *The Cocktail Party?*). His criticism and scholarship are the air we breathe and, like the air, they are being taken for granted by the young and clever. Admitting, in one of his essays, that we know more than the men of the past, Eliot adds: 'But they are what we know.' He has joined their number. It was delightful to know Mr Eliot. Eliot—the great bare name like Donne or Milton— is someone we go on knowing, not only in the cerebral cortex but in the digestive tract. And are grateful to go on knowing.

Kipling and the Kuch-Nays

IN SINGAPORE, a few years ago, there was a slogan com-petition, run by the 'Tiger' beer company. One of the winning entries was:

> If all Malaya's rivers
> Could run with 'Tiger' brew,
> How grand to be an *ikan*,
> For think what *ikan* do.

Ikan is the Malay for a fish. This kind of bilingual punning was very common in British colonies and protectorates. The interaction between English and a non-cognate native language could produce, at its highest, quasi-literary pleasure; at its lowest, it was the facetiously macaronic dialect of a tribe. When an Englishman was repatriated from the colonies, he had not so much to relearn a mode of communication as to cauterize a whole communicative area of his brain. Coming home meant the abandonment, except in memory, of a whole area of experience and the language to go with it. When Malay calls a curry hot, it distinguishes between *panas* (temperature, as of tea) and *pedas* (spiciness), just as rice in the field is *padi*, in the store *beras*, on the table *nasi*. Of what use is this linguistic knowledge in England? A writer who learned his trade in a colony was bound to feel deprived when he came home to practise it. This was my experience; how much more must it have been Kipling's.

This point about language is not made in Dr Cornell's book,* but it seems to me as relevant as any other factor in the analysis of Kipling's highly idiosyncratic contribution to British literature. Kipling used more of the English lexis than any writer except Joyce and Shakespeare, and it was because of his bilingual upbringing in India. The literary dialect as he found it had, when it could no longer be enriched by India herself, to be referred back to its earlier historical phases ('I'm all o'er-sib to Adam's breed') or peppered with the colloquial and the technical. The Kipling additives are a substitute for lost Hindi.

Dr Cornell concentrates on other matters, and perhaps we ought to start by summarizing the facts of Kipling's early life. He was born in Bombay and spent his first six years there. His sensuous development was in terms of heat, gold and purple fruits, Hindu gods, the vultures from the Parsee Tower of Silence dropping the hand of a dead child into the garden, tree-frogs, the night-wind in the banana-leaves.

It was not all idyllic. One of Kipling's 'Nursery Rhymes for Little Anglo-Indians' ends: 'When the hot weather comes / Baby will die— / With a fine *pucca* tomb / in the ce-me-te-ry.' Kipling's moral development was not helped—nor was that of any Anglo-Indian

* *Kipling in India* by Louis L. Cornell (Macmillan, 1966).

KIPLING AND THE KUCH-NAYS

child—by the feudal deference of *ayah, jhampani, mehter, dhobi* and *sais.* Sent home with his sister Trix to lodge with strangers—the Holloways in Southsea—he found himself rudely thrust out of his snaky Eden. The story 'Baa, Baa, Black Sheep' describes the horror of the change—the murky Victorian Christianity he'd never met before, full of threats of hell; the demotion from infant despot to very ordinary middle-class boy; the white *ayah* ('Aunty Rosa') who doesn't call him *sahib* but beats him. It was the first and perhaps the most lacerating of the Kipling traumata: it confirmed him in Anglo–Indian attitudes which he never lost. One can always sniff either snobbery or inverted snobbery. He could identify with the *raj* and the sweeper, the colonel and the Tommy, but never with the English middle class.

J. I. M. Stewart, in his fine general study of Kipling,* goes so far as to suggest that a fear and dislike of women was a more fundamental consequence of the Southsea days. Mrs Holloway is often just 'the Woman', and Mr Stewart sees 'something savage about the capital "W." ' Taking time off from Dr Cornell's specific examination of Indian Kipling, and looking ahead with Mr Stewart at Vermont Kipling, P and O Kipling, and Burwash Kipling, one can see how 'the house of Desolation went further than the inculcation of class-feeling and intermittent misogyny.' Blake said that a tear is an intellectual thing. 'Aunty Rosa' made hate an intellectual thing: she was herself a Blakian emanation, symbol of the darkness in a child's cosmogony. Kipling's later hates can be frightful, even unclean. And we can accept with Mr Stewart that his view of life was 'as sombre, in essence, as was the vision of his great elder contemporary among English writers, the poet and novelist Thomas Hardy'. It is not pure fancy to find the roots in Lorne Lodge, Southsea.

But he was thrust by Mrs Holloway into the protective life of the imagination, enclosed by a fence and ruled by magic; he was to become what Auden called 'the poet of the encirclement'. He was predisposed to literature by his Pre-Raphaelite parents and Burne-Jones relatives and, despite 'Prooshian' Bates in *Stalky & Co.*, found

* *Rudyard Kipling* by J. I. M. Stewart (Gollancz, 1966).

another Morris-Burne-Jones enthusiast in Price, the real headmaster of the United Services College at Westward Ho! in Devon. If he kept his verses to himself at school, it was because they were private, not because he might be ragged for being a poet. Back home in India (for it really was home), the infra-literature of colonial journalism presented the only possible career for a word-troped young man unfitted for business (unthinkable), army (bad sight) or the ICS (too competitive). And so the years of sub-editing for the *Civil and Military Gazette* in Lahore.

We are familiar with the newspaper galley-slave who dreams of literary fame with the verses and novels he writes off-duty, keeping his art and his sub-craft separate. The remarkable thing about Kipling is that he moved to art through his journalism and, to the very end, kept something of the journalistic in his art. Had not his parents shown Victorian prudence, he might have stayed in London, writing moony poetry on the Bohemian fringe. In Lahore one conformed. After all, one needed an audience, and that audience was in the club.

Kipling's early achievement was to raise the level of taste in his local Anglo-Indian readership by contriving a verbal intensity that could avoid the mawkishness of the imitation Rossetti and Swinburne that flourished back in London. He used parody on various levels. 'Sing a Song of Sixpence / Purchased by our lives — / Decent English gentlemen / Roasting with their wives' was on the lowest. Much more subtle, foreshadowing the really mature Kipling, was:

> Mother India, wan and thin,
> Here is forage come your way;
> Take the young Civilian in,
> Kill him swiftly as you may ...

That is from 'A Vision of India', which parodies Tennyson's 'Vision of Sin'. As Dr Cornell says, the parodic element 'has become a rhetorical device to heighten our sense of the speaker's lack of "poetic sentiment" about life and death'. The Anglo-Indian's stoic approach to the horrors which qualified the glory of the *raj* is finding a voice.

Kipling's first published story, 'The Gate of the Hundred Sorrows', found its way into the *Civil and Military*, despite the editor Stephen Wheeler's discouragement of 'literary' journalism. But what Kipling, who had abandoned all efforts at what he thought of as 'serious' poetry, regarded as prose literature was little more than sub-Poe fantasy. It was the sub-editorial eye, the need to notate the actual and give it hard unrhetorical compression that turned Kipling into the master of a unique short-story form. 'The Gate of a Hundred Sorrows' has its smoky, opium-tainted, Poe-like elements, but it is much more the prototype of the Conrad study (imitated but debased by Maugham) of the white man going to pieces on Black Smoke. In other words, it is a new kind of naturalism, and it could only come from a writer working in the East.

Dr Cornell reminds us that, though Zola and Maupassant were still not much read in England, it was not too hard to get hold of them in India. And, even when they were not translated, Kipling had enough French. But Kipling, unlike the home-based writer, did not need to get his realism and irony from foreign models. He had developed the ironic approach through verse-parody and straight-faced reportage; the subject-matter—not available to sweet stay-at-homes—was in the province of a journalist. The thing we have to remember about the first really mature story collection—*Plain Tales from the Hills*—is the primary Anglo-Indian audience. Kipling was not exploiting the exotic for the titillation of readers back in England; he was presenting a mirror to the people who took a regular Simla holiday and knew Mrs Hauksbee well. That Kipling was able to communicate with an audience bigger than Lahore may be ascribed to the great artist's insight, which sees the universal in the local; he wrote for Anglo-Indians as Shakespeare wrote for Elizabethans.

Kipling's vision of the India that made him a writer was—as we know from all his Indian writings—far from liberal. He did not like the English middle class and he did not like the Indian middle class either. He preferred the pre-Mutiny India, with high and low fixed immutably in a formal frieze. It was perhaps his unwillingness to see how a new India was already emerging from an articulate middle class that prevented his doing more than composing merely fragmentary pictures of India, and not some epic prose or verse work that should be animated by a sweeping historical insight.

There remains something of the Lahore journalist about all his work—the magazine stories, the 'occasional' verses. And, in all the repatriate years, whether in New England or East Sussex, the urge to find a place and a mythology in which to feel at home—as he had felt at home in Bombay and the Punjab—strikes with great pathos. He was the product of a system which could accept the unequivocal terms of feudal loyalty, the language of parable and prophecy; he wrote for a minor autocracy. But a member of that autocracy, back home in England, is nothing more than a *kuch-nay*—a middle-class nonentity. By a terrible irony, the *kuch-nays* of England, praying for ten per cent, made him their own poet.

Kipling: A Celebration in Silence

THE Kipling centenary (1965) passed as quietly as the paws of a fieldmouse whisker-twitching through the grounds of a Bateman's which seems to dream—so little of him is left there—of incumbents earlier than its most famous one. That is a Kipling sort of trick—the image that gets out of hand and fails to illuminate. In 'The Return of Imray', as Dr Tompkins reminds us,* lightning 'spattered the sky as a thrown egg spatters a barn-door'. In 'The Light that Failed' (a good title for an essay on the Kipling simile), the camel-guns open up lanes in the Mahdi's forces, and these are compared to 'the quick-closing vistas in a Kentish hop-garden, seen when a train races by at full speed'. What applies to the simile applies also to the thing plainly described. At the beginning of 'Love-o'-Women', a spot of blood on the parade-ground is dried and then pulverized and then blown about by the wind. I doubt if ever

* *The Art of Rudyard Kipling* by J. M. S. Tompkins (University Paperbacks, 1965).

Kipling really saw that happen, but it is the sort of thing a myopic man might imagine as being available to normal sight. This is not just Beetle peering on the touchline; it is the eye of Allah. Visual fancy often takes the place of straight observation. That business of the egg on the barn-door has nothing to do with lightning; it belongs with the green digressions of Milton's hell or Homer's bardic cadenzas—the epic simile which is not a concentration on the thing in hand, but a temporary release from it.

Kipling had much of the epic poet's equipment, but he could not write an epic. I don't, of course, mean a verse epic; I mean a great novel. The novels he did write are interesting, but they are structural failures: even *Kim* is pasted together. Kipling did not have the architectural gift. Looking at a collapsed empire, we feel that it ought, in its greatest days, to have been recorded in some huge Tolstoyan unity, and that Kipling ought to have been the man to do it. He was too small, however; the halo of greatness which his devotees make sit on him is really an emanation of that vast wasted subject-matter. Many of us want him so much to have sung that finished empire—Britain's only epic theme in a thousand years—that we sometimes dream he actually did it. Perhaps the centennial silence is a sending to Coventry: Kipling let us down.

Or did he? Literature, like history, is what was done, not what might have been done. If Kipling had not been born, there would not have been even a fragmentary record of the Indian Empire from the viewpoint of the men who maintained it; the soldier would have had no voice; warnings about British *hubris* might never have been delivered in public language that suggests ceremonial robes hastily put on over a sandfly-bitten body. And yet he is the pendent to his age, not the encloser of it. Some of his insights remain astonishing, but he does not ride above history. One does not have to be Hamlet to understand Shakespeare, but Kipling makes most sense to men who have been Private Ortheris or to women who, repatriated with their husbands, find the blasted English drizzle genuinely waking the fever in their bones. The expression of 'general truths' was not Kipling's business as a poet; he was a poet of a sector of life, and this diminishes him.

But it is as a poet that he must ultimately be judged, not as a writer of *contes à clef*. He must be read entire in the Definitive Edition of his verse,* not in that dangerous Eliot selection which restored Kipling's name (reassuringly chaperoned on the book's spine) to the shelves of intellectuals. What emerges from a total re-reading of the whole vast verse corpus is an unfailing technical professionalism which—one of art's horrible anomalies—proclaims him as indubitably minor. With a great poet, technique fails along with inspiration; with a minor poet, technique has to get used to subsisting on very little. Kipling could do anything—free verse, couplets, Wesleyan hymns, ballads, sestinas, Sapphics—and he never sank to Wordsworth's level at its lowest. When he had nothing to say, he could still simulate the accents of the gnomic or profound, invoking Biblical phraseology or contriving neat antitheses or alliterations (form as a substitute for meaning). And yet there is something heart-lifting about the resourcefulness and virtuosity, just as there is something admirable about the stretching of vocabulary to incorporate the exotic and demotic. This is an engine-room more than a poet's bower; Kipling is a sort of MacAndrew.

This easy stigmatization of Kipling as a minor poet begs, I admit, too many questions. It is not enough to say that the greatest poets are introspective and complex; *Lycidas* and Marvell's 'Horatian Ode' are public utterances, true 'occasional' pieces, but they are magnificent. When Kipling addresses the Americans on their taking up of the white man's burden, or asks for God's mercy on an empire-building nation, he is performing feats of emotional engineering no less remarkable. But look again at Milton and Marvell, and you find a personal quirkiness, a conscious subjective qualification of a required public sentiment. Kipling does not dare let himself go, even on the margin, in this way. He has to assume a persona, whether of tommy, high priest, or bard, before he can speak; otherwise he may betray neurosis. What he needed to do, and never could do, was to fuse the poet and the story-teller. The stories are full of schizophrenic imagery, and their very subject-matter has become a mine for amateur psychiatric investigation. The split, myopic Kipling was

* Hodder & Stoughton, 1940.

scared of seeking catharsis in verse; reading his verse, we always feel vaguely cheated.

Yet, with some poets, we must always be willing to forgo depth for the sake of breadth, to accept that the scholar's selection or the bunch of anthology pieces cannot admit us to their essence; they are existential poets. Kipling's best-known poems are a sort of gloss on the daily papers, and there is a great deal to be said for a kind of writing which exalts the ephemeral or finds an exact articulation for our inchoate attitude to the current of events. But when the events are over, we look to their poet for a residue of lasting rhetoric—a distillation from fruit that most of us leave to rot in the trees. Kipling's rhetoric cannot match that of another poet who followed the news and who shares his centenary—W. B. Yeats. At best, Kipling is pub-gnomic, hymnal, Bible-echoing; at worst, Yeats is always himself, whatever orts of decayed Dublin oratory he is chewing. Kipling only gave us something of himself, he withheld. That partly explains the silence.

Said Rudyard to Rider

KIPLING, like the subject of Auden's 'penny life', kept none (or, at any rate, few) of the letters he received, long, marvellous, or otherwise. Nevertheless, Morton Cohen's redaction of an apparently one-sided correspondence with Rider Haggard* is so skilful that it doesn't look one-sided. The relationship between these two some-how complementary writers is of interest, though—on the evidence of Kipling's letters and Haggard's journal—it can't be classed among the great illuminatory margins of English literature. There are various reasons for this, but they all boil down to a lack of obsession with art. Both writers skirt, with a kind of British embarrassment, Paterian obscenities like aesthetic values; their skills are in the service

* *Rudyard Kipling to Rider Haggard: The Record of a Friendship.* Edited by Morton Cohen (Hutchinson, 1965).

of entertainment or national and imperial reform. Fronting the public and the politicians, seeking the ears of both, they are not much concerned here with any posterity but that which would bless them for afforestation. Their enlargements, naturally, look like a diminution.

Of course, we cannot expect Kipling to go into the agonies of the sestina-form when corresponding with a writer of romances. He brings himself down to Haggard's level, though at first—Kipling is ten years younger, unknown, while Haggard has already published *She*—he has to climb to it. Professor Cohen spends much of his introduction on the power and glory of the Savile Club, 'where, over pipes of tobacco and glasses of sherry, a handful of men casually, even haphazardly, helped steer the ship of English letters for a quarter of a century.' Kipling's election to it, and consequent first meeting with Haggard, was promoted by Andrew Lang, who—the Ezra Pound of his day—helped everybody. It was at the Savile that J. K. Stephen wrote the poem ending:

> When the Rudyards cease from kipling
> And the Haggards ride no more,

and referring to the literary politics of the club, the professional jealousies which condemned two scribblers alike in popularity, preferred—as the columnist in *Harper's* said sadly—to the 'artistic and important books in our reach'.

Both Kipling and Haggard were clubbable men, and a kind of yarny masculinity (tales of India and the Zulu wars) pervades their post-Savile relationship (the men getting down to literature while the women suffer pregnancy or menopause at home). The phase of greatest intimacy shows Kipling beginning his letters with 'Dear old man' and ending with 'ever thine'. But did they have much in common, apart from their complementary imperial concerns—Africa the one, India the other—and their attempts to import a kind of imperial planning to the motherland that seemed sometimes so foreign? If they did, it was not the community of artistic equals. Kipling could plan a story for Haggard and frequently did, the two sharing the big table in the study at Bateman's. But what Haggard gave to

Kipling he gave early. The British public seemed to be outgrowing Haggard at the very time when it was recognizing Kipling's true stature. And yet both continued to be aware of a shared loneliness—strangers who knew an empire that others merely pontificated about, writers whom the reviewers never took seriously, gentlemen who tried to put their estates in order.

But if neither was an abstract imperialist nor, in the sphere of home affairs, a mere writer to *The Times* (Haggard received his public honours not for literature but for the innumerable commissions he served upon), both remained remote from the immediate community. My country home is at Etchingham, a couple of miles from Bateman's, and its station still serves—as it did in the Kipling–Haggard time—travellers in search of Kipling. Haggard must have been met there often. And yet neither Etchingham nor Burwash (from which Bateman's stands remote) has much to remember about either man.

In his straitened times, after the First World War, Haggard gave up Ditchingham House in Norfolk and went to live in St Leonards (no ghosts there either) to be near Kipling. Old yokels in Adderbury, my former Oxfordshire home, talk of the Earl of Rochester as though he died only yesterday, but Burwash shopkeepers mention mainly the Kipling cheques that used to be sold to tourists. Ultimately, Kipling and Haggard must be seen as sharing visions, not easily distinguishable from the story-teller's fancies, in a house well off the main road.

The Kipling letters are often touching, sometimes very interesting, but rarely memorable. Where we find something of himself it is usually in the form of a no-nonsense manly persona which goes in for the slangy: ' ... one realizes what a toss-up it was that our creed hadn't taken a dominantly oriental twist (might have been better if it had, p'raps!).' But the prose stylist can come out, too: 'Not a sign of spring yet except in the winter wheat and a certain staring hardness—as it might be the coat of a horse before moulting —in the texture of the wayside grass.'

Professor Cohen was right to bring these together in this centenary year; his notes and links are admirably full, and we don't have to look anywhere else for the literary and historical backgrounds. Yet, finally, one is depressed rather than elated by the revelations, or lack of them—colloquy without dialectic, unfailing niceness, a friendship eerily without qualifications:

> 'That's just what I say,'
> Said the author of *They*.
> 'I agree; I agree,'
> Said the author of *She*.

5

Making de White Boss Frown

SENTIMENTAL and didactic, sub-Dickens with the American South as one big Dotheboys Hall (though no satisfying thrashing of Squeers-Legree), *Uncle Tom's Cabin** expended its ration of serious attention in its own day, leaving the slush and not the anger for posterity. That is the general view, at least in England. American organs like the *Bulletin of the Historical and Philosophical Society of Ohio* can produce scholarly papers like 'Eliza Crossing the Ice — A Reappraisal of Sources', and students of the Civil War — like Edmund Wilson in *Patriotic Gore* — accord it the attention due to any book that helped to change history. Only in the USSR, whose bookshops parade it next to *Three Men in a Boat*, *Hatter's Castle*, and the novels of Messrs. Braine and Sillitoe, is it still purveyed as a piece of literary socialist realism, a device of confirmation. But, if we are to take seriously the literature of the South, from Mark Twain to Faulkner, and if we are to accept that our own age shows the true flowering of the novel of protest, we cannot afford to neglect Mrs Stowe, who was the mother of both.

'The little woman who made this great war' — so proudly she was hailed by President Lincoln in 1862. She didn't, in fact, quite make it, but she made it possible for the making of it to seem the only way out of the North-South impasse. First serialized in the abolitionist *National Era*, her masterpiece came out as a book in 1852, two years after the Compromise which satisfied no one but held off war for a decade. Though California entered the Union as a free state,

* *Uncle Tom's Cabin* by Harriet Beecher Stowe. Edited by John A. Woods (O.U.P., 1965).

that Compromise did not expressly forbid the extension of Negro slavery to the territories gained from the Mexican War, but neither did it condone expansion of so lucrative a trade and so restful an institution. Southern acceptance of the Compromise depended on how far the North was willing to enforce the Fugitive Slave Law: men north of the Ohio had to dull their consciences to keep the peace and the Union. *Uncle Tom's Cabin* appeared as a whetstone; it did not argue, it showed. There was the brilliantly articulate escaped slave George, prototype of James Baldwin but far handsomer and not so black: walnut-juiced to temper the Euro-African yellow, he could be taken, in his Italianate cloak and with his brace of pistols, as some Byronic rebel wholly acceptable to the ladies' reading circles of Concord; there was his wife Eliza, palely beautiful with a beautiful child, running, by God's grace, over the ice-blocks of the Ohio. No more sympathetic refugees could well be imagined. Southern readers picked up a Scott-looking romance ('Late in the afternoon of a chilly day in February, two gentlemen were sitting alone over their wine, in a well-furnished dining parlour, in the town of P—, in Kentucky') and found that what they had there was a bitter attack on a constitutional right; their anger helped to sell three hundred thousand copies of the American edition in the first year alone. *Uncle Tom's Cabin* helped to start the crumbling of the 1850 Compromise and to show that no further one was possible. In that sense it did what Lincoln claimed it did.

Apart from a literary style that recalls (and probably influenced) the phthisic Sunday-school prizes which reconciled working-class children to malnutrition and a premature transfiguration, *Uncle Tom's Cabin* has been chiefly neglected—in our own age—because it is hard to accept that an instrument of historical change should also be a work of art. The Victorian men of letters who were also liberals had to swallow *Uncle Tom's Cabin* whole without meanly regurgitating the style. But the book's popularity soon made it possible to discount the literary content altogether. It was eaten in fragments—tract-abridgements, school-selections, dramatic adaptations. As a barnstorming melodrama on tour (little Eva dragged heavenwards on a pulley), as a silent film (accompanied by the tunes of Stephen Foster), it held a large public till late in the nineteen-twenties. Even in Catholic Lancashire, where I was brought up, it was part of the pop-art of childhood, though the Church had placed it on the Index and enfranchisement had raised the price of cotton in our grandfathers' hard times. The vitality of the work is considerable. It survived its debasement as a bogus Siamese *wayang* in *The King and I*, recalling that Anna Leonowens had written to Mrs Stowe about the Lady Sonn Klean's liberating all her slaves, saying: 'I am wishful to be good like Harriet Beecher Stowe, and never again to buy human bodies, but only to let them go free once more.' Now, it seems, we have to take the whole book again, since there is little relevant to our age that can be taken out of it. Today's Negroes, who reject martyrdom and intend to overcome, are ashamed of bible-thumbing Uncle Tom; George Harris, prophet of a vital Africa, has become a demagogue with two gold Cadillacs. If the book is to mean anything now, a good deal of the meaning must reside in the art.

Reading it, we find that all we have to forgive is the style. This is an un-American activity, a cluster of fashionable importations—chiefly from Scott and Dickens, though, in the Simon Legree episodes, Mrs Stowe draws on that earlier Gothic which continues, in more sophisticated forms, to exert its appeal for Americans. Structurally, the book is very sound, and it even has a visual skeleton provided by the geography of slavery. Kentucky is the middle earth, a vale of tears but with the Jordan–Ohio as its northern frontier, Canaan—Illinois, Indiana, or Ohio—on the other side. Then come the Great Lakes and the haven of Canada. George and Eliza make the journey and, in freedom, George is able to deliver a manifesto on the secular glory of a new Africa. 'I go to Liberia,' he says, 'not as to an Elysium of romance, but as to *a field of work*.' And Mrs Stowe comments: 'If we are not mistaken, the world will yet hear from him there.' As for Uncle Tom, who has the other half of the story, his way lies south from Kentucky, down the Mississippi to the precarious earthly paradise of New Orleans, then north-west to martyrdom on the Red River. He has no Liberia to look forward to, only the Christian heaven.

What may look like self-indulgence frequently turns out to be structural necessity. The death of little Eva, whom Tom saved from drowning, thus earning a cushy billet with the St Clare family, is usually picked out as the limit in slush: 'A bright, a glorious smile passed over her face, and she said, brokenly,—"O! love,—joy,—peace!" gave one sigh and passed from death unto life!' But the image of a good Christian death is what sustains Tom when he is suffering not from phthisis but from Simon Legree. Lashed first to labour and at last to death, Tom needs Eva to keep him steady in belief and resolve, a sort of animated hagiograph. The sugar lilies and the weeping Topsy may be intolerable, but Mrs Stowe makes up for that—Faulknerian realism begins here—with those protracted sufferings on the old plantation. There is, anyway, a balance, no gratuitous feeding (as so often in Dickens) of a necrophagous appetite. As for Tom's forgiving Christianity—'O, Mas'r! don't bring this great sin on your soul! It will hurt you more than 't will me! Do the worst you can, my troubles'll be over soon'—it doesn't deserve the sneers of the Negro intellectuals, or white ones either. What palliative ought a progressive slavery novel to make available to the victims of Legree—a bundle of abolitionist pamphlets, gems from Tom Paine? The visions of secular reform have always been the real pie in the sky; a man entering the gas chamber needs heaven. What may have disturbed Christians in Mrs Stowe's own day—apart from cries like 'Oh my country! these things are done under the shadow of thy laws! O, Christ, thy church sees them, almost in silence!'—is the implication that Christianity only really works as a slave religion.

Even in his hammiest postures as a slave with a soul, Tom is totally convincing. Indeed, all Mrs Stowe's characters, who might well have been mere morality fascias, have a remarkable roundness—even the 'good' master Shelby, whose implausible sale of Tom and Eliza's child sets the plot working. Her triumph is Augustine St Clare, the indolent and indulgent New Orleans gentleman who lets his Negro butler bully him and Tom preach his hind leg off. Attractive as he is, Mrs Stowe doesn't hide from us that his paternalism is as misguided as Legree's proprietorialism is vicious. St Clare's slaves are, for the most part, a great deal happier than many a free-born white, but his free and easy welfare state cannot, and does not, survive his death in a café fracas. Tom has been promised his manumission (it is only a matter of asking), but the papers are still unsigned when St Clare dies, and Tom is sold down the river. St Clare has made the mistake of assuming that personal benevolence can turn bad law into good; but, in effect, good law comes to mean no law at all, and without law we are, however paternally coddled, wholly vulnerable. As for benevolence, that is precisely well-wishing, not acting. For all his weaknesses, St Clare is a sort of voice of history; he knows perfectly well that the slave-owning mentality is not confined to the Southern States of America. How about the British labourer? His New England cousin, Miss Ophelia, will not have it that British factories are another kind of plantation: 'The English labourer is not sold, traded, parted from his family, whipped.' St Clare replies:

> He is as much at the will of his employer as if he were sold to him. The slave-owner can whip his refractory slave to death —the capitalist can starve him to death. As to family security, it is hard to say which is the worst—to have one's children sold, or see them starve to death at home.

American slavery is no more than

> the more bold and palpable infringement of human rights; actually buying a man up, like a horse—looking at his teeth, cracking his joints, and trying his paces, and then paying down for him—having speculators, breeders, traders, and brokers in human bodies and souls—sets the thing before the eyes of the civilized world in a more tangible form, though the thing done be, after all, in its nature, the same; that is, appropriating one set of human beings to the use and improvement of another, without any regard to their own.

It is St Clare, more than the Northern abolitionists, who sees that a '*dies irae*' is coming everywhere. Like any Marxist, he regards the process as ineluctable, but he is an aristocrat who calls himself a democrat and feels neither regret nor elation at the impending change in the order. He plays the *Dies Irae* from Mozart's *Requiem* on the piano, pushing back his very prophecy into an art that serves a religion he cannot accept, despite Tom's humble but importunate evangelizing. It is as complex a portrait as any in nineteenth-century fiction.

Mrs Stowe's resistance to the technique of the morality (a far stronger resistance than is evinced in much present-day protest literature—Baldwin's *Blues for Mister Charlie*, for instance) is attested by the divisions built into her characters. Miss Ophelia has a New Englander's abhorrence of Southern slavery, but also of the slack-ness, the reversion to tropical torpor, which her cousin's indulgence seems to encourage. She wants Negroes to be Christianized into the austere patterns of the North, educated and turned into free wage-earning Americans, but (and here her crime is, in its way, as great as that of the slave-owners) she cannot bear the touch of a black skin. Paradoxically, to be surrounded by slaves may be a means of accept-ing them as a sort of human beings; it will rarely—since these black bodies are your property—mean physical revulsion. The atti-tudinizing of the North, the work of enlightenment delegated to missionaries, will not do; Miss Ophelia (whom the slaves, with prophetic insight, call Miss Feely) must learn to cherish dark flesh with her own hands. That is why Topsy is brought in, Miss Ophelia's own charge and passive, or resistant, educatrix; eventually she will be taken to New England as a living witness that Negroes are real touchable people.

The whole book sometimes seems to resolve itself into a protest, not just against slavery, but against the forces—law or prejudice—which destroy simple affection or break family ties. The real horror of slavery is that it separates mothers from their children: it is a horror that Mrs Stowe, a bereaved mother, is qualified to express: no amount of abstract, diffused abhorrence of slavery—appropriate to a male writer—could have given *Uncle Tom's Cabin* its peculiar bitterness. And yet the book is far from being a mere mono-thematic exercise, and that is where much of its distinction lies. We are given a picture of mid-nineteenth-century America which is as cosy as Mrs Gaskell's England: tea is taken, chicken pie is cooked, the crinolined ladies are subject to the vapours, the calm legislative processes go on in the capital. But a system is accepted which is more than mere hypocrisy. Hypocrisy is allegiance to the letter and denial of the spirit; in the American South the letter itself has to admit ambiguous values. There are men and women to whom, since they are only chattels, Christian institutions cannot apply. One of the most sickening episodes in the book is the recollection of the marriage between George and Eliza, sentimentally arranged by Mrs Shelby with all the bijou trimmings, presided over by a real clergyman. But this marriage can mean nothing, since slaves are sold as individual bodies: the slave family just does not exist. Mrs Stowe will allow husbands to be separated from wives, but the wresting of a child from its mother cannot be tolerated by nature: the mother will kill herself, escape with her child (but only, as with Eliza, through a kind of miracle) or—improbably, as in the dénouement of the book —achieve reunion in freedom. It is through the disruption of nature that slavery is shown as not merely evil but mad.

Mrs Stowe is prophetic in that she implies no real hope for the integration of the races in America. The future of the Negro lies in Africa, and the future of the world may lie there too:

In that far-off mystic land of gold, and gems, and spices, and waving palms, and wondrous flowers, and miraculous fertility, will awake new forms of art, new styles of splendour; and the Negro race, no longer despised and trodden down, will, per-haps, show forth some of the latest and most magnificent revelations of human life. Certainly they will, in their gentleness, their lowly docility of heart, their aptitude to repose on a superior mind and rest on a higher power, their childlike simplicity of affection, and facility of forgiveness ... Perhaps, as God chasteneth whom he loveth, he hath chosen poor Africa in the furnace of affliction, to make her the highest and noblest in that kingdom which he will set up, when every other kingdom has been tried, and failed; for the first shall be last, and the last first.

It is straight from Revelations, the Holy City, with no tse-tse flies or dysentery; it's the other side of the Jordan, no more. Charles Dickens, for one, would not have it:

> I doubt there being any warrant for making out the African race to be a great race, or for supposing the future destinies of the world to lie in that direction; and I think this extreme championship likely to repel some useful sympathy and support.

And certainly, since only Uncle Tom looks 'respectable enough to be a Bishop of Carthage' and only George Harris shows any intelligence, the rest of Mrs Stowe's Negroes exhibiting few of the virtues of a God-chosen race, we find it hard to reconcile the prophet with the novelist.

It is the novelist who counts. Mrs Stowe's primary gift to Southern fiction derives from an ability to take the Negro seriously as subject-matter, and to render—for the first time—the involutions of the Negro character through exact transcription of speech. Mrs Shelby's Sam, sent out to 'help this yer Mas'r to cotch Lizy', explains why he hindered instead:

> Dat ar was *conscience*, Andy; when I thought of gwine arter Lizy, I railly spected Mas'r was sot dat way. When I found Missis was sot the contrar, dat ar was conscience *more* yet—cause fellers allers gets more by stickin' to Missis' side,—so yer see I's persistent either way, and sticks up to conscience, and holds on to principles. Yes, *principles*,' said Sam, giving an enthusiastic toss to a chicken's neck—'what's principles good for, if we isn't persistent, I wanter know? Thar, Andy, you may have dat ar bone—'tan't picked quite clean.

The speech is the speech of a whole tradition of fictional Negroes, not excluding film and music-hall, but the argument is that of the modern African politician. And here is the voice of modern Negro protest:

' ... What country have *I*, or any one like me, born of slave mothers? What laws are there for us? We don't make them—we don't consent to them—we have nothing to do with them; all they do for us is to crush us, and keep us down. Haven't I heard your Fourth-of-July speeches? Don't you tell us, once a year, that governments derive their just power from the consent of the governed? Can't a fellow *think*, that hears such things? Can't he put this and that together, and see what it comes to?'

It is the impact of the characters, and what they say, that excuses the frequent ineptitude of the *récit*, the hollow prophecies, and the tedious moralizing. *Uncle Tom's Cabin* works well as fiction, but the fiction is also the feather of the dart. It has, whether we have read it or not, done more than any work of literature to make Negro servitude in the South seem not only the type of all slavery but the only one we ought to feel guilty about. We can forget what happened to the Jews, or what is still going on under Islam, or that a greater white novelist than Mrs Stowe was a galley-slave. Thanks to her, colour has become for all time the colour of the oppressed.

He Wrote Good

I WAS in Russia when Ernest Hemingway died. *Pravda* had a headline: *Smert Gemingvaya*, I think it was. Many young Russians I drank with asked me, as if I had any chance of knowing better than they, whether it was murder or suicide: their Russian souls saw right through Mary Hemingway's very sensible announcement that it was an accident, that he had merely been cleaning his guns.

One girl cried into her *konyak* and said: 'We were all lovers of Ernest Gemingvay.' It was a good tribute. She added: 'He was very much similar to Jack London.' And so he was. He sailed in boats, shot things, caught big fish, fought for the right causes, turned imaginative writing into an aspect of the physical life. But London's death at forty was untimely; Hemingway's suicide at sixty-two came when his brain was decaying, when pleasure in the functions of the body, which included writing, was no longer possible. It was the only way. The senile ex-writer, the shell of whose body is honoured like a monument, is all very well for England; it will not do for America. Hemingway was all-American.

A. E. Hotchner's book* presents the last years with ruthless compassion. The boxer, drinker, bull-fight *aficionado* who didn't give a damn suddenly became petulant, a worrier about money and excess air baggage and shooting in somebody's field with only the wife's permission. He developed persecution mania: those two men at the bar were feds, after him; don't let Bill drive the car, he's trying to kill me; I'm not making enough money this year (despite the annual hundred thousand dollars in royalties, the stock, the property). The decline is not merely pathetic; it's embarrassing. That premature announcement of his death on safari was recording the true poetic event; if he had not written so well afterwards we should want to accept it.

But even the decade or so before Hemingway's suicide—from 1948, when Hotchner first met him—has a kind of odour of approaching nemesis, for, though Hemingway was sailing, swimming, shooting, following *corridas* all over Spain, he was living more and more on his past and, as writers will, effortlessly inventing some of it, or at least giving some of it a more satisfactory shape. Perhaps the gods of true enactment are at war with the muses of fiction and, when they inhere in the one being, they have to destroy it. It was in keeping with his *persona* for Hemingway to say that he had slept with Mata Hari and enjoyed it, though she was a bit heavy in the thigh; cold historical dates show that she was dead before he could have got to her. The long streams of reminiscence over wine, running far into the night, had to be taken on a plane where the imagined and the actual became acceptable as the same thing. No reason

* *Papa Hemingway* by A. E. Hotchner (Random House, New York, and Weidenfeld & Nicolson, 1966).

why not; Pontius Pilate asked one of the great questions of all time, though his choice of occasion was infelicitous. Take Hemingway as one of his own works and we shall all be happy.

But, as Hotchner's book seems to show, life itself had a tendency to become Hemingway fiction, and when life acts something already written it takes on a ritualistic quality. Put Hemingway in a bar in Venice and a chapter from *Across the River and into the Trees* starts to play. The American students in Pamplona were there because that was the scene of the *corrida* in *The Sun Also Rises*. Not that life necessarily becomes any meaner or less flavoursome when fiction starts to shape it; after all, art is there to make sense out of life. But, for all the immense and admirable variety of the historical, as opposed to fictional, Hemingway saga—if it is possible to separate the two—there is a sense in which he was a man less expansive than contractive, that he could really only take life if it was cleansed and blood-let into a ritual.

Ritualize violence and you get the big shoot, death in the afternoon, the grave courtesies of men who respect each other's trigger-finger. To see Hemingway as a sort of Catholic (which he was) admits no inconsistency in the image. His early story about Christ's crucifixion, in which one of the soldiers says: 'He was pretty good up there today,' puts Christ among the great bullfighters and men who seek death fighting for lost causes. The ritual is always tragic and stoic; when you drink wine, think of the blood of fallen men. Papa Hemingway is a tribal figure, presiding over solemn ceremonies. He addresses Ava Gardner and Ingrid Bergman as 'daughter', and we're no more embarrassed than when Jack London, writing to his wife, signs himself 'Wolf man'. The drums are beating; the frontier hasn't pushed back all that far. The safer the civilization, the less need for ritual.

Hemingway's prose, which has the tone and rhythm of liturgy, was developed at a time when Western man was unhappy at the civilization he had made. After all, it had produced the most terrible war in history: there was an instinctive tendency to associate progress with destruction; the horrors of war were, in a sense, products of the highly refined intellect. Both D. H. Lawrence and Hemingway revolted against the higher centres; the subject-matter of both was instinctual, or natural, man. But Lawrence's prose was stuck in the pre-war age of rhetoric. it suggested intellectual organization, the liberal era; Hemingway's achievement was to create a style exactly fitted for the exclusion of the cerebral. He didn't, as we know, forge it *ex nihilo*; he got it from Gertrude Stein, in whose books it seems more *faux-naïf* than a genuine return to the roots of language. But Gertrude Stein didn't know what to do with it; Hemingway did.

That it was the product of prolonged meditation and hard work on Hemingway's part seems implausible to those writers who can hammer out yards of it on the typewriter: Hemingway made it seem as inevitable as all good writing, and, once the rhythms had been sounded, it was not difficult to pick them up and reproduce them. Faulkner said of him that he had no courage, that he had 'never been known to use a word that might send the reader to the dictionary'. Hemingway's reply was, according to Hotchner: 'Poor Faulkner. Does he really think big emotions come from big words? He thinks I don't know the ten-dollar words. I know them all right. But there are older and simpler and better words, and those are the ones I use.'

That was a fair statement of the position. Hemingway was a very bookish man, always reading and, moreover, always sensitive to what other men were doing with language—perhaps more sensitive than any of his contemporaries, not excepting Joyce. When he talked as he thought a prizefighter or baseball-player ought to talk he was really creating a vernacular for them (such men can become bloated and turn sesquipedalian): they should all talk about playing good, just as he talked about writing good. He was acting as Instinctual Man, just as Elgar used to act as Racing Man. Whether the act became second nature we can never really know. Hemingway rarely dealt with the products of real introspection; he invited the study of the behaviourist.

The five volumes by Hemingway now published by Penguin* exhibit the range and possibilities of that very original prose. There

* *Green Hills of Africa, Across the River and into the Trees, The Torrents of Spring, The Fifth Column, A Moveable Feast.*

is no better medium for the expression of action, since there are none of those highly intellectual structural devices which suggest manipulation, the ordering of memory, rational analysis. There are few subordinate clauses: 'and' or 'but' is the most-used conjunction. There are few synonyms; there is no avoidance of repeated forms: ' ... the trail was easy to follow. Droop and McCola trailed one on each side, leaving the trail between them, pointing to each blood spot formally with a long stem of grass. I always thought it would be better for one to trail slowly and the other cast ahead but this was the way they trailed ... '

A trail is a trail is a trail. Because of the falling cadence which follows on the avoidance of periodic sentences, there is often a curious overtone of regret, as if the good things of life were rapidly passing away: 'It was early and we sat on my raincoat on the fresh-cropped grass bank and had our lunch and drank from the wine bottle and looked at the old grandstand, the brown betting booths, the green of the track, the darker green of the hurdles, and the brown shine of the water jumps and the whitewashed stone walls and white posts and rails, the paddock under the new-leafed trees and the first horses being walked to the paddock.' In his least satisfactory book, *Across the River and into the Trees*, the rhythms of regret sometimes seem to be without content. The Hemingway music, heard in a void, is as limpid and potent as branch water. It needs the stiff bourbon of action.

The masculine action doesn't always please: too much shooting at things and people; too many boy's book gestures of loyalty and honour; too many camp-fire rituals. But the blood was a cleanser, and after the expatriate American Henry James the expatriate Ernest Hemingway was needed—a thrust of the old *yang* to ginger up the flaccid *yin*. But the dangers of flaccidity and decadence could hit his ritual prose as easily as the fatter liturgy against which he rebelled. In *Across the River* he fell; in *The Old Man and the Sea* he recovered—beautifully and triumphantly. Reconciling literature and action, he fulfilled, for all writers, the sick-room dream of leaving the desk for the arena, and then returning to the desk. He wrote good and lived good, and both activities were the same. The pen handled with the accuracy of the rifle; sweat and dignity; bags of *cojones*.

The Postwar American Novel: A View from the Periphery

I HAVE given up trying to look at literature as the emanation of a language rather than of a racial or national or regional consciousness. To be honest, I think that it has always been a little disingenuous of me to expect Americans to accept the term 'English Novel' as meaning 'the Novel in English'. We in England have wanted too long to regard the American Novel as a regional aspect of the English (national, not linguistic) Novel. We can still contrive to see the Australian Novel as leaping out of D. H. Lawrence's *Kangaroo*, or the Anglo-Indian Novel as the terminus of *A Passage to India*, but the American Novel has (if we will be honest with ourselves) always been a distinct genre from Hawthorne onward. In the last twenty years the English have been prepared to admit as much, but also to go further than is either healthy or necessary. We know we are on the periphery of world power, but there is no reason for us to regard ourselves as being on the artistic periphery as well. Yet we tend to look to the future of the Novel in English as belonging wholly to America, with our Waughs and Greenes and Powells as provincial satellites, their art charming but calligraphic.

This is not solely because of America's status as one of the two world dynasts, nor because of a wealth that is able to give writing men prizes, sabbaticals and huge advances, as well as—America being the only English-using country that has literary magazines—chances of highly paid serialization. It is rather that American novelists seem to possess the courage to deal with big themes thrown up by contemporary history, whereas we in England tend to be too satisfied with provincial subject matter—class, hypergamy, suburban adultery. Our World War II was longer than America's, yet no substantial British novel came out of that war. It had to be left to Norman Mailer with *The Naked and the Dead*, Gore Vidal with *Williwaw* (and he was only nineteen when he wrote it), John Horne Burns with *The Gallery* and, most recently, Joseph Heller with *Catch-22* to make the big statements about war's mess and futility. Perhaps we in England failed to see any mythic content in that six-year grey struggle: we wanted it to be a parenthesis, not part of that current which gives themes to artists. If so, we were wrong. Only Evelyn Waugh, with his *Sword of Honour* trilogy, recorded the European conflict at any length and in any depth, and he recorded less the war itself than the death of a British social class, an incidental casualty of that war. Like Ford Madox Ford before him, he was primarily concerned with seeing how a 'gentleman' behaved in camp and battle. Our class system continues to get in the way of the basic human truths; the Americans are not so inhibited.

Many of the American novelists who continue to interest British readers started off with war books. Gore Vidal, nourishing the seed of the male community theme—a gift of wars, as of monasteries—went further, in *The City and the Pillar*, than any British author had yet dared to do in portraying homosexual love. Mailer took up the theme of the power struggle, finely and disturbingly expressed in *The Naked and the Dead*, and developed it in a novel that said more to Europeans than to Americans, if one may judge by American reviews—I mean *Barbary Shore*, which seemed to us to be in the Koestler-Orwell tradition with a flavouring of Kafka. Away from this theme, he has floundered badly: *The Deer Park* was disappointing; *An American Dream* plays with evil without being quite sure what evil is. J. D. Salinger, in his short story 'For Esmé with Love and Squalor', was, in a war context, already adumbrating his theme of innocence (a regenerative spring in a bad world) beset by adult forces which are either malevolent or phony. *The Catcher in the Rye* was as important to us as to young America; it gave us a dialect of candid and innocent protest, healthier than the shouts and batterings of our own angries. But, looking back at Holden Caulfield from the Glass house which is being built so slowly, we begin not to be too sure how genuine Holden is; sometimes now the candour looks contrived and the innocence seems sentimental. We cluck and tut over Mailer and Salinger quite as much as their compatriots do, worrying about their development. There are too many *homines unius libri* among the younger American writers, we feel; we want to see signs of an *œuvre*. What is Ralph Ellison doing after *Invisible Man*; what is Heller planning after *Catch-22*? Vidal is safe; *Julian* is a superb historical novel. John Horne Burns wrote *Lucifer with a Book*—a fine, vigorous indictment of the phony in American education—then died. In England we still admire the shelf builders; the romantic figure with the single big work—cut off from fulfilment of huge promise by death, discouragement or inanition—has become very American. Herman Wouk was, I think, trying to say something about this in his interesting but uneven *Youngblood Hawke*.

The massive single novel, of Dickensian or Proustian or Joycean dimensions, is something that England has almost ceased to produce. Apart from their subject matter, I cannot imagine an English novelist achieving the sweep of William Styron in *Lie Down in Darkness* or *Set This House on Fire*. I am not being old-fashioned in regarding length itself as somehow admirable in the novel. Even the mediocrities of James Jones have at least the courage to charter a big boat for a big sea, however unprosperous the voyage. I think again it is the assumption of the American novelist that he can, if he wants to, always find a large theme, whereas we in England have few large themes left. We missed our opportunities when we had an empire: only in one man, Kipling, did mystical belief in empire and great literary genius come together, but Kipling was no novelist. The *romans-fleuves* of Snow and Powell seem to limit themselves to the chronicling of class—no epic subject. America still has itself, and the Whitmanesque expansiveness can reappear in the most unexpected places—in Kerouac, for instance. Even the examination of a racial consciousness outsidethe pale of the WASP can have a vigour which we can only call American. I am thinking of James Baldwin's novels and the works of those writers whom we must call Jewish-American—Bellow, Malamud, Herbert Gold.

England has her racial problems, but no novelist with Baldwin's

fire—which I, in my tepid English way, sometimes think too hot
for its subject—has yet come forward here. Our West Indian writers
are sooner or later drawn into the English tradition, so that V. S.
Naipaul—one of our best novelists, and a Trinidadian—comes closer
all the time to E. M. Forster. We are, of course, a great nation for
compromise, whereas America is a great nation for juxtaposition.

One of the problems that face the outsider looking at the American
novel is in deciding how far the recent exile can justly claim to have
entered its tradition, whatever—Whitmanesque breadth and revolutionary fire apart—that tradition is. Christopher Isherwood's *A
Single Man* seems to me an American novel, whereas Aldous
Huxley's *After Many a Summer* does not. Huxley assumes that
American culture is on the periphery of Europe, while Isherwood (whose hero is as British as Huxley's) comments on American
civilization as an American would. I think there is also a matter
of prose rhythm, hard to analyse and not just a matter of locutions
like 'gotten'. Auden's postwar poems sound best when delivered
with an American accent, and the prose of *A Single Man* calls
for a similar dryness, an eschewal of orotundity: it is something
to do with the difference between the flavour of port and the flavour
of a martini. Or, put it another way, the sweetness of nostalgia
seems missing from American prose, whereas we British writers are
still bedevilled by it. Faulkner can get away with the poetic peroration at the end of *The Mansion* because it doesn't relate directly to
the British romantic tradition: it fits easily into the Faulknerian
turgidity but one is aware of it as a deliberate importation, a rather
cold fastening-on.

Whether to call Vladimir Nabokov an American novelist is one
of the biggest of our problems. The narrators of both *Lolita* and
Pale Fire are civilized foreigners self-conscious about their American
exile, and they tend to a creative pedantry which, as in James Joyce,
seems a mark of the *émigré* European: lacking a country, he clings to
a language. But when I say that neither *Lolita* nor *Pale Fire* could
have been written outside America I do not just mean that the anno-
tation of American *mœurs* from the inside is central to them both.
I mean rather that experimentation in English is now tolerated in

America to an extent no longer possible in England, and that literary or philological scholarship conjoins with creative writing in—so far as I can judge—a perfectly natural way. Our British scholars may (like J. I. M. Stewart) produce intellectual thrillers in their spare time, but we have hardly a single instance of a scholar who is also a serious novelist or poet. Again, the British ideal of a novelist is to be found in Lord Snow, whose approach to language is strictly utilitarian and no-nonsense. Once admit the exciting pedantry of a Nabokov, and the public and the publishers shy. The state of academic scholarship and the state of the novel are of necessity related, but that social dynamism which inevitably modifies language must also have something to say to the literary artist. The Americans have to invent a new vocabulary and new rhythms in order to make articulate new approaches to the world; America is increasingly expansive while England tends to contract. Thus linguistic experiment in art must, in America, seem an integral part of the social process, not mere coterie preciousness.

I must not let it appear that we are masochistically prepared to yield primacy to America in the art of fiction totally without a struggle, indulging in that typically British disparagement of the home product which foreigners can so easily misunderstand. I think more bad novels have come out of America in the past twenty years than out of the British Commonwealth—best-selling sexstuff (we all believe that America produces the best pornography), books about political corruption whose apparent honesty is really cynical sensationalism, historical panoramas in ghastly prose. But the bad novels are rarely bad in a niggling cheap way: they all subscribe to the doctrine that massiveness is a virtue in itself; they are horrible not like a squalid shack but like a vulgar skyscraper. Again, a country that has great opportunities for satire has not taken them often enough: *The Loved One* should have been written by an American. When satire *has* appeared it has frequently been too muscle-bound to move quickly—this is true of *Catch-22*. There has not been enough writing of intricate delicacy—although here I except Nabokov and Peter De Vries: the latter is surely one of the great prose virtuosos of modern America. But if we attempt a catalogue of important world fiction published since World War II, we shall find that America will lend it an inordinate number of names. Above all, the novel is taken seriously in America, even if the seriousness occasionally approaches the solemnity of Hemingway's bloody owl.

The novel is taken seriously because criticism is taken seriously. No American novelist of any stature, knowing he has done bad work, can expect to be let off with a few disparaging epigrams at the foot of a seven-hundred-word article devoted to five or six authors. American journalism holds on to the tradition of the long review; Britain lost it during the war, along with the literary periodical. When a British critic reviews, he knows that his appraisal is too brief to be true criticism; an American critic finds space—and the leisure bought with a good fee—to write for a kind of posterity. Posterity may not greatly interest the American novelist, but those qualities posterity might be expected to be interested in tend, far more than with his British counterpart, to find their way into his work—massiveness, the panoramic vision, a sense of history and (perhaps most of all) a powerful national awareness.

The Jew as American

MR A. ALVAREZ, writing on Lenny Bruce's autobiography, reminds us how that sick scourge or WASP-swatter jumped from a second-storey window shouting: 'I'm Superjew!' A joke that falls as flat as its maker fell when you consider that Superman was the creation of two Jews, and that he could not so easily have been contrived by Gentiles. For the modern American hero, pop or highbrow, belongs not to the rivers and the prairies but to the towns, and the Jew is America's great urban expert. He migrated not from failed potato-land but from an over-civilized continent crammed with neurosis and dialectic; he was weary with the burden of city-lore and yet recognized that it was only in the city that man could come to self-realization. When America turned its face from the fully-expanded West and looked East again, it found the Jew ready equipped with the materials of a sophisticated literature.

One can call a long roll of Jewish-American fiction and find that the European wisdom and the mythopoeic genius are not well matched by staying-power. Pre-war Jewish writers had the death-urge; after the sustained European pogrom they were neurotic, obsessed, self-pitying, paralysed. Daniel Fuchs, Henry Roth, Nathanael West, Isaac Rosenfeld, H. J. Kaplan, Delmore Schwartz have wit, dialectic, compassion, but not muscular vitality. Self-doubt, and doubt about the Jew's role in an Anglo–Saxon society, can produce single important books and stories, but they cannot build a shelf.

It is only with Bernard Malamud and Saul Bellow that a positive voice is sustained, and this does not mean a self-assertive one: it means rather a willingness to make the American Jew the spokesman for all Americans. Malamud promises an *œuvre*; Bellow, at fifty-one, has already achieved one. His importance can be judged from any single book, since the vitality seems uncontained by it, long though some of the books are; but he is best approached as a developing novelist with themes that assert themselves more and more strongly as he progresses. Penguin Books have already reprinted *Dangling Man*, his first novel; now, in one bulky parcel, the rest appear.* Bellow is an intellectual and uncompromising writer, but it is probable that the paperback public will take the opportunity of discovering what serious contemporary American fiction is really about.

A common theme animates all the American fiction that British readers find interesting, and that theme is the success or failure of the innocent, the misfit, the minority to adjust to a complex, vital but ruthless urban society. In the works of Salinger and Baldwin the theme is simplified to sheer morality: there is a demand that sympathy be given to the desperate teenager or Negro or sexual invert. In 'popular' novels like *Focus* and *Gentlemen's Agreement*, the nastiness of anti-Semitism is played up sensationally. Such books tend to

* *Dangling Man, The Victim, The Adventures of Augie March, Henderson the Rain King, Seize the Day,* and *Herzog* (Penguin Books).

shrillness and the vitiation of that objectivity without which there can be no genuine literary values. Bellow, on the other hand, is primarily concerned with creating literature, and the extraction of social messages from his works is not easy.

In *The Victim* he seems to be playing the 'popular' anti-Semitic tune, but we soon become aware of ambivalent counterpoint. Asa Leventhal is accused by the psychotic anti-Semite Allbee of losing him his job; he asserts that Leventhal's material success was gained at the expense of a downtrodden Gentile. Leventhal responds with the stock complex feelings of the baited Jew. Allbee becomes parasitic; Leventhal nurses guilt and wonders who the victim really is. The two men become engaged in a kind of hostile symbiosis; they need each other, fulfilling the primal condition of man as a social animal. Jew and anti-Jew only blazon themselves as such because they have not yet learned to define themselves as men. Self-pity gets in the way of self-realization.

When the American Jew achieves self-realization it is not in ancestral terms. Tommy Wilhelm, in *Seize the Day*, is a re-working of Arthur Miller's failed salesman (but how much more rich and subtle). He is another kind of victim, with a messed-up marriage, a tendency to be exploited by financial sharks, destined to lose what little money he has, faced daily at the breakfast table with an autocrat of a father. The wretched single day which the book describes ends with Tommy weeping over a stranger's corpse (it is, of course, proleptically his own) in a funeral parlour. The self-disclosure is horrible, but there is a kind of elation in it—the elation of having achieved a definition. Tommy knows what he is—a failure in a world that worships success; his relationship with society is clarified and celebrated with tears. But we are not to share the tears: this is not the stock pitiable Jew whom an alien community rejects; it is a big, well-set American (all Bellow's heroes are of heroic build, none of your bowed starved tailors) who has failed to make the grade. To fail to make the grade is a human achievement that teaches us what we are; it is an aspect of the myth that sustains America.

As Bellow takes the standard themes of two tough-sentimental 'popular' works—*Focus* and *Death of a Salesman*, both by the same author—and uses them to a literary end, so his aim in his major novels seems to be to write success stories, but not as the world knows them. The hero of *Henderson the Rain King* is an all-American tycoon who has had everything and yet still cries 'I want, I want'. What he wants is to descend into the dark continent of the unconscious, fulfil himself as primitive man, then emerge to become something useful—doing, not being. So, after fantastic adventures in an Africa of Bellow's own invention, Henderson, a millionaire in his middle fifties, turns himself into a medical student. We recognize the existential motif—self-definition through action. *The Adventures of Augie March* is a vast picaresque book which lauds success as the rejection of success. Augie deliberately eschews the American gods of power and money in a kind of Mark Twain quest for the primal Columbian freshness. The daring of the book lies in its making a Jew into a superman Huckleberry Finn—the Jew as American folk-hero, though not one for juvenile readers. For Augie fulfils one aspect of the American dream by being a sexual success—a fertility god, as well as a searching Columbus.

More recently, the eponym of *Herzog* demonstrates how the qualities that make for failure can, by a perhaps typically Jewish paradox, be the positive definers of a man's worth. Moses Herzog (the name seems to come from *Ulysses*) has, like Tommy Wilhelm, made a bad marriage; he has little money; he has not fulfilled his promise as a scholar. He has grudges against the makers of the modern world, and he expresses these through the medium of highly articulate, but unposted, letters. His brain is preposterously alive, questioning, doubting, re-defining. He is man becoming; the set institutions of the community—including marriage—cannot hold him. He is a good lover, and a highly successful one, but bad as a husband. He appears comic, but that is perhaps because he is too big to engage the pigmy stairs and doorways of made, set, congealed society.

The vitality of Bellow's creations owes everything to the language in which they are presented. If Augie and Herzog ever stride the cinema, they will be much diminished as heroes. They are essentially literature. Bellow's 'rich, crazy poetry, a juxtaposition of high and

134

low style, elegance and slang' (so Professor Fiedler calls it) can be regarded as the contribution of the cultivated American Jew to the American language—a natural literary dialect whose extravagance is the true answer (Nabokov's artificial dandyesque being the false one) to the careful etiolations of writers like Hemingway. The dialectic of Jewish city-dwellers is urgent, passionate, as tangible as physical action; English is refreshed through the rhythms of Yiddish; a 'descriptive lust' (Ellmann's term) is lavished on common objects. When the abstract enters Anglo–Saxon writing, the concrete lumbers out; in Bellow an idea provokes the same salivation as roast meat. It is easy to see this as a product of the ghetto—agoraphobic eyes looking in to the overstuffed living room, ventures into argument not out to the dissipating world. But it is easier still to see it as the old synthetic tradition to which Shakespeare belongs—life before it was parcelled out by the Enlightenment, conserved by a conservative people.

Perhaps the Bellovian richness will displease some palates. And the relish for detail—minute dirt from Tommy Wilhelm's fingers on the white of his peeled egg; Herzog's vision of a bed coverlet as a coated tongue; the fully reported monologue of a Puerto Rican taxi-driver—inevitably clogs the action. But action is not all that important to the fictional tradition which Bellow exemplifies. Every novelist must sooner or later make up his mind about the kind of fiction his temperament hovers over, happy to be undecided. Either detail must give way to action or a fictional centre must be found which will justify the minute examination of the external world—or its mirror-image, the mind. Bellow could be both kinds of novelist, but in his maturer work he has opted for the delineation of a complex dissatisfied personality, a heaving centre with a periphery glittering with near-hallucinatory detail. Man seeking self-definition is plot enough.

Contemporary British fiction looks very shoddy in comparison with the work of this polymath, sensuous, compassionate American Jew. We can, if we stretch a point, call him British: after all, he was born in Canada. But, though all Europe is in his work, he was made for America. The American city is the arena where contemporary

Western man must find himself. That he achieves his best expression as a Jew is not one of the ironies of history. This is what history has been working towards.

Blood in the Matzos

IN MATTERS of art the categorizing urge is a dangerous one, but it is born into us, like Original Sin. Talk of Bernard Malamud leads to talk of Saul Bellow and Isaac Bashevis Singer; comparison follows, and it is rarely to Malamud's advantage. This is only because he has, unlike Bellow, failed to turn the American Jew wholly into an American, and, unlike Singer, failed to stay uncompromisingly in the East European ghettoes. Though he writes an English very nearly as fine as Bellow's, his spirit is closer to Singer's. This is as much as to say that he is not primarily a secular writer: he is interested in sainthood, while Bellow is interested in success. He doesn't go as far as Singer, who unashamedly makes the next world trade with this, but his occasional surrealism looks like a compromise with the supernatural, and his two best novels resolve, if you strip them down, into studies of miraculous conversion.

The Assistant is set in a New York slum full of very poor Jews, one of whom, a grocer called Morris Bober, is beaten up by a *goy* hoodlum. Actuated by a mysterious remorse, the hoodlum returns to the shop to run it while Bober is recovering from his injuries. The remorse doesn't lead directly to a desire to be good: the wretch remains himself, kicking against the pricks. But imperceptibly the yeast of grace starts to work, and the *goy* ends up as an orthodox Jew, complete with circumcision. It is a new life. *A New Life* is the title of what is perhaps Malamud's best book, in which a comic, foolish, accident-prone college lecturer becomes a saint not through the denial of the flesh (eventually the way of the *goy* penitent in *The Assistant*) but through the assertion of its rights. Levin, the lecturer, commits adultery. Adultery is a sin, but it is a sin that leads to love. At length it leads beyond love to the disinterested responsibility of true sanctity. Such themes sound sentimental, sweetly pious tract-stuff, but Malamud's approach is through irony and a kind of bitter naturalism.

His most recent novel, *The Fixer*, has a Jew for its hero, but the American setting has been changed for a Singerian one—a place of snow and pogroms. The time is Singerian, too—the period of the western migrations of the oppressed Ashkenazim. Yakov Shepsovitchy Bok, a fixer or handyman, sickened by lack of opportunity in his village and by the defection of a barren wife, goes to Kiev, 'the Jerusalem of Russia'. The sobriquet is ironic, since the Jew-hating Black Hundreds, with their two-headed-eagle badge, are very active here. Ironic, too, is the fact that Yakov finds opportunity for bettering himself (changing his name and dissembling his race) by helping a drunken Black Hundred snoring in the snow. Set up as supervisor of a brickyard, reading Spinoza in his spare time, he knows, with Jewish fatalism, that all this cannot last long. And, indeed, the blow falls.

The body of a murdered Russian boy is found in a damp cave near the brickworks. It has been bled white and is covered with stab-wounds. At once the Jews are accused; the double-headed-eagle pamphlets rain down. It is put about that the killing was ritualistic and that the blood is being used for the making of Passover matzos. The usual concatenation leads to Yakov's arrest—he chased the boy off when he trespassed into the brickyard, his subordinates dislike his just dealing and anti-graft watchfulness, he gave shelter to a rabbi who was being persecuted by hooligans, the rabbi ate part of a matzo and left it behind, Yakov had a jar of strawberry jam on the table which peerers-in took for Gentile blood. It all adds up. But the important thing is that Yakov confess to his prosecutors that he is a mere tool of a great Jewish conspiracy. This he refuses to do.

The book is mostly an account, masochistically detailed, of Yakov's long season in prison as he awaits trial. Few books, not even *Darkness at Noon*, have dwelt so fully on incarcerative miseries. This is Imperial Russia, and the refinements of the NKVD are still unknown. The concentration is not on coldly administered torture but the wretchedness of cold, solitude, near-starvation, brutal anti-Semitic insults. Yakov has a humane-seeming counsel, but he is eventually discredited and commits suicide. The periodic interrogations are conducted by men who will believe anything of the Jews—that all the males menstruate, that blood-eating is ordained by the Talmud, that the systematic slaughter of all Gentiles has been long planned. Here is Father Anastasy talking:

It is said that the murder of the gentile—any gentile—hastens the coming of their long-awaited Messiah, Elijah, for whom they eternally leave the doors open but who has never, during all the ages since his first coming, bothered to accept the invitation to enter and sit in the empty chair. Since the destruction of their Temple in Jerusalem by the Legions of Titus there has been no sacrificial altar for animals in their synagogues, and it has come about, therefore, that the killing of gentiles, in particular innocent children, is accepted as a fitting substitute. Even their philosopher Maimonides, whose writings were suppressed in our country in 1844, orders Jews to murder Christian children. Did I not tell you they think of us as animals?

He goes on to enumerate the various Jewish uses of Gentile blood —sorcery, love potions, well-poisoning, as an ingredient in 'fabricating a deadly venom that spreads the plague from one country to another', a panacea which will 'heal their women in childbirth, stop haemorrhages, cure the blindness of infants, and to alleviate the wounds of circumcision'. It is an incredible performance (and let us admit it, it must have been great fun to write).

In his extremity of pain, years after his committal, Yakov learns that he is at last to be brought to trial. The book ends with his delirious ride over the cobbles towards the Court of Justice, the crowds shouting, some weeping, some calling his name. In a typical Malamud near-surrealist sequence, Yakov confronts a naked Czar, 'his phallus meagre, coughing still,' and shoots him in the name of all the Russian oppressed. 'Nicholas, in the act of crossing himself, overturned his chair, and fell, to his surprise, to the floor, the stain spreading on his breast.' Yakov has learned that there's no such thing as an unpolitical man, especially a Jew. 'You can't be one without the other, that's clear enough. You can't sit still and see yourself destroyed ... Where there's no fight for it there's no freedom. What is it Spinoza says? If the state acts in ways that are abhorrent to human nature it's the lesser evil to destroy it.' We don't need the mock-trial; a few more years will bring the Revolution.

That this is a moving and harrowing book need not be further demonstrated. We respond instinctively to the theme of Jewish oppression, and sometimes one must feel that much of the slow unwinding of tribulation is otiose: mention the one word 'pogrom' and we react as to a bulky thesis. But this historical area of anti-Semitism has, admittedly, not been so well explored fictionally as the later German one. Schwarz-Bart, in *The Last of the Just*, set himself to cover the entire phenomenon, from the Hugh of Lincoln affair (evoked painfully in Malamud's epigraph from Chaucer) to the gas chambers, but he homed to Nazi Germany after a few introductory chapters. Malamud here gives us the finest fictional summation yet of Slav Jew-hatred, in firm objective prose which will admit no self-pity, sentimentality, or even gratuitous horrors. But still one has reservations about the whole project, and these reservations are somewhat complicated.

It is, of course, stupid to be disappointed that Malamud has not given us again what he has already given us so well—the working of the spirit in an exactly rendered contemporary Jewish-American scene. Novelists must try new things. What worries me about *The Fixer* is a suspicion that Malamud is indulging in an exercise rather than exploring a fresh zone of human experience. His book, despite the modern Americanisms and the revelations proper to a permissive age, reads like an imitation translation from the Yiddish (Singer again). The conjuration of a dead era and city is brilliant, but it is the brilliance of the cold and deliberate technician that is displayed. *The Fixer*, one feels, is a pastiche of a writer who never existed but, in order to fill a historical gap, ought to have existed.

Some of the dialogue, especially the honest opinings and self-exculpations of Yakov, reads like essays in colloquial translation, though there was never anything to translate. To move Malamud from the Yiddish stream to one less sectarian, one has the impression that he is turning himself into a Russian novelist, without the bore of having to write in Russian: there are Gogolian elements in the early part, and a sufficiency of Dostoievskian in the main body of the book. This is not necessarily to be condemned. Sometimes the only way in which to write a novel about a particular theme, time and place is to project oneself into an alien body or hand over to a sort of mediumistic 'control'. Gabriel Fielding had to do this in *The Birthday King*, which reads like a brilliant translation from an unknown liberal survivor of the Nazi regime. But there remains with Malamud's book a suspicion of the deliberate exercise, the self-indulgent craftsman showing off certain magical tricks of evocation.

The earlier novels are small glories of American literature, and the later ones will be too. This present novel disowns America (except as a vague promised land) and is suspended nowhere except in the historical consciousness of the Jewish race and a country made out of books, old newspapers and the creative imagination. The result is superb, needless to say. But it should have been an agonizing book to write, and I'm pretty sure that it was not. The elation of contriving a trick piece of Jewish-European literature must have cathartized in advance the anguish of the subject-matter. The pity and terror, totally unpurged, are left to us.

Caprine Messiah

THAT this is a book* there can be no doubt (ah, how delightful it must have been to be Arnold Bennett, making and breaking reputations in the *Evening Standard* of the 'thirties). That it is a long book may easily be verified (742 pages, to my computation). It is by an American, and Americans take—which may have something to do with their heroic geographical horizons—to long books like herrings to the proverbial herring-pond. The necessity of reading the book is less apparent than with most books, especially those of

* *Giles Goat-Boy* by John Barth (Secker & Warburg, 1967).

less gargantuan dimensions, since its publishers have provided a very useful brochure entitled 'Blueprint for a Bestseller'. This contains a synopsis, a selection of gnomic laudations, and copies of American reviews. In spite of all temptations to take the easy way, I have read the book. Indeed, I have read a great deal of the book. It is unquestionably by an author.

When *The Sot-Weed Factor* appeared in Britain, reviewers were wary of committing themselves, especially when they had not found time to wade through its immense spoof history of early Maryland to the exhausting finish. A Rabelaisian book, not only in its rank humour but also in its outrageously perverted erudition, it seemed to many, including myself (who briefly noticed it first and then, during an enforced retirement from journalism, read it for pleasure), to represent one direction the novel might take in order to progress or stay alive, which is the same thing. It followed Sterne in mocking not only its subject-matter but itself. It took an existential approach, assuming that the novel-form was dead and then seeing what could be constructed out of the ruins. *Giles Goat-Boy*—Barth's fourth novel but second to be published here—seems to imply that now the form must revert to its mixed origins and mock even those. The book is allegory, parody, didactic treatise, fable, religious codex, and the taking of it seriously involves the taking of it unseriously.

You need a kind of eighteenth-century parsonage leisure, appropriate for a book that breathes Swift, Sterne and Cervantesque picaresque. Before you begin the story, you have to read a series of fake publisher's readers' reports on the book itself (ironic frame, like that of *Don Quixote*). Then you dive into all too intelligible allegory. George has been brought up among goats by a Professor Spielman who, out of love with the world with its suicidal perversions of pure science, has become a tragophile, believing that 'der goats is humaner than der men, and der men is goatisher than der goats'. Equipped with a salvatory basic animality, George goes to New Tammany College to learn to be human. Tammany College is the most important establishment on West Campus, which is in rivalry with East Campus. There have been terrible riots, but none since Tammany invented WESCAC to destroy its enemies. All clear so far?

The university is a universe of deadly initials—WESCAC can EAT people (Electroencephalic Amplification and Transmission): it has been turned, because of the danger from EASCAC, into a computer-annihilator of immense power. George himself is a product of a Grand-tutorial Ideal: Laboratory Eugenical Selection; hence GILES. His striving towards becoming a messiah or Grand Tutor (like Moishe, Enos Enoch and T'ang—work those out at leisure) gives the book its plot. He rejects NOCTIS (Non-Conceptual Thinking and Intuitional Synthesis), even science itself, and—we have to have a parody, full-length, of *Oedipus Rex* to make the point—the Panglossianism of the Chancellor which, untragic, is also not tragoid. I don't think I need go on.

An impressive achievement, but one bred by the peculiar and happy circumstances of Great Contemporary American Writers, who have university sinecures and can spend (as Barth did) six years on a novel. If we want this sort of king-size artefact in Britain, we shall have to look, not to our professional writers, but to our dons. *Giles Goat-Boy*, like the architecture of a skyscraper, would be less impressive on a reduced scale. When Dr Johnson said of *Gulliver's Travels* that it was only a matter of thinking of little men and big men, sir, he threw out a seed of nasty truth along with the prejudiced fatuity. *Giles Goat-Boy* impresses more with its concept than (sheer mastery of length apart) its execution. And the concept is available to any clever undergraduate. On the other hand, self-criticism is built into the book, and any disparagement of mine has already been well taken care of. It makes much contemporary British fiction look very lightweight. Interpret that in what sense you like.

Poet and Pedant

FRANT is the first station out of Tunbridge Wells on the line to Hastings. I've never inquired into the etymology of the name.

All I know is that, should Vladimir Nabokov ever decide to leave his rare Swiss air and come to settle in England, Frant would be the only place for him. For, whatever Frant is in English, in Russian it means 'dandy'. Nabokov is, with the possible exception of Raymond Queneau, the last of the dandies of literature. What, in *Pale Fire*, looked to some like fashionable *avant-gardisme*, the deliberate fragmentation of a traditional form in the service of a new aesthetic concept, now appears much more old-fashioned: plot is a bourgeois vulgarity, like work; it's the words that count—the *mot juste* sitting like a Brummel cravat, locutions as rings, puns winking like Fabergé curiosities. I know it is customary to call the Nabokovian waywardness by the name of pedantry, but pedantry and dandyism are no more disparate than glamour and grammar (which ultimately are the same word), and when readers are repelled by the pedantry they should try converting that feeling into admiration of aristocratic chic.

Nabokov is one of the few living writers I honestly admire and would, had I the equipment, like to emulate. But his approach to English is essentially a foreign approach; he does not play cricket but chess; he doesn't appreciate any of the unwritten laws about rhetoric and reticence. He is ridden by cerebral passion, which is indecent. But he is yet another sad exemplification of the truth that literary English in this century has owed most to foreigners (which, of course, includes Irishmen and Americans). The special task of the English-writing Slav has been to remind us of the gorgeousness of our language—a gorgeousness repressed by puritans and pragmatists —and it is probably right to bracket Nabokov and Conrad. But whereas it was Conrad's vocation to be an English writer, Nabokov became the author of *Lolita* only by historical accident.

This accident is at the core of Nabokov's autobiography, *Speak, Memory,*★ which has just—March 1967—been reissued in a revised form. It first appeared in 1951, when it caused small stir: the *Lolita* case was to be the ironic launching-pad of a fame more general than was perhaps fitting, Nabokov being one of the most rarefied writers alive. On the other hand, this fame (and how mad it is to see all

★ Weidenfeld & Nicolson.

143

those paperbacks of *Pale Fire*—the ultimate in rarefaction—on Tunbridge Wells Station's bookstall) is a kind of historical justice. The new Russia drove out the Nabokovs, but even the coarsest reader in the West knows Vladimir's name, and how many Soviet writers have they heard of? *Speak, Memory* (which, typically, he wanted to call *Speak, Mnemosyne*) tells a bad tale of treachery and dispossession, but with not one grain of self-pity, with aristocratic *hauteur* rather, and a stoicism which defies the reader to suppose for one moment that he minds, or ever minded, the loss of an inheritance of a huge estate and two million dollars. His eye is keener than the axe's edge, but the courage is too inhuman for admiration, just as the mastery of an alien language is too inhuman, sometimes, for anything but admiration.

The whole glittering orchestra of words is put in the service of a remembered idyll which is bound to bring out the Jacobin in even the most reactionary of us. There was this great and wealthy family, close to the court, Vladimir's grandfather a Minister of Justice, and there were uncountable servants, English governesses, all the spoils of Bond Street spilling into a mansion where Russian was a remoter tongue than French or Italian. Vladimir chased butterflies all over Europe, and St Petersburg was a suburb of Paris or London or Cannes or Biarritz. The butterflies had to be broken; the big historical processes had to bring about what they did; dare one regret anything? Only, perhaps, the death of a liberalism that, anyway, could not survive in either Czarist or Soviet Russia. Nabokov's father was one of the great democrats, leader of that faction which tried to act as reasonable buffer between Czar and Bolshevists. Both sent him to prison; in exile he was assassinated. He combined a large soul with what can only be called stoic style; through the elaborate prose of the son a simple, adoring devotion shines out.

The young Nabokov took into his own exile all of his father's stoicism; he had to forge a new style of his own. But first a barrier of pride and scorn had to be erected, and the habits of uncharitable despication developed. One of the least likeable aspects of Nabokov's writing is the tendency to throw off a summary condemnation of some man or other concerned less with style than with soul—

Dostoievsky, for instance, or Balzac. Pushkin, for whom Nabokov has built a vast and beautiful monument in the four-volume *Eugene Onegin* apparatus, is perhaps impossibly exalted, but the ornamental pool and rococo statuary recall an external aristocratic butterfly summer; the soul is earnest and vulgar. Analyse the soul, as Freud did, and you will be called a quack. This is perhaps going too far.

The exterior life of Nabokov in exile must seem ungrateful and unedifying, but we can be charitable if Nabokov can't (not that he asks us to be). He got nothing out of Cambridge, except a degree gained through the self-confessed carelessness of turning in good papers, a maturer practice of lepidoptery, and a fair reputation as a goalkeeper. On the Continent he wrote nine novels in Russian for an audience of émigrés like himself; he married, but into the old in-grown world. Eventually he went to America and, as he is always telling us, pulled the whole engine to pieces and rebuilt it. It was hardly foreseeable that so exquisite and scholarly an artist should become America's greatest literary glory, but now it seems wholly just and inevitable. *Lolita* is the study of an obsession in which a European sensibility cultivated to a pitch of ultimate Oneginism slavers over American false innocence. For the first time in literature America is seen, as it were, absolutely. Henry James committed *il gran rifiuto* (so Maugham's Driffield puts it), turning his back on one of the most important processes of the age—the making of a new civilization; Nabokov restored the balance, bringing all of James's fineness of perception to the recording of America, but blessedly lacking his spinsterish scruples and quirky habits of over-qualification.

One can put it another way, noting that native American novelists can produce jumbo artefacts like Bruckner or Mahler symphonies but have shown little aptitude for the rococo concerto: they lack exquisiteness, they can show off like tycoons but not like dandies. Nabokov's works revel in cadenzas. The most memorable passage in the Cambridge chapter of his autobiography is totally irrelevant to the narrative substance:

So I would heap on more coals and help revive the flames by spreading a sheet of the London *Times* over the smoking black jaws of the fireplace, thus screening completely its open recess. A humming noise would start behind the taut paper, which would acquire the smoothness of drumskin and the beauty of luminous parchment. Presently, as the hum turned into a roar, an orange-coloured spot would appear in the middle of the sheet, and whatever patch of print happened to be there (for example, 'The League does not command a guinea or a gun,' or ' ... the revenges that Nemesis has had upon Allied hesitation and indecision in Eastern and Central Europe ... ') stood out with ominous clarity—until suddenly the orange spot burst. Then the flaming sheet, with the whirr of a liberated phoenix, would fly up the chimney to join the stars. It cost one a fine of twelve shillings if that firebird was observed.

That is typical Nabokov. Life is not the progress of the soul, and international politics serves only to draw the fire. Literature must concern itself with the meticulous observation of moments, rendered as cadenzas. But is it possible to create books in this way, or any word-structure at all larger than the brief lyric? Yes, if the structure of an obsession is laid down first. Butterflies can be caught, mounted, classified, described at length. Passion for a nymphet will draw together all the delirium-sharp notebook-jottings of America observed. John Shade's poem of 999 lines can be wrongheadedly annotated, with a pedantry that contains its own self-parody.

And there are those twin pastimes on black-and-white-squared diagrams—chess and crosswords. Nabokov made the first Russian crossword, and he devotes many pages to his exilic passion for chess problems ('Inspiration of a quasi-musical, quasi-poetical, or, to be quite exact, poetico-mathematical type, attends the process of thinking up a chess composition of that sort'). The ultimate *frant* literature moves like a chess game and has all the verbal ingenuity of a very highbrow crossword. But what of the soul? That was a commodity that could not be exported from Russia. And perhaps, anyway, it was always an overrated property, like money. Love is better, and intelligence, and erudition, and elegance, and pride.

6

Koestler's Danube

As a sixtieth birthday present, Arthur Koestler's works have been brought out in a uniform collection, very well printed and bound, though rather expensive, each volume headed or tailed with a hindsight comment from the author.* There is a kind of resolution of antinomies in the name given to the collection—the Danube Edition. To the British, who have been Mr Koestler's frightened audience since the late 1930s, the Danube means Strauss and *Goodbye Mr Chips*; to Mr Koestler it is a river that has written his early biography in Hungarian and German; it also symbolizes the God that Failed.

These three books—two novels and a volume of essays—belong to the end of the war and the period of Orwell's perceptive article on Koestler. Koestler frightened us not just because he brought in the freezing wind of totalitarian experience in Europe; he used his third language with as much confidence as Conrad; he virtually invented the 'political novel'; his intellectuality was ferocious, earnest, not just a donnish game. He humbled the British, who had taken neither ideas nor politics seriously; his gift to English literature was a horse's-mouth authenticity that no one would dream of looking into. And yet that phase of his career which these three books celebrate has a strong smell of failure about it. He has, I think, recognized that a novel like *The Gladiators* and an essay like *The Yogi and the Commissar* are too much rooted in a stage of personal development to strike with that perennially fresh surprise we expect from a true work of art or a piece of genuinely creative thinking. We who were never

* *Thieves in the Night; The Gladiators; The Yogi and the Commissar* (Hutchinson, 1965).

147

European Communists have missed the prisons and the concentration camps (we apologize to Mr Koestler for that), but we have also been unshaken by the failure of a Utopian revolution. Mr Koestler quotes Pascal almost with surprise: 'Man is neither angel nor brute, and his misery is that he who would act the angel acts the brute.' If one had never had a Utopian faith one could never be disappointed, nor, in *The Gladiators*, could one see what all the fuss was about.

Thieves in the Night is about the Jewish settlement of Ezra's Tower. Its theme, Koestler reminds us, is 'the ethics of survival. If power corrupts, the reverse is also true: persecution corrupts the victim, though perhaps in subtler and more tragic ways'. The book is not a mere morality illustrating this; it is a genuine novel smelling of a sharply observed Palestine, the characters totally credible, and 'the peaceful growth of Ezra's Tower', rising above the terrorism and savagery and injustice, the sort of symbol a novelist thanks God for. But *The Gladiators*, which is about Spartacus and his slaves' revolt, fails for several reasons. Koestler is not sure whether he wants to bring ancient history to life or, by using a technique of alienation, merely allegorize the dilemma of the modern revolutionary leader. The slaves' City of the Sun is, if we want a lesson on ends and means, not so compelling as Animal Farm (though we must remember that Orwell had the advantage of having read Koestler): it is not so simple, not sufficiently a blackboard drawing. At the same time it is not sufficiently a work of the historical imagination. And Spartacus, if we are to take him as a modern revolutionary, is incredibly unaware of the dilemma of power. Can we, then, take him as an ancient liberator of the oppressed, fired by an Essene vision? If we can, the allegory collapses.

Very occasionally in his novels (*Darkness at Noon* is the obvious, and magnificent, example), Koestler achieves a balance of the literary and the didactic, which, like Plato's horses, want to pull different ways. In his essays one is sometimes fascinated by a self-defeating desire to use images to clarify an intellectual thesis: as in a metaphysical poem, the image takes over; the conceit has to be worked out to the limit in a compulsive literary lust: the lesson is choked in the foliage. Nothing is more admirable, in *The Yogi and the Com-*

missar, than the presentation of the Commissar (who believes in Change from Without) at the infra-red end of the spectrum, and the Yogi (who 'believes that the End is unpredictable and that the Means alone count') at the ultra-violet. But the image is deployed with such powerful consistency that our shock at reading about 'pendular changes in the mass-psychological spectrum' is very different from our cringing at other people's mixed metaphors.

One of the chilling things about Koestler's war-time writings, untempered by twenty-odd years of lagging, is his apparent acquiescence in 'the tragic barrier which separates the progressive intellectual from the educated working class'. To a man in the 'Thoughtful Corporal belt' (unpromotable) he says: 'Read for pleasure, man, and don't both about Péguy and *Finnegans Wake!*' The naivety accords ill with the polymathy, and if we find Orwell, also a highbrow, more sympathetic, it has nothing to do with the Danube being a long way from the Thames. Still, Koestler has done us a lot of good. When the black-out in London was relaxed and he let out his light to the dark street, a little girl of seven, brought up to regard light-spilling as a sin, sobbed: 'Uncle Arthur does not believe in God.' Such Yogi-ethical outbursts are the price he must pay for being a light-bringer.

Treasures and Fetters

OLIVIA MANNING has inveighed against the stupid people who say that they 'never read women novelists'—as though male and female fiction constituted two distinct and recognizable categories of art. All novelists, says Miss Manning, are really a sort of a blooming hermaphrodite. I would like to agree all the way there, but I can't. Apart from the practical utility of the division, it's valid as the Taoist *yin-yang* duality is valid: it roughly works. The woman novelist comes well out of the division, though—as Lilith rather than Eve; forget the big Tolstoyan or Joycean architectonic gift, and you will find that women have a better natural fictional equipment than men. They notice surfaces, which is what novels are made out of; they have a phenomenal semantic range when it comes to dealing with texture, colour and nuance of speech; being the primal order of creation, they *enclose* men and see through them. Their faults are the faults a man finds in a woman: they chatter, they are deficient in moral values, they are too empirical, they fall in love with the accident and miss the essence, they are distracted by a golden apple. Naturally, there is a way of looking at these vices which turns them into virtues.

When Elizabeth Bowen's name is mentioned, other women novelists are mentioned too—often ineptly: Mr Pritchett's comparison with Virginia Woolf won't really work. To fit Miss Bowen into a group is one thing, to find her origins quite another. Having subscribed above to the big male-female opposition, I am not really reneging if I bring in Henry James as her true progenitor. James is the unique example of a writer who (and there is no Western substitute for these terms) allowed the *yin* principle to overcome his *yang* when he settled in Europe. Those endlessly qualified sentences with their spinsterish scruples were a bequest not only to Edith Wharton, but to a whole line of woman novelists, of whom Miss Bowen is one:

> He more than looked, he continued to look, he stared at this person, so disingenuous, of a so impassioning wish to be in the right. So strong had become his habit of mind that he saw no behaviour as being apart from motive, and any motive as worth examining twice.

> Deep and beautiful on this her smile came back, and with the effect of making him hear what he had said just as she had heard it. He easily enough felt that it gave him away, but what in truth had everything done but that? It had been all very well to think at moments that he was holding her nose down and that he had coerced her: what had he by this time done but let her practically see that he accepted their relation?

One of these passages is from *The Ambassadors*, the other from *The Heat of the Day*.

The involutions of James's prose, the torturings of natural syntax to avoid the cliché, the enthroning of the cliché where the cliché is not even enlightening—all this was James's substitute for poetry. But, paradoxically, if there had been more poetry in him there would have been a less massive image of a civilization. In Miss Bowen there is a great deal of poetry: it is what lightens her involutions, and if it sometimes drops to mere fancy (the French clock 'busy ... on the chimneypiece, amid idling china'), that is appropriate—it serves her concern with 'atmosphere'. Where James articulates a whole culture, Miss Bowen conserves a particular place at a particular time; this is a feminine gift. The theme of *The Death of the Heart* is the massacre of innocence, but what we remember best is the scenery through which young, betrayed Portia passes—frosty Regent's Park, dingy hotel furniture. *The House in Paris* is really about its eponym; *A World of Love*, in which the real protagonist is the sensibility of the author, seems to be nearly all 'atmosphere'.

It is the 'atmosphere' of war-time London, encapsulated so miraculously in *The Heat of the Day*, that survives the strange story of Stella Rodney and her lover. I've always found him hard to take—the man who, discharged wounded from the services, becomes a traitor; Stella can't swallow the treason either, but her incredulity is of a different order from the reader's. There's a parallelism in *The Heat of the Day* which is perhaps typical of all Miss Bowen's work—a world of intense and highly credible detail which conjures one's own sensuous and emotional memories, though so heightened that it feels like a re-living (remember Louie, who 'had, with regard to time, an infant lack of stereoscopic vision; she saw then and now on the same plane; they were the same'); a world of people who are never quite real and often unmemorable. A miracle makes the parallels meet: while the weaving of atmosphere and the accumulation of detail proceed, the illusion of solid existence holds. But, behind the whirl of phenomena, there doesn't seem to be much of a thing-in-itself.

*The Little Girls** is Miss Bowen's first novel for nine years. She hasn't, apparently, been using those nine years to plot new departures, though her observation of the contemporary world is, as we

* Cape, 1964.

expect, very sharp: 'atmosphere' is still her business. But the contemporary world is only part of it. Three women of sixty—Dinah, Clare and Sheila—were schoolgirls together in 1914 (Dicey, Mumbo and Sheikie). Dinah, an ageless beauty, summons her friends from the past by means of newspaper advertisements. A great burier-for-posterity, she wants to know what's happened to a box the three of them buried at St Agatha's all those years ago ('We are dead, and all our fathers and mothers. You who find this, Take Care. These are our valuable treasures, and our fetters ... Here are Bones, too ... '). This gives Miss Bowen an opportunity for a delicious recall and a fine scenic set-piece on what's become of the school's site now:

> ... The revenants stood back, backs to the balustrade—above them, ten or a dozen nice-looking houses, spaced out over the hill's face, harmlessly contemplated the Channel; garages, their doors painted pastel colours, sat on ledges surrounded by landscape gardening ... In general, the gardens were veiled in the thinly dusky yellows and coppers and bronzy purples of mid-autumn ...

And so on. This, I think, is authentic flavoursome Bowen.

The box, when they find it, is empty. The warning comes too late for the three, but not for the reader; the story is, in fact, an easy morality: 'Gently dip, but not too deep.' The intensities of a childhood relationship are invoked in middle age at one's own peril. Never choose to call back past time: choice, anyway, is dangerous. 'We were entrusted to one another, in the days which mattered, Clare thought. Entrusted to one another by chance, not choice. Chance, and its agents time and place. Chance is better than choice; it is more lordly. In its carelessness it is more lordly. Chance is God, choice is man.' Moral profundities swirl about, among the aubergine jerseys and the coloured scenery-motifs on cups and bowls. They are of much the same order as the discrete elements of the sensuous world that Miss Bowen proves, so lavishly, to exist. What James made terrifying is here rather charming.

Confronted by so much technical brilliance, even when not awed by reputation, the reader may well blame himself for being, as he thinks, insufficiently moved. But what Miss Bowen has achieved is less the peopling of time and place with entities which, like Emma Bovary or Charlus or Bloom, have a human validity which bursts their literary bonds, than the furnishing of time and place with the conditions which might enable such beings to exist—and this means not only 'atmosphere' but the texture of skin and hair and bags under the eyes. There are times when, seduced by the miraculously caught cadences of feminine speech, one wakes to the shock of thinking it all a contrivance—a device for moving spheres (if one may use the old metaphysical imagery) which in themselves have no intelligence. Perhaps all this is going too far: the book is, after all, a comedy, a pleasant warning against the dangers of nostalgia, a demonstration of the allure which informs a sensuous world uncoloured by nostalgia. It is a wonderful artefact, a triumphant Female Novel by one whose gifts release her from the more male duty of being just among the Just, among the Filthy filthy too, and of suffering dully all the wrongs of Man.

What Now in the Novel?

'THE future of the novel? Poor old novel, it's in a rather dirty, messy tight corner. And it's either got to get over the wall or knock a hole through it. In other words, it's got to grow up.' That was D. H. Lawrence in 1923. He was not, of course, thinking of his own novels, but those of 'Mr Joyce, Miss Richardson and M. Proust', as well as—Lawrence always being a great man for the whole hog— 'the *Sheiks* and *Babbitts* and Zane Grey novels'. Demonic novelists are ill-qualified to deliver judgments on the fiction of their own day, since the sun of their personal aspirations must always be in their eyes. But I sometimes think that a resurrected Lawrence might crow with pleasure at the way the British novel has gone in the last ten years. The pale Galilean has conquered; the world has grown grey with his breath. We have got over that infantile concentration on streams of consciousness; we don't worry overmuch about form; we take the provincial lower orders seriously; we clear people's minds of cant; we try to make new myths out of the deep dark bitter belly-tension of man and woman, man and man; we go abroad.

We? I am somewhere in this decade of hope, since I took seriously to novel-writing in Malaya in 1955. New themes seemed to be coming into British fiction then. The old colonies were seeking self-determination, and Britain herself was one of the old colonies. The Labour régime of the post-war period held back the street fights and drawing-room belches of revolt but, after the Festival of Britain and the end of meat-rationing, it was seen that there was plenty to revolt against and that—thank God—the new writers were not, after all, to be the voices of the Establishment. If the classless society had come into being, the subject of hypergamy (i.e., bedding a superior woman) could never have been exploited by Kingsley Amis and John Braine. The social order was changing, but the changes were to be minimal—no more academic cant, no more cultural pretentiousness (whether filthy Mozart or imbecilic hey-nonny-nonny), regional accents for all who wanted them, more liberal opening-hours, a sufficiency of beer and fags, booby-traps or a damn good crack on the chops for the enemy, the enemy's woman abducted.

It was a soldier's dream over sausage and chips in the Naafi, but it was a dream that partly came true. The so-called 'redbrick' novelists (who had all been to Oxford) prophesied the end of the hegemony of the East Midlands and sponsored the Albert Finney accent, the jazz columns in class journals, even *The Times* article on the art of the Beatles. Bliss was it in that dawn—*Lucky Jim, Hurry On Down*: they strike one's senses today with a lavender nostalgia. The question is: what can their authors do now? *One Fat Englishman* has a punching randy hedonist who is a kind of consummation of Jim Dixon. The fags have become cigars and the pints of bitter New York State champagne, but physical self-indulgence, as well as schoolboy vindictiveness, becomes disgusting when it ceases to be a dream. *One Fat Englishman* is a brilliant exercise on the medieval theme of the Seven Deadly Sins.

Is that the way the novel is going to go—all moral? William Golding has only one subject—the primacy of evil—and his power derives from its non-sectarian presentation. Evil is not just a Church doctrine. It grows wild; it is, as the hero of *Free Fall* reminds us, as immediate as gamboge or the taste of potatoes. Perhaps novelists neglect evil (as opposed to wrong) at their peril. Iris Murdoch once seemed concerned (in *The Bell*) with an eschatological subject, but she took the dangerous way of making her own myths. *A Severed Head* drains both the comedy and the morality out of a Restoration dance of all the sexes; the result is a ghostly paradigm with no spume of life playing on it. Her recent attempts to put back heart into her art have produced a kind of raw melodrama tricked out with rare stylistic jewels. But, if the time for lashing at society is over, and we lack Golding's concern with the moral profundities, what has the novelist to write about? Our senior novelists are morphologists, recorders—often in the serial form of the *roman fleuve*—of changing social patterns: I think particularly of C. P. Snow's *Strangers and Brothers*, Anthony Powell's *Music of Time*, the war trilogy of Evelyn Waugh and the shamefully disregarded sequence of Henry Williamson. But how about the junior novelists?

I think there is evidence among these already of a dissatisfaction with the subject-matter inherited from the 'fifties. The big social themes were set then and have hardly changed—the acquisitive rat-race, apartheid, youth's need of a voice, the splendours and miseries of post-war provincial life, the jazz-man as hero, the revelations of urban puberty, and so on. The new wave from France has douched us; Lawrence must have groaned in his sleep ('And, oh, Lord, if I liked to watch myself closely enough, if I liked to analyse my feelings minutely, as I unbutton my gloves, instead of saying crudely I unbuttoned them, then I could go on to a million pages instead of a thousand'). If you cannot make your theme out of the flux of society itself, then you will find the day-to-day details of social change too ephemeral. I feel that we are already swinging to a new interest in form rather than content, and that that is where the significant pattern of the next ten years must lie. Of writers in English, surely Vladimir Nabokov must seem to present the sharpest future auguries

—not in *Lolita*, but in *Pale Fire*. We shall have to cease to feed on our native Lawrentian fat and look abroad again.

Perhaps the young novelists who are growing up now will be the more encouraged to experiment with form and language as they see that there is little future hope for the novel's competing with the other mass media. Instead of trying to become best-sellers, they may be driven back to the consolations of art. This does not mean mere verbalizing, composing a novel in the shape of an encyclopedia or *apparatus criticus*, or going back to the macaronics of *Tristram Shandy*. It means expending the resources of literature in an attempt to find out more about the whole human complex, the roots on which societies are built. Only through the exploration of language can the personality be coaxed into yielding a few more of its secrets. The novel, said Lawrence, has 'got to break its way through, like a hole in the wall ... then, of course, you're horrified when you see a new glaring hole in what was your cosy wall. You're horrified. You back away from the cold stream of fresh air as if it were killing you. But gradually, first one and then another of the sheep filters through the gap and finds a new world outside.' Well, we're waiting to be horrified.

7

In Search of Shakespeare the Man

ANECDOTES are no substitute for biography. They can even be terribly misleading. Take the following, for instance—an entry in the diary of John Manningham, student at the Middle Temple:

> 13 March 1601–2 ... Upon a time when Burbage played Richard III, there was a citizen grew so far in liking with him, that before she went from the play she appointed him to come that night unto her by the name of Richard the Third. Shakespeare, overhearing their conclusion, went before, was entertained and at his game ere Burbage came. Then, message being brought that Richard III was at the door, Shakespeare caused return to be made that William the Conqueror was before Richard the Third.

One would probably be very wrong to deduce from this that Shakespeare was a nimble satyr, quicker into adulterous beds than bulkier Dick Burbage (he was playing Hamlet about this time, fat and scant of breath). One would be right, though, to conclude that Shakespeare was well known in the Inns of Court as a kind of film-star myth, somebody to tell dirty stories about. In my own school-days there were rather more scabrous jokes about Mae West and Hore-Belisha; in the 'twenties there was a rhyme asking if one would like to sin with Elinor Glyn on a tiger-skin. Such little libels were good-hearted. Sex was in Mae West's films, Elinor Glyn's books, Belisha beacons. Sex of the same guiltless order was in Shakespeare's plays—those of the 'sweet Master Shakespeare' period. It was thus legitimate to employ sexual references to symbolize admiration.

The image of Shakespeare the man that comes to the fanciful

researcher—somebody who, like myself, wants to write a novel about him rather than a Rowse-type tome—is not at all like the witty lecher of Manningham's anecdote. Where sexual transports are celebrated in his work, there is very little of the purity of lust: 'love' tends to mean what it means today, not what it means in Beaumont and Fletcher ('Lady, will you love and lie with me?'). In the 'dark' works he was engaged on when Manningham made his diary entry, sex is already becoming unclean. Shakespeare is our greatest thunderer against the snares of physical passion (I am thinking of the Lear speech about the fat rump and the potato finger); in the sonnet beginning 'The expense of spirit in a waste of shame', with the dog-panting of 'had, having, and in quest to have', revulsion is hardly tamer—it is merely checked by the exigencies of the form. In the final plays, with the achievement of a sort of purgation of fleshly attachments, the ideal relationship between a man and a woman is the father-daughter one.

In trying to build up a picture of Shakespeare in his dealings with women, the woman we turn to first is his own wife. I cannot see their ménage as a very happy one, nor this marriage as being of Shakespeare's own choice. He was a boy, she a mature woman; the first child was born six months after the wedding. The inescapable image of Shakespeare the negative, the passive, the put-upon—this begins here. He perhaps, with a certain irony, idealizes a situation in which she was the wooer, he the wooed, by writing *Venus and Adonis* and dedicating it to the lord with whom he is to have a perfumed, Hellenic, essentially metropolitan homosexual relationship. The lengthy pleading of the goddess is ominously eloquent, the shrewishness of Adriana and Katherina, the litigiousness of Portia in the making. Adonis escapes a torrent of physical love and chatter by dying in earnest, not in sex; Shakespeare, too decent to evade his obligations, marries but eventually leaves Stratford. He leaves not only a wife, armed with a second-best bed from Shottery (her father's bequest to her?), but also three children—the first-born Susanna and the twins Hamnet and Judith.

When variorum editions peel away at the words of the texts, like so many large potatoes, it is forgivable for the fanciful inquirer to find significance in these children's names: Susanna—a pure girl in a bedroom full of adult lust; Judith—decapitatrix of Holofernes, Nebuchadnezzar's general (Nebuchadnezzar can be the male organ). Holofernes is also Gargantua's tutor in Rabelais, hence the pedant of *Love's Labour's Lost*. I associate him less with John Florio (Southampton's secretary) than with Shakespeare himself—word-boy, reader in a non-literary home, perhaps even schoolmaster. After Judith's birth no more reading (there is the need to work hard to keep a large family) and no more begetting of children. The initials of the three he has are those of Noah's sons—his own son is called Ham. Shakespeare sees himself ironically as Noah, drunken patriarch riding a sea of troubles. Later, when he has made money and comes home from London to see his only son buried, there is no thought of begetting another son to carry on a name which will soon be confirmed as a gentle one, and *non sanz droict*. I smell out adultery, his wife's not his own, adultery committed on that second-best bed. The form of marriage continues to the point where Anne lays pennies on his eyes, but it has no further physical meaning. And, after the laying on of the pennies, Anne gets back the second-best bed she herself brought as her dowry. It is a final irony.

The life of Shakespeare then, from beginning of manhood to the reading of the will, may be thought of as being enclosed in a protective caul of irony. The gentle and sweet character we hear of—open and honest, attached to a 'facetious' wit and a fluent pen (too fluent, said Ben Jonson: '*sufflaminandus erat*')—sounds like a deliberate creation, a disarming mask put on to prevent engagement with the world. For the world cannot easily grapple with the smooth and pliant—the man who smiles but refuses to come out on a debauch 'because he is in pain' or, smiling still, will not lend money out of friendship, only at high interest. Shakespeare's main aim was, I think, to make money, not to bequeath deathless plays to posterity. Ben Jonson was much concerned with the redaction of his 'Works'; Shakespeare left the collection and publishing of his own to Heming and Condell, a posthumous job. Making money was a means of becoming a gentleman, and to be a gentleman with a fine cloak and a coat of arms was a means of twofold redemption—a bad marriage and an improvident father were aloes to be sweetened by the purchase of New Place, former home of Clopton, prototype of Stratfordians who leave home to make good in London.

If your imaginative gifts are great you can leave the living of life to your servants. Oscar Wilde said that major poets are duller people than minor ones—to meet, that is: the major poets are fulfilled and sleepy; the minor ones try to enact the poetry they cannot write. I feel that Shakespeare was both shy of involvement in the world (there is a lot of blushing in his plays) through natural timidity and unwilling to act in it because it was best, from the point of view of his art, to be a quiet observer. But he rushes at the world with his sword when he wants money and advancement. Hence the fervent embracing of the golden chance of securing the Earl of Southampton as his patron. But he is human, and the postures of love and devotion are perhaps suddenly and shockingly revealed as no mere postures. Twice, I should think, Shakespeare lost his heart when he was least willing to lose it—once to a golden-haired boy with a vulpine face, once to a dark woman. Both attachments ended wretchedly. Shakespeare was not able to meet Southampton on equal terms, despite the gentling of his condition with a grant of arms; nor could he follow the Essex faction, in which Southampton was a big name, when it came to the enacting of treason. As for the dark lady—perhaps the revulsion was less out of *tristitia* than out of disgust and despair at finding himself stricken by the *morbus Gallicus*, love's disease—named by Fracastoro for the pretty shepherd Syphilis. The plays of the 'dark' period that begins in 1599 draw some of their imagery from sickness, sickness suffered not just observed. The general theme of the tragedies is the breaking of order—as expressed in the state (Elizabeth feeble and the succession unsecured, treasonmongers like Essex), marriage (his own?), the body itself.

I need not, like Sellar and Yeatman, warn scholars of the unsoundness of all that. But the image of a man not well able to involve himself in the dirty world persists despite the lack of firm evidence. Money, though, is a different matter; money is not dirty as love and friendship may turn out to be. Ultimately there is nothing there. Disturb the bones to find what spirit animated them, and the curse comes upon you—you are face to face with emptiness. That is why any man's image of Shakespeare both works and does not work, and that is why it is best to stop playing these games of reconstruction from a few bones and get down to reading the plays again. So, anyway, reason tells us. But is there one person living who, given the choice between discovering a lost play of Shakespeare's and a laundry list of Will's, would not plump for the dirty washing every time?

Dr Rowstus

I MAKE no apology for not having read Dr Rowse's book on Shakespeare. When it came out I was struggling away at my own contribution to the quatercentenary celebrations—the novel called *Nothing Like the Sun.* I understood from the reviews that Dr Rowse had done something original and important: he had brought the hard disciplines of the historian to a subject traditionally monopolized by fanciful critics and uninformed *belles-lettristes.* This I did not want. I had learned by heart a calendar of Elizabethan events, compiled from the works of Prof. G. B. Harrison, and I did not wish these to be disturbed by any new findings. I wanted Mr W. H. to be Wriothesly, Harry, Earl of Southampton, and the Rival Poet of the Sonnets to be George Chapman—dull and orthodox identifications which should be a foil to daring speculations about the Dark Lady. I gathered that Dr Rowse had more or less proved that Mr W. H. was Sir William Harvey, and that the Rival Poet was Christopher Marlowe. About the Dark Lady he had, thank God, established nothing. The time for reading his Shakespeare book was, I suppose, when my own page proofs were past tinkering with, but by then I was temporarily sick of the subject.

And now here is Dr Rowse on Christopher Marlowe,* a poet

* *Christopher Marlowe: His Life and Work* (Harper & Row, Macmillan, 1964).

who has haunted me for thirty years and, since I do not propose writing a novel on him (the celebratory occasion has passed, anyway), is not likely to make me sick. And presumably, so I thought, the technique so admired in Dr Rowse's Shakespeare book would, whetted by extravagant praise, be even sharper here; I would be absolved from reading the earlier study. This sounds cynical, but Dr Rowse has that effect on me.

To be honest, I did once write something about Marlowe—in Manchester, England, 1940, when the bombs were dropping. It was a graduation thesis, but my own feelings about the poet were stronger, more personal than can easily be understood in a context of mere academic study. I was a renegade Catholic who mocked at hell but was still secretly scared of it, especially as it might come any night now. I felt, despite all the biographical evidence, that Marlowe himself might be such a man, his blasphemies and beery jags the true voice of imperfect emancipation. I regarded him as a sort of proto-Joyce, and this perhaps made me a sort of proto-Harry Levin. The peculiar urgencies of 1940 (how about repenting before the bombs drop on this typewriter?) dragged Dr Faustus out of the Elizabethan theatre and dumped him in bed beside me, under a roof which might suddenly crash down like the vengeance of God (disguised as the vindictiveness of the Nazis). Would he, when the air-raid sirens sounded, feel like saying: 'Come, I think hell's a fable'? Hell was very near, not 'xxiv yeares' off: the devils, with fireworks, had the trap door ready open.

This sense of intimacy with a great Marlovian theme engendered, even then, a sort of contempt for the academic text choppers. And, though Rowse is not one of those, I am out of sympathy with a scholar who talks about the Reformation's sweeping away the 'junk' of medieval devotionalism from Canterbury (Marlowe's birthplace) and describes the cathedral itself as a 'veritable holy factory manufacturing grace'. I have a feeling that the Rowse eschatology does not contain a hell and is perhaps even impatient with the concept of a soul. He seems closer to Henslowe than to Marlowe, eager to make inventories of copes and chasubles and chalices, but not so ready to tell us what it may have been like to be a young Renaissance intellectual unable totally to free himself from the grip of what Dr Rowse might call medieval superstition.

Dr Rowse, in fact, subscribes to the romantic view of Marlowe— 'with mouth of gold and morning in his eyes'. To me, Marlowe's fascination lies in the fact that he stands at the crossroads—Janus-faced, with morning in one set of eyes but night in the other. The character of Hamlet has a cognate fascination. Here is a young man caught between the opposed forces of medievalism (which has ghosts and hell in it) and the rationalism of Montaigne and Machiavelli. Thus caught, he is unable to act: his fires are ineffectual. Marlowe *can* act, but most of his action is bluster. His poetic gift turns verbal bluster into genuine rhetoric (this art had not yet been debased by demagogues); his intellectual sympathies draw him to glorification of the world of Hamlet's stepfather—a *Realpolitik* which, however, finds its myths and images in a rediscovered Golden Age.

Looking at *Tamburlaine*, *The Jew of Malta* and *Dr Faustus*, we see a kind of Renaissance trilogy so neat that we cannot help thinking that Marlowe is working to a deliberate plan, the delineation of three kinds of power seeking. First, the Scythian shepherd-con-queror wants to take over the rule of the world, daring God out of His Heaven in the process. Next, Barabas the Jew looks for power through wealth. Finally, Faustus wants the ultimate power—not over men's minds and bodies but over time, space and causality. Tyranny, wealth, knowledge, all unbounded, are—severally or conjoined—the big Renaissance dreams, and Marlowe creates super-human poetic symbols out of idealized Renaissance dreamers.

But the dreams have a flaw in them. Divine Zenocrate has to die, and so does semi-divine Tamburlaine. The divinity is bluster: both are, after all, only too mortal. Barabas hates and is hated by the Maltese Christians: he falls cursing into a vat of boiling oil prepared for his enemies. Faustus finds that God is not mocked. He may wish to confound hell in Elysium ('his ghost be with the old philo-sophers'), but the medieval hell, with its Bosch or Dürer furnishings, exists, however Dr Rowse or Dr Faustus may rationalize it away. In the terrible final scene, the Pythagorean doctrine of metempsy-chosis is a mere comfortable tavern speculation: the reality is Christ's blood streaming in the firmament, and the cry of the Roman lover in bed with his mistress—'*Lente, lente currite, noctis equi*'—finds its true meaning in the shriek of a damned soul pushing off midnight with his bare hands. In other words, Marlowe's Renaissance attitudes are very heavily qualified by older, less intellectual convictions.

And yet the qualifying is not all one-sided. William Empson, in 1930, pointed out that the negatives in 'Ugly hell, gape not. Come not, Lucifer' are very weakly placed, so that a positive desire for hell to gape and Lucifer to come is implied: the Renaissance hunger for ultimate knowledge is here even at the end, and the scholar, as the first flames lick him, thinks to put everything right by shouting: 'I'll burn my books!' In other words, blame everything on the desire for knowledge: go back to prelapsarian innocence, before the *felix culpa* which brought a Redeemer, and then there will be no hell. The subtlety of all this is the concern of the mere literary speculator: Dr Rowse, being a historian, is above it.

The greater part of this book is a literary commentary on Marlowe's plays and poems and, since we can buy better commentaries in other, more specialized shops, Dr Rowse may be said to be wasting our time, if not his. But it is hard to see what else he can do if he wants to produce more than a mere pamphlet on Marlowe. He promises us an account of the poet's life, but he cannot do better than John Bakeless nor, for that matter, Dr William Urry, whose biographical revelations in *The Times Literary Supplement* of February 13th, 1964, are honoured by a briefer reference than they merit. All we get is a chapter on Canterbury and one on Cambridge, which will do for any Elizabethan born in one place and educated in the other. Then, with a kind of relief at finding something solid to discuss, Dr Rowse gives us the works.

For a scholar, Dr Rowse asks us to take rather too much on trust. For instance, we have to assume with him that *Dido, Queen of Carthage* is prentice stuff, perhaps interesting for its Jupiter-Ganymede prologue (Marlowe as pederast) but for little else. Eliot thinks differently. Admitting that *Dido* is 'a hurried play, perhaps done to order with the *Aeneid* in front of him', he yet sees in it a 'newer style', the development of a technique of near-caricature altogether idiosyncratic, hardly imitable even by Shakespeare:

And after him, his band of Myrmidons,
With balls of wild-fire in their murdering paws ...
At last, the soldiers pull'd her by the heels,
And swung her howling in the empty air ...

What at first looks like pleasure in violence here (as also in *The Massacre at Paris* and *The Jew of Malta*) resolves, on closer examination, into a kind of comic diminishing of man, most un-Renaissance-like. A fair analogy would be the harmless lethal tricks of some film cartoons, the use of violence for a laugh. Barabas starts as a heroic capitalist, with his infinite riches in a little room, but ends in his scalding vat—'Die, life! fly, soul! tongue, curse thy fill, and die!'—as a cartoon animal, with neither nerves nor soul. The pricking of the heroic, the cutting down of Renaissance man to medieval size, is as Marlovian as the great Tamburlaine inflations, but it was something that had to be learned. If Dr Rowse wants us to believe that *Dido* is tyro work, he must use the historian's privilege of feeding us a date or so.

At one of the points where literature and biography meet, Dr Rowse both disappoints and reassures. I refer to his chapter on the Rival Poet of Shakespeare's Sonnets where, by antedating the composition of these and adducing comparisons from the work of both poets, he tries to establish that Shakespeare's rival was also his predecessor in greatness. His evidence is insufficient: thus he disappoints. He reassures by this same insufficiency: there is no need for us, after all, to pull down the statue of George Chapman. The 'affable familiar ghost' of Shakespeare's key sonnet refers us, says Dr Rowse, to Mephistophilis: Marlowe is his own Faustus. But one has only to read the dedication of Chapman's *The Shadow of Night* (published the year after Marlowe's murder) to see that Shakespeare was not getting at Marlowe (whom, anyway, he loved and admired; how otherwise explain that gratuitous reference in *As You Like It*?). Chapman believed that a nocturnal spirit (nightly gulling him with intelligence, says Shakespeare) fed his inspiration; there is even a reference to a 'heavenly familiar'. And, in this very poem of Chapman's, there's a nasty dig at the *'Pocula Castalia'* of the dedication to *Venus and Adonis*: Chapman mentions 'flesh-confounded souls that cannot bear the full Castalian bowels', meaning Shakespeare. I think Dr Rowse will have to try harder before he can convince us of an enmity, however good humoured, between Shakespeare and his two-month-elder master.

If Dr Rowse is writing a popular book, a general introduction to Marlowe (and it is at least charitable to take his book this way), he would do well to draw our interest by making our flesh creep— Marlowe is an eminently fine subject for that. There has been some scholarly speculation, of fascinating import, about Marlowe's death, but Dr Rowse gives us the coroner's facts and no more. If he wants us to know more about the impact of *Dr Faustus* on popular audiences, he could at least refer us to the Bakeless biography. He tells us about the appearance of 'one devell too many' during the performance at Exeter. A more interesting story is about the 'apparition of the Devel' on the stage at Dulwich, which so worked on the fancy of Alleyn, who was playing Faustus, that 'he made a Vow, which he perform'd at this place'. The vow was to build a college at Dulwich, and it is there to this day—Alleyn's College of God's Gift, which I pass every time I travel by road from Sussex to Chiswick. Marlowe tapped, in this play at least, a great popular artery of belief (or, if Dr Rowse prefers, superstition). It is the chemical action set up in Marlowe's imagination by the clash of the old and the new that makes him unique—not greater than Shakespeare, but different.

I think Marlowe's quatercentenary, cast into deep shadow by that of his longer-lived junior, called for a better book than Dr Rowse's— something less opinionated, more sensitive, more—in a word— Marlovian. Will we have to wait till 1993, quatercentenary of a dagger through the frontal lobes and a swearing death, before we get it?

The Milton Revolution

THE twentieth century debunking of John Milton has, because of the critical energy entailed in his reinstatement, done nothing but good to his reputation. Two centuries of official Christian piety had to genuflect before a poet who wrote an epic to justify the ways of God to man, but it was not obligatory to enjoy reading him: a sort of Sabbath duty was enough. When Middleton Murry, Pound, Herbert Read, Eliot and Leavis removed his bust from the embrasure it had traditionally shared with Dante and Shakespeare, they were affirming two doctrines which may still be regarded as salutary — first, that we should never be bemused by subject-matter, however elevated; second, that a dead poet's claim to our devotion rests, in some measure, on his power to help us solve our own problems of thought and language. To read and understand Milton, they argued, involved the rigidities of historical perspective. Shakespeare, Donne, Marvell, Chapman did not require us to put on period costume: the width and unity of their sensibility, also their concern with language as a living current and not as a special stylized diction, were in tune with our own (or should one say Eliot's?) conception of what literature should be. They were modern; they spoke to us directly. Milton was not and did not.

Some of Milton's detractors went perhaps too far, but extravagant words are appropriate to a revolution. Pound said that Milton's real place was not with Shakespeare or Dante ('whereto the stupidity of our forebears tried to exalt him' — why, that might have come out of *Areopagitica*) but with poets like Drummond of Hawthornden. His subject-matter was attacked, as well as his 'asinine bigotry, his beastly hebraism'. If young modern poets tried to learn from him, they would end 'trying to pile up noise and adjectives'. Eliot was more moderate than old Uncle Ez. He said that the real attack was to be levelled less at Milton and his work than at 'the idolatry of a great artist by unintelligent critics, and his imitation by uninspired

167

practitioners'. Eliot accepted, then, that Milton was a great poet, but he denied that he was a good one. This was one of those dangerously seductive distinctions that Eliot propounded in reviews (later to be called Critical Essays) and left it to others to follow up. And there was that even more dangerous seduction of the term 'dissociation of sensibility'—meaning a disastrous and irreversible schizophrenia that overtook the British mind in the seventeenth century and for which Milton had to be accounted largely responsible.

Patrick Murray's wholly admirable book, *Milton: The Modern Phase*,* traces the history of the anti-Milton movement and those processes of reversal which have led us to a saner—less idolatrous, more critically appreciative—view of our greatest, or perhaps only, epic poet. It is astonishing, when one looks back, how unquestioningly the word of Eliot was taken on the matter of Milton's alleged failure to work in the 'English tradition', his perversion of language, his erection of a 'Chinese Wall' of versification which stultified later poets' attempts to write good blank verse, his inferiority to Donne in the manifestation of 'wit' and 'tough reasonableness', his stubborn and misguided devotion to a 'conceptual' view of diction. When the shattering of Milton's reputation was completed, it only remained for Leavis to announce, in 1933, that his dislodgement had been effected 'with remarkably little fuss'. It was then that the fuss really began. The old guard weighed in with righteous anger. But it was Eliot himself who, changing his critical tune and also his poetic practice, initiated the re-revaluation. And, more recently, younger critics like Frank Kermode, Bernard Bergonzi and Christopher Ricks have revalued the re-revaluers.

What did Eliot, Pound and the Scrutineers really have against Milton? They had, in fact, very little against the poet of *Comus*; it was *Paradise Lost* which they reviled as a monstrosity of genius, a diabolically skilful engine for the torturing of English and the elevation of sound above sense. Milton, they said, turned English into a kind of Latin, forcing an uninflected tongue into the agonizing postures of a highly inflected one. That the dialect of *Paradise Lost* behaves like Latin nobody will deny, but the Miltonic miracle seems

* Longmans, 1967.

to lie in the attainment of a compressed Virgilian effect without undue syntactical ambiguity. We have to remember that the style was conceived auditorily and the ear is the only true arbiter of sense. There are few who will complain of not understanding Milton when he is read aloud, and his concern with right emphasis is attested by his 'creative' spelling—the stressed *hee* and *their*, the unstressed *he* and *thir*. It is true English, but an English which deliberately exaggerates its Romance elements. The Scrutineers never complained that Gerard Manley Hopkins, quite as deliberately and far more bizarrely on occasion, exaggerated its Teutonic elements.

Milton seems deliberately to point the Latinate exaggeration by suddenly homing, after a cluster of polysyllables, to a native word of domestic simplicity: 'The Sun, that light imparts to all, receives / From all his alimental recompense / In humid exhalations, and at even / Sups with the ocean.' And, as Helen Darbishire pointed out, it is no self-denial for him to avoid 'percussed' in echoing Virgil's *ingenti percussus amore:* 'Smit with the love of sacred song.' It is surely in the Shakespearian tradition to shock by suddenly turning the other face of English. The common way is to interpolate a Latinism in an Anglo–Saxon context. Eliot himself did it, but his most famous example has inept Latinity in it: 'In the juvescence of the year / Came Christ the tiger.' Milton's practice in the later poems is to reverse the process, assuming a Latin norm, jolting with sudden Saxonisms. You call the chessboard black, I call it white. The Romance vocabulary of English has a status as legitimate as the Teutonic one. Milton exploited it because it proclaimed the Virgilian tradition he was working in, also because it evoked a generalizing remoteness altogether appropriate to his theme.

This kind of language would be intolerable in Elizabethan drama, and the Miltonic vocabulary was in fact used farcically in those eighteenth-century pastoral poems which needed real spitting shepherds, not Damon and Lycidas, and real nettles and cowdung, not an odourless and conceptualized nature. The condemnation wholly earned by Milton's followers was, unfairly, transferred to Milton himself. Milton was writing about things unattempted yet in prose or rhyme: he needed as specialized and artificial a diction as Joyce needed for *Finnegans Wake*. To the unprejudiced reader of *Paradise Lost*, the wonder must always be that, with the special artistic problems raised by the subject, Milton deviated so little from the traditions of English poetry.

I imply above that Milton has been disliked for his subject-matter. This means that he is disliked for his theology, ethics and politics. Hopkins, who wanted to 'purify' his style towards the Miltonic, wholly rejected what Milton the man stood for. Anglicans, royalists and Tories like Johnson and Eliot have been equally revolted. Empson thinks that Milton's God is the Devil. The man's beliefs are all wrong; the man himself is bad. Nobody can like his regicidal republicanism or the arrogance of his hates, but the other vices, Mr Murray suggests, have been much exaggerated—writing on the need for divorce while on his honeymoon (untrue: it was at least a year after), turning his daughters into long-playing language records, beating his nephews. The picture of a thin-lipped Brownist, intolerant of fleshly indulgence, does not tally with the praise of married sex in *Paradise Lost*. The false image of militant self-denial has been transferred to his work, converted into a 'limited range' or the solitary euphoria of a man playing loudly on the organ.

Mr Murray's survey of Milton's comparatively recent rehabilitation appears at the same time as the revised edition of E. M. W. Tillyard's indispensable long study, *Milton*,* to which an Eliot-answering epilogue has been added. One of the values of this work lies in its power to rewhet relish for the 'marginal' writings of Milton. I have been sent back to the polemical books, particularly *Areopagitica*, wherein Milton inveighed against the press-muzzlers and presented the image of 'a noble and puissant nation rousing herself like a strong man after sleep, and shaking her invincible locks'. Milton, thou shouldst be living at this hour, having a crack at our own 'timorous and flocking birds, with those also that love the twilight'. The Miltonic image, seen against the history of his own age, continues to be heroic, and the two great works of his blind maturity, taken as autobiography elevated into myth, strike with a super-Byronic romanticism. It is impossible not to be moved

* Chatto & Windus, 1966.

by this Samson beset by Philistines, fury tamed into resignation, sniffing the corruption of a Gaza that has brought him low, the hopes dead whereon he expended his sight to the utmost. The roof has come down on our own distinguished Philistines, but, with another revolution in taste, it will undoubtedly be rebuilt. Meanwhile, it is quite in order for us to admire once again those pillar-shaking feats.

Bagehot on Books

THERE was a time when reviewing was a branch of criticism; but nowadays criticism is only a branch of reviewing. We can spare whole plains of esparto grass for books, but only the odd inch to say just how and why those books are good or bad. A couple of slow sessions with a contemporary equivalent of the old *Edinburgh Review*, and some of our jauntier reputations would go sprawling. As it is, the exiguity of reviewing space in the journals, and the paucity of periodicals, which, granting space, are not uneasy at talk of values, have a great deal to do with our present literary debility. Writers get away with too much because reviewers get away with too little— a few orts of jargon from sociology or depth-psychology, highly emotive clichés, boutique novelties, cold scraps from public-relations luncheons, the daring of a sneer if a book has been read, the caution of praise if it hasn't. As for critical principles, these have all been deposited in the bank, and the lack of space declares a perpetual moratorium.

Reviewers would like reviewing better if they could engage their whole personalities on it, revel in real exhibitionism: the art of love is best learned at night in a big bed, not through a furtive ten minutes in a back alley. Victorian England had the big beds (which have all now gone to America), and the *Economist* cordially invites you to watch Walter Bagehot at work in some of them. These first two volumes of his Collected Works★ are devoted entirely, after Norman

★ *The Collected Works of Walter Bagehot.* Vols I and II (*The Economist*, 1966).

St John-Stevas's editorial preface and biography, and Sir William Haley's literary appreciation, to Bagehot's literary essays. The *Economist* is to be warmly commended on so courageously (perhaps quixotically) undertaking this act of homage to the memory of its third editor. The quality of the production is superb, the choice of editor less inspired than inevitable, since Mr St John-Stevas has made the life and work of Bagehot his peculiar province and has already exhibited, most brilliantly, the extent of his sympathy with Bagehot's personality and aims and understanding of his achievement. The whole edition will be a great act of scholarship. My present question is: has Walter Bagehot anything to say to the ordinary literati of our own age?

It has to be confessed that Bagehot's literary criticism has been suspect to a large body of men of letters, and for two reasons—the fact of Bagehot's polymathy, which makes literature merely one of his interests, and the evidence of his enjoyment of reading books and writing about them, which smacks of the amateur. But it is doubtful whether criticism has ever been a professional art in the sense that, say, the writing of fiction has been and still is; and the aesthetic philosophy of Aristotle is not invalidated, but rather given more authority, by the fact of its forming part of a bigger corpus of specu-lation. Matthew Arnold seems to many to be the one Victorian critical voice we ought to listen to, chiefly because his approach to literature anticipates those wider, social and cultural inquiries which the Cambridge school, as well as T. S. Eliot, has taught us to regard as a proper concern of criticism. Arnold rings with the authority of a 'professional' (perhaps because he was an Inspector of Schools and a very serious poet); Bagehot merely seems to fill great tracts of space in the various *Reviews* (*National, Prospective* and *Saturday*), as well as the *Spectator*.

It has been held against Bagehot that his taste was not sound, but this is perhaps solely on the grounds that he found both Hartley Coleridge and Bailey's *Festus* worth writing about. Now, everybody was taken in by *Festus*, which was commonly mentioned in the same breath as Goethe's *Faust*, just as everybody was once taken in by Christopher Fry; as for Hartley Coleridge, his 'gentle and minute genius' was worth examining out of devotion to his father and his father's friends. Anyway, Bagehot gets over these enthusiasms—if they can really be called that—in his two earliest essays, and then he is ready for Shakespeare, Bishop Butler, Dickens, Milton and Shelley. He is also ready, or rather unready, for Arthur Hugh Clough (Clough influenced him greatly; his essay on his poems was occasioned by Clough's premature death), and it is his examination of poems like *Amours de Voyage* which must commend him to modern readers—specifically, those modern readers who owe a great deal to Michael Roberts's *Faber Book of Modern Verse*, whose introduction, quoting Clough at length, cannot avoid also quoting Bagehot. It does not quote the following summation of Clough's talent:

> By fate he was thrown into a vortex of theological and metaphysical speculation, but his genius was better suited to be the spectator of a more acting and moving scene. The play of mind upon mind; the contrasted view which contrasted minds take of great subjects; the odd irony of life which so often thrusts into conspicuous places exactly what no one would expect to find in those places—those were his subjects.

That is the kind of thing Bagehot is capable of, but only after protracted examination of the work, and much quotation. You are not allowed to take anything on trust.

The essay on Dickens was written before the publication of *A Tale of Two Cities* and *Great Expectations*, yet its tone suggests not just a posthumous assessment but a revaluation in a cool time, long after the settling of the turbid pool of popular worship: 'Mr Dickens was too much inclined by natural disposition to lachrymose eloquence and exaggerated caricature. Such was the kind of writing which he wrote most easily. He found likewise that such was the kind of writing that was read most easily; and of course he wrote that kind.' I don't think any later critical judgment on Dickens—not even Orwell's—adds anything to Bagehot's, and the occasional Johnsonian stricture—'there was a weakness of fibre unfavourable to the longevity of excellence'—is usually qualified by a rather un-Johnsonian charity: 'No other Englishman has attained such a hold on the vast populace; it is little, therefore, to say that no other has surmounted its attendant temptations.'

The presence of this charity in Bagehot may be taken by some, later and harsher, critics as a weakness, but the essence of his approach to an author is human: he sees the works as an emanation of personality. It is perhaps significant that his most telling essays are those whose subjects have what we may call a pre-literary appeal—Lady Mary Wortley Montagu, Laurence Sterne, Shelley and Gibbon. His study of Shakespeare anticipates Frank Harris and, for that matter, the Dublin symposium of June 16th, 1904, in concentrating on the enigmatic personality (his title is 'Shakespeare—The Individual'). Where Shakespeare and Scott are brought together, we do not have to excuse Bagehot's Victorian taste, since on the level of humanity (a love of field sports, shoulder-rubbing with the low, affability with servants, and so on) the two may legitimately be compared. The danger of becoming 'mystical and confused' over the greater genius is admirably, and consciously, skirted. Bagehot was brought up on the Romantics but, at the time of writing on Shakespeare, he had published 'The Currency Monopoly', been called to the bar and to Stuckey's Bank, and was only eight years off his editorship of the *Economist*. It is good to read, in 1853, that 'Shakespeare was worldly, and the proof of it is, that he succeeded in the world ... It was a great thing that he ... should return upon the old scene a substantial man, a person of capital, a freeholder, a gentleman to be respected, and over whom even a burgess could not affect the least superiority'. Bagehot doesn't let this satisfaction at a poet's financial success condition his aesthetic judgments (any more than in the Dickens essay), but he evidently admires the integrated man who can beat both the aesthetics and the magnates at their own games. 'Why did Mr Disraeli take the duties of the Exchequer with so much relish? Because people said he was a novelist, an *ad captandum* man, and, *monstrum horrendum*! a Jew, that could not add up. No doubt it pleased his inmost soul to do the work of the red-tape people better than those who could do nothing else. And so with Shakespeare ... ' So, also, in reverse, with Bagehot.

As for what Bagehot thought of the reviewer's art, it is all in 'The First Edinburgh Reviewers': 'The modern man must be told what to think—shortly no doubt—but he *must* be told it. The essay-like criticism of modern times is about the length which he likes.' Our response to this is a wry one: 'shortly' can mean as much as 20,000 words. How Bagehot would have responded to an invitation to consider, say, Lord Jeffrey or Sydney Smith in just over one thousand words can easily be guessed at. It was essential to his leisurely craft to be able to work out his general principles in full view of his audience and, so far as their practical application to the subject in hand was concerned, to be able to lay before the reader ample specimens of the author's style and content. There is in Bagehot a sufficiency of the epigrammatical and the gnomic, but these are the seasoning of, not a substitute for, the long-drawn expatiation of a summer afternoon or a winter evening. There is room enough for the disclosure of foibles and the hinting at fields of experience beyond the immediate and nominal; there is all the time in the world for the digression which eventually is shown to illuminate the central theme. It is civilized and humane writing, of a kind that has long disappeared. One is glad to have it eternized in this altogether admirable edition, a gift to literature from men to whom literature is not a primary concern. Perhaps all the best things are done on a sort of margin.

The Democracy of Prejudice

'WE' is the most treacherous of the English pronouns. The Malays, who have an honest language, distinguish between *kami*, which means us as opposed to you, and *kita*, which takes in the spoken to as well as the speaker. The Borneo Malays—and this is an interesting analogue to Old British nanny-usage—push the 'you' aspect of *kita* so far that the 'we' element totally disappears. Now what does the 'we' of this title* signify? B.B., M.L. and C.O. say,

* *Fifty Works of English Literature We Could Do Without* by Brigid Brophy, Michael Levey and Charles Osborne (Rapp & Carroll, 1967).

in their 'Address to the Reader', that 'the critic who lets you know that he always looks for something to like in works he discusses is not telling you anything about the works or about art; he is saying "see what a nice person I am".' (Conversely, if you don't want to be known as a nice person, which seems to be one of Miss Brophy's masochist aims, knock hell out of anything you review, provided that it is by a male author.) See what a nice person I am: I've been trying to find in this book the properties of an idiosyncratic profession of faith or unfaith. But the 'we' can't be *kami*, because the authors are doing without the fifty books already and don't have to justify their rejection to themselves. It must be *kita*, and a *kita* closer to Brunei than to Johore Bahru. We're being told what to dislike and, on the margin, like, and the telling is half-disguised as the showier sort of WEA teaching. But it is really an inept kind of con-trick, based on irrational appeals to rationality, pushed along with sneers, dirty sniggers, the snobbishness of the ill-bred. I've never in all my reading encountered such bloody arrogance.

This deplorable little work has been duly deplored in the literary reviews and the 'class' papers: only the *Sunday Express*, I think, found anything to praise. The authors are now rubbing themselves in an ecstasy of the kind granted only to Exclusive Brethren. In *Books and Bookmen* they have, abusing or counter-abusing their critics, re-affirmed their role of three-tailed scourge of the weak and triple pillar of the strong. They are having a rather shrill good time. And, my dear, there are still the Commonwealth and American reviews to come. If everybody says we're wrong, why then we must be right, along with Robert Pitman. I don't propose to help inflame the delicious abscess. I merely want to express my disquiet that this is what British literary criticism should have come to. Miss Brophy, who is Mrs Michael Levey, was awarded a Jubilee Scholarship at St Hugh's College, Oxford. The merit of her novels is widely recog-nized, and she has won two important literary prizes. Mr Levey is a master of arts of both Oxford and Cambridge; he is a distinguished art historian, has been Slade Professor and is second-in-command of the National Gallery. Mr Osborne is respected as a music critic, an authority on Italian opera, a hard-working magazine editor and a responsible officer of the Arts Council. Here, then, are three people of large culture and considerable social standing. They have enough fame and they are presumably not short of money. What then has impelled them to publish so ill-conceived, ignorant and vulgar a book?

One answer, a shameful one, is a hunger for notoriety. Their book, far from being ignored (if it had been the work of uneducated people that would have been a just response), has had wide newspaper coverage; they themselves have been interviewed at length on commercial television. Like children, they have shown off, and the showing-off has provoked attention. They have even angered a number of people, and anger, like sexual desire, can be flattering to its object. What they regard as iconoclasm can also be seen as the indiscriminate destructiveness of infants who will do anything to get notice. They kick *Hamlet*, *Pilgrim's Progress*, and the poems of T. S. Eliot. Very naughty, most smackable. But they also pulverize the already broken pieces of *Aurora Leigh* and *Lorna Doone* and *Tom Brown's Schooldays*. They're still in the nursery, cut off from the big world. In the nursery are a few books, many of which they don't like. They have still to engage libraries and the systematic study of literature.

Their first target is *Beowulf*. I take it that they must all have read this in the original, since, in their preliminary address, they say: 'We have ... excluded translations. That is why the Bible is not listed' (that would have been naughty fun, wouldn't it?—having a crack at all those dreary patriarchs, the trite proverbs, the one-sided sexuality, the bloodthirsty tribal god, as though the world outside Old Brompton Road actually liked them). I don't think students of *Beowulf* have ever really preferred its eponymous hero to Grendel and his mother, though the crunching-up of the Danes because they drink late and loud seems to be going too far. And I don't think the passing of value-judgments much concerns them either. Nobody, in fact, tackles *Beowulf* merely because he wants a good read: he can get that, can't he, from *Flesh*, which still sells well in the bazaars. We go to *Beowulf* out of curiosity, a very reasonable motive, and for the sort of special pleasure to be gained from watching the manipulation of a language both alien and familiar. Doubtless, as we are told, 'we need some respectable pseudo-Homeric epic from which to make Northern literature evolve', but, unless one of these three can do a Macpherson, we have to be content with what's already there. And we can't hope to understand the evolution of English literature without knowing something about the aesthetic behaviour of English before French and Latin got into it.

Ah, but I'm on the wrong track, aren't I? We're concerned not with historical monuments but with books as isolated instruments of pleasure and enlightenment. Nonsense: literature is a continuum. Ignore Anglo-Saxon literature and the technique of headrime it bequeathed to Middle English literature, and you're able to talk, à propos the York Mystery Plays, of drunken monks writing doggerel: 'They *must* have been drunk: the preponderance of alliterative verse in the plays points to this. Alliteration is most frequently resorted to in intoxication.' The jettisoning of history enables you to see the Middle Ages spatially—an island no one wants to visit, what with its 'crudity of life and religious thought' and the mean 'intellectual capacities of the credulous citizenry'. Soon you will reach the state of scoffing at old writers because they lived before the Enlightenment or before Freud. After condemning *Pilgrim's Progress*—a 'monstrous tract … a curious monument to frightened conformity'— the trio give us some of Bunyan's verse, which—'*For having now my method by the end, / Still, as I pulled, it came*'—provides us at least with a dirty laugh. But we have, presumably, to be respectful in the presence of tool-swinging Roderick Hudson.

Apart from unwillingness to look at literature historically, Osborne and the Leveys are above being ashamed at their own ignorance. We can ignore small gaffes like the retitling of 'Kubla Khan' as 'Xanadu', but we're entitled to ask for evidence when we're told that Ben Jonson's verse is laboured, that he is 'the great Elizabethan non-poet', that his intelligence is 'arid' and his language lacks vigour. This sort of evidence, perhaps:

> See, a carbuncle
> May put out both the eyes of our St Mark;
> A diamond would have bought Lollia Paulina,
> When she came in like starlight, hid with jewels,
> That were the spoils of provinces; take these,
> And wear, and lose them: yet remains an ear-ring
> To purchase them again, and this whole state.

Or, as their special concern is *The Alchemist* ('the plot is uninteresting, and is hardly animated by the pedantry of the verse in which it is expressed'), this:

> My foot-boy shall eat pheasants, calver'd salmons,
> Knots, godwits, lampreys: I myself will have
> The beards of barbels served, instead of salads;
> Oil'd mushrooms; and the swelling unctuous paps
> Of a fat pregnant sow, newly cut off,
> Drest with an exquisite and poignant sauce;
> For which I'll say unto my cook, *There's gold,*
> *Go forth and be a knight.*

But the reference to meat-eating, with its exaggerated tincture of cruelty, must certainly put Miss Brophy off. Pedantic or horrid, which is it? Both? Put meat-eating in your work, deprive your female characters of orgasms, present religion as something other than superstition, chase the odd fox, and you can be sure—however exquisitely you write—of earning Brophy censure or condemnation. She, they, subscribe to the hersey of subjectivism: literature is not there to modify your (mainly irrational) convictions but to confirm them. And if a book doesn't confirm them, the Life Force help it.

The most summary of all the condemnations is of Gerard Manley Hopkins, and it can be quoted in full:

> Hopkins's is the poetry of a mental cripple. Sympathize as one
> might with his confusion, with the absurd struggle that went on
> within him between priest and poet, it is impossible not to end
> by feeling completely exasperated with the disastrous mess he

made of his life. The muscle-bound, determinedly 'difficult' verse that he produced is really abhorrent. It may have a sentimental appeal to his co-religionists, but to others Hopkins is surely the most unrewarding of the Victorian poets. The interior war in his permanently bared breast between aesthetic and ascetic is a blatantly uneven combat: the aesthete scarcely exists. The man is all metaphysics, mysticism and neurotic longing for the cross. Add to these disabilities the baleful influence of Dante Gabriel and Christina Rossetti, and it is immediately apparent that poor Hopkins hadn't a chance.

In his groping attempts to find his own mode of expression, Hopkins is not unlike Browning, but he lacks completely Browning's sudden illumination. Hopkins is at the mercy both of his superstitions and of his theories. It was the theories that proved the more dangerous to his verse. His meaningless and arbitrary definitions of 'inscape' and 'instress' serve to underline the almost Nihilistic emptiness of his thought. In a letter, Hopkins wrote: 'You know I once wanted to be a painter. But even if I could I would not, I think, now, for the fact is that the higher and more attractive parts of the art put a strain on the passions which I shd think it unsafe to encounter.' No wonder his poetry is so cringingly irrelevant. There is nothing brave about his obscurity: it is that of weak-mindedness and theology.

In answering this, it is, one might think, possible that we're falling into the trap of a somewhat heavy-handed spoof, but the subtler forms of humour are evidently beyond this earnest trio. Can it be answered? Probably not, since most of the terms used are loaded with the connotations of private prejudice: 'metaphysics', 'mysticism' (unless used in connection with St Teresa, one of the few women in history to be sculpted in orgasm), and 'theology' are altogether pejorative. This kind of imposition could be amusing in a Samuel Butler way, but the whole passage goes beyond the mere registration of anti-clericalism. There are far too many statements demonstrably untrue. In Hopkins there was no struggle between poet and priest, however these three like to think that the two vocations are incompatible. His early work had Keatsian rather than Pre-Raphaelite qualities; his true voice is raised after ordination. He was never 'confused', though he was conscious of failure in his mission and, in his last poems, expressed the horror of the dark night of the soul (indigestion really, these three will say: 'I am gall, I am heartburn'). He formulated his theories only after composing his first long poem in sprung rhythm. There is not one poem which embodies 'neurotic longing for the cross'. He has never made much of an appeal to Catholics: his great followers in the 1930s were the young left-wing poets Auden and Day Lewis. His verse expresses no 'ascetic' urge. Far from not existing, the 'aesthete' in him tends to over-richness. He never 'groped' for a new mode of expression: 'The Wreck of the Deutschland' is mature and assured writing. We grant that he was superstitious, if to be superstitious is to be a Catholic. No amount of good-humoured acquiescence in semantic distortion can, however, reconcile the contradictory sneers—'mental cripple' and 'muscle-bound', 'permanently bared breast' and 'cringingly irrelevant' (irrelevant to what?); 'all metaphysics' and 'almost Nihilistic emptiness of his thought'; 'meaningless' and 'arbitrary' (an arbitrary meaning is still, presumably, a meaning). If 'poor Hopkins' is confused, what shall we say of poor Brophy, Levey and Osborne?

This sort of half-literate and more than half-ignorant pseudo-criticism would be harmless enough if its perpetrators did not profess an anti-philistine and reformist aim. The danger is that students, bemused by the status, reputations, and qualifications of the authors, may reproduce this kind of waffle in their examination papers. No examiner objects to reasoned abuse, but evidence of failure to read the texts is unforgivable. 'Discuss the work of Gerard Manley Hopkins.' Off we go then: 'Hopkins's is the poetry of a mental cripple ... ' Could the examinee possibly hope for a pass? And yet he might seem justly aggrieved: after all, if printed books by leaders of British taste can get away with it, why not a mere candidate for a degree?

The really worrying thing is that this work exemplifies, however grossly, abusively and pigheadedly, the state of British criticism today. Reviewers, especially, mistake the parading of prejudice for the objective appraisal of a book.

Catholic novelists are becoming something of a bore ... the imagery resolves into an unappetizing fester of camp tat ... we're all sick of lesbian *ménages* ... as soon as I see that a book has a provincial setting I run a mile ... puffed-up pseudo-masculinity with a show-off of erections that are merely piss-proud ... it's about time novelists dropped good and evil ... Miss A's good literary manners are merely spinsterish prissiness ... another saga of the avocadau pair belt ... the trouble with Mr B is that he can't write ... it isn't his hero that's confused but his prose-style ... jogtrot traditionalism ... abortive experimentalism ... '

See, for the last time, what a nice person I am. When I don't like a writer my first instinct is to look for the fault in myself. I don't like Jane Austen, though many people do: this must be because of a failure in my own temperament. Really, of course, I should write something like this:

Let Austen have her swink to her reserved. Was it worth while, this sedulous setting-down of tedious flirtations, drawing-room intrigues, pompous avowals? There's no intellectual content (only Kotzebue seems to be mentioned, though not even by name), no attempt at rendering sensuous immediacies—only the interminable record of insipid courtship and venal marriage brokerage. Outside the smug little parsonages and *rentier* retreats the Napoleonic wars—the real world of change and history—thud and boom away, but there is no mention of them here: the hermetically sealed life of the boudoir and parlour—with occasional healthful toddles round the rose garden—twitters on in blessed self-sufficiency. And even inside the twee miniature world only one human stratum is taken seriously: the maids and coachmen and cooks are nameless, faceless, beneath notice, the sub-human helots who sustain the simpering misses, the mothers given to the vapours, the valetudinarian parsons and slippered bookmen. Miss Austen (as we must affectedly continue to call her, along with her fellow-spinster admirers of both sexes) has the bitchy capacity for remembering exactly what she hears and reproducing it exactly, but she has no mastery (or mistressy— no, on second thoughts, a shocking word: how her readers would blush) of the *récit*. Her prose-style has a school-exercise flatness; her little *mots* are pathetically inept; her descriptions are woolly. Like her twentieth-century counterpart, Miss Brophy, she is distinguished only for a splendid insularity of thought and manner, and an extraordinary infelicity of expression.

I understand that Mr Osborne and the Leveys are next going to tell us what pictures to get rid of. I look forward to the same bizarre mixture of the misunderstood great and the non-starter— the unbelievably disparate brought together only by irrational dis-like, the democracy of prejudice. If we can have *Hamlet* and *Lorna Doone* in the same gallery we can also have 'The Last Watch of Hero' and the Botticelli Venus. Hogarth will be rejected because he ate too much beef (or accepted because his dog is in the forefront of his self-portrait?). And then, with Mr Osborne in the lead, they can have a crack at music. Already, in the margin of this present book, *The Bride of Lammermoor* is slated so that Donizetti's opera can be called 'a valid work of art', and Brahms and Dixieland jazz occupy the same slot of rhythmic ineptitude. I don't expect anything like the following in *Fifty Musical Works We Could Do Without*:

The emasculated elegance of Mozart could be regarded as over-compensation for his ridiculous butch name Wolfgang. His reputation is based on such extra-artistic factors as his child-prodigy beginning and his macabre-romantic end. Add to these his sickening fecundity—the pouring-out of notes is, to the uneducated, the inspiration of genius when it is in fact nothing but phonorrhea, an incontinence the more morbid for being sugary—and you have a sufficient explanation for the gawping indiscriminating awe or head-wagging joy which is accorded his very ordinary music. His fortieth sympathy in

G minor (a very ordinary key) is as good or as bad an example as any of the so-called major works of his rushed and excessive output (he wrote rapidly because he needed the money, but he was not even a good businessman: he died in debt). The tunes of this symphony, if tunes they can be called, are four-square nursery jingles, made portentous by being put in a minor key, though even here he shows the inconsistency of the weak-minded, for sometimes they also appear in the major, where their vapidity is embarrassingly apparent. He is repetitious and rhythmically unadventurous (contrast this work with Stravinsky's *Le Sacre du Printemps*!) and his orchestration is thin—only two horns, and those without valves; no trombones. He fails even to make the most of the instrumental resources he has: the double-basses invariably double the 'cellos.

His third movement is a minuet—the most stilted dance-form imaginable. He attempts to disguise its inadequacies by peppering it with *Sturm und Drang* huffing and puffing, but his artistic impotence is pointed by the fact that this movement is in the same key as the first and last (yes, G minor). The other movements are silly and ill-written, codpieces filled with air. We've got rid of the Austro-Hungarian Empire; isn't it about time we got rid of Mozart as well?

The trouble is that, since Miss Brophy loves him so much, one almost feels like saying yes.

The Steinerian Agony

I APPROACH George Steiner's major collection of essays* *in*, to borrow from Kafka, *grosser Verlegenheit*. My respect for Dr Steiner as scholar, critic and novelist is as considerable as my admiration of him as a human being. I wonder how far, ill-equipped in

* *Language and Silence* by George Steiner (Faber & Faber, 1967).

scholarship as I am, I have the right to find him frequently wrong-headed. And there is the more general embarrassment of, in the context of Dr Steiner's main thesis of the need for more silence and fewer words, my adding, however minimally, to the least defensible body of noise of the lot—the noise of the reviewer who reviews reviews. For Dr Steiner's essays are, many of them, in the tradition of what T. S. Eliot wrote in *The Criterion* and then persuaded the whole world to regard, when cunningly grouped in a volume, as contributions to scholarship: I mean the submission of tentative ideas, however novel, unbacked by little except the personal hunch, the small arrogance of conviction. Anything that stimulates the duller, more plodding mind to the erection of large critical structures is to be cherished, but we must not pretend that a collection of reviews, even when given unity by a common theme and dignity by hard covers, is much more than a bundle of salutary irritants or, more digestible, trayload of cocktails flanked by pretzels. Dr Steiner starts things, but he does not finish them; nor do we expect more from reviews. I am most particularly *in grosser Verlegenheit* when faced with reviewing Dr Steiner reviewing Dr Leavis, who shares with Lévi-Strauss and Marshall McLuhan the section in this volume entitled *Masters*. I am put in the position which Dr Steiner regards, rightly, as the most ridiculous with which any writer can be confronted: having to write about a man who writes about a man who writes about men who write.

Still, Dr Steiner has a separable message which ought not to be met by the silence which appears to be acquiescence. This message relates to the ultimate failure of language to provide an apparatus of adequate expression for the horrors of the contemporary world. Dr Steiner is a Jew, and it is as a Jew, not as a detached aesthete or philologist, that he reproaches language with its inability to cope with the referents that modern history submits to it. All that is left, after Auschwitz and Buchenwald, is silence. Monsieur Beckett, as he calls him, is on the right track here. Dr Steiner envisages a stage on which characters grope for expression foredoomed to inadequacy; at length a word is squeezed out; then the curtain descends. Beckett has, of course, recently given us a *dramaticule* on those lines.

There is a better man in Cocteau's *Orphée*, who exhibits a titled book with totally blank pages. And, some years ago, in the public bars of England, a similar book went the rounds of the customers. Its title was *What the Labour Government Has Done for the Working Man*. It would be irrelevant here to call for a new edition.

Dr Steiner has, of course, a special right to be horrified by what the Nazis, and the other, lesser, anti-Semitic states have done to a whole race. There is the guilt of his own escape, there is the subtler guilt of having brought children into the world. He exhibits some of his horror and incredulity very movingly, and adds to German guilt the guilt of the Allies, who inexplicably failed even to attempt to destroy the gas-ovens or the railway lines which brought doomed freights of Jews to die in them. Particular horrors are ghastly enough —like the rabbis forced to clean out latrines with their mouths—but the true ghastliness seems to be quantitative. Now the tradition in which I was brought up has always discounted the quantitative argument. To make one Jew, or Catholic, or Lutheran, or free-thinking intellectual, drown, flayed, in a bath of human ordure is as much a token of the existence of evil as the world needs. To repeat this act a million times adds to the sensationalism of the evil but not to its quantum, since evil, by its very nature, cannot be quantified. To wish to destroy a race or sect is strictly no more evil than to wish to destroy a single man or woman. The amount of evil in the world has not increased since the days of the Inquisition: this is self-evident. It would seem to follow that language is as adequate today for the symbolization of evil, or the expression of abhorrence at it, as it was when Shakespeare saw kites gnaw at heads on Temple Bar or hang-men pluck out still-beating hearts at Tyburn.

But Dr Steiner is right when he refuses to accept literature, which is the aesthetic exploitation of the word to the end of presenting a *Vorstellung* of a presumed ultimate reality which is wholly 'good', as a mode of activity or communication to which the fact of evil is irrelevant. I personally have always found it difficult to think in terms of the 'Humane Literacy' which provides the title of Dr Steiner's first, and basic, essay, but the civilization of the Protestant

West has taken as axiomatic literature's power 'to broaden and refine the resources of the human spirit'. As Dr Steiner indicates, the seed-beds of the highest literary culture have frequently been the forcing-grounds of hate, intolerance and persecution. 'Barbarism prevailed on the very ground of Christian humanism, of Renaissance culture and classic rationalism. We know that some of the men who devised and administered Auschwitz had been trained to read Shakespeare or Goethe, and continued to do so.' This again is nothing new, but only an age able to subscribe to the heresy of literature as a moral teacher is likely to be shocked by it. It is cognate with another heresy, that liberal one propagated by H. G. Wells, which taught the attainment of human perfection through scientific education. Evil, said the liberals, was only another name for ignorance. The Germans, the least ignorant people in the world, exploded that fallacy with typical thoroughness.

And yet it is the reformed liberals who are most Augustinian in the presentation of evil as ontological reality, though, being reformed liberals, they do not backdate this reality. In *What is Literature?*,★ Sartre said:

> We have been taught to take Evil seriously. It is neither our fault nor our merit if we lived in a time when torture was a daily fact. Chateaubriand, Oradour, the Rue des Saussaies, Dachau and Auschwitz have all demonstrated to us that Evil is not an appearance, that knowing its cause does not dispel it, that it is not opposed to Good as a confused idea is to a clear one ... In spite of ourselves, we come to this conclusion, which will seem shocking to lofty souls: Evil cannot be redeemed.

Evil was not the children blowing up a frog or tearing the wings off a fly at Le Havre or Laon, when Sartre was a schoolmaster there: evil had to wait for Dachau and Auschwitz. In other words, evil, like gin, is not a spiritual fact in the drop, the hardly tastable globule:

★ By Jean-Paul Sartre. New edition (Methuen, 1967).

you need a good swig before you can start believing in it. Dr Steiner seems to accept, with Sartre, that new responsibilities were presented to literature in 1945; the truth is that, if those responsibilities are viable, then they were always so. But I do not believe that literature has ever been anything but a limited exploration of such sensibility as its practitioners are gifted or poisoned with. Aware of Dachau, we can rage at the charming Pelagianism of *Under Milk Wood*, but we shall be wrong to rage. And we shall probably be wrong to make our aesthetic evaluations in terms of the artist's width of moral sensibility. For literature is, in fact, art, and it would be pure form if it could.

Viewed in Thomastic terms, literature becomes something that merely pleases. Dr Stainer is wrong when he says: 'There is some evidence that a trained, persistent commitment to the life of the printed word, a capacity to identify deeply and critically with imaginary personages or sentiments, diminishes the immediacy, the hard edge of actual circumstance. We come to respond more acutely to the literary sorrow than to the misery next door.'

The truth is that the responses are qualitatively different. 'Men who wept at Werther or Chopin moved, unrealizing, through literal hell.' The tears of aesthetic rapture belong to different ducts from the ones stimulated by real-life agony. The man who is indifferent to the pain of others is not made more of a monster by his ability to weep at the slow movement of Beethoven's Pastoral Symphony. Art has little to do with life, which merely provides raw material for sonatas and sonnets. To enjoy *Macbeth* is pretty close to enjoying an apple, and we continue to enjoy apples even though Nazi torturers enjoyed them too. The fallacy that literature is essentially different from the other arts derives from the fact that it uses language, not pure sound, shape, or colour, and it shares this medium with modes of social action that can be viewed morally. But language is given meaning only by contexts, and the contexts of art are not those of the living-room or the death-chamber.

Of one language Dr Steiner has a good deal to say. What he says is dangerously seductive, and I think it ought to be resisted:

... let us keep one fact clearly in mind: the German language was not innocent of the horrors of Nazism. It is not merely that a Hitler, a Goebbels, and a Himmler happened to speak German. Nazism found in the language precisely what it needed to give voice to its savagery. Hitler heard inside his native tongue the latent hysteria, the confusion, the quality of hypnotic trance. He plunged unerringly into the undergrowth of language, into those zones of darkness and outcry which are the infancy of articulate speech, and which come before words have grown mellow and provisional to the touch of the mind. He sensed in German another music than that of Goethe, Heine, and Mann; a rasping cadence, half nebulous jargon, half obscenity ... A language in which one can write a '*Horst Wessel Lied*' is ready to give hell a native tongue. (How should the word '*spritzen*' recover a sane meaning after having signified to millions the 'spurting' of Jewish blood from knife points?)

This is all very intemperate and unscholarly. I refuse to accept that German ever had the unique and horrid privilege of pre-ordination as the language of evil. To be fanciful, as Dr Steiner is, one might regret that German always refused to drink of the humanizing Mediterranean, but the same may be said of the Scandinavian languages, whose associations are with candour, cleanliness, and winter sports. The romantic pursuit by Jacob Grimm of the Aryan sources of German is commonly regarded as noble rather than sinister: if there was primordial savagery to be unearthed, it was not far from the cadences of the *Rig Veda*. The German language, like every other language, has always been morally neutral, with no greater propensity for corruption than its neighbour languages of the pogroms. Its apparent brutalizing under Hitler was no more than the dragging of it into new contexts of obscene belief and filthy action. Like the pigeons that roost in blessed indifference on the Berlin Wall, its words are beyond good and evil.

*

Context is all, and perhaps it is only the foreigner, with a rare and superficial contact with German, who is likely to delimit its words to small personal areas of significance. Reading a German shirt advertisement, which undertakes to replace any garment found unsatisfactory, I took in with a shock the term *Ersatz*. The guns-not-butter connotation swiftly faded, however, and the word settled into its primary and neutral denotation of 'replacement'. On the Kurfürstendamm, a week or so ago, I saw a motor-van advertising *'Striptease für Jedermann'*. I had recently been thinking of the German morality play, and the *Jedermann* suddenly struck, in that context, with a factitious smack of blasphemy. Then it slid out of the zone of narrow and specialist denotation and merely came to mean 'everyone'. The same thing has, surely, happened with *spritzen*. When a girl fondly introduces her big brother, the Orwellian associations are automatically excluded. Language is like that. There are several Berlin telephone subscribers with the name Streicher (though, admittedly, there is no Hitler), and one expects them to be decent family men who would never harm a fly.

Unhappy about the fancied culpabilities of language, Dr Steiner nevertheless does not call for its liquidation and the immediate supervention of heavenly silence. Like virginity, silence must be opted for in full awareness of the richness of experience (however dangerous) which it replaces. He is appreciative of the achievement of Günter Grass, who has thrown whole dictionaries at a West Germany whose linguistic life must, so we are invited to suppose, have been first diseased and then etiolated. Among modern British novels, he finds especial virtue in Lawrence Durrell's *Alexandria Quartet*, whose rather old-fashioned orotundities belong to the same rhetorical school as Dr Steiner's own expository style. I think he's misled by a wayward ear although he is acute enough to descry a certain emptiness under the coruscations. On Shakespeare's language (in an occasional essay written for the quatercentenary) he speaks admirable and moving sense. It is a virtue in Shakespeare to seem to use English radically—that is, with a full awareness of etymology and paronomastic tensions. One might purge what Dr Steiner says of Hitler of all its pejorative content, affirming of Shakespeare that 'he plunged unerringly into the undergrowth of language, into those zones of darkness and outcry which are the infancy of articulate speech, etc., etc.' Again, a matter of context.

The great author fills the world with sound but, like the great musician, he knows the virtue of silence. Kafka, whom Dr Steiner reveres, asked for the suppression of all his works after his death. Rimbaud and Hölderlin went suddenly silent. Sylvia Plath died young, and this was a kind of opting for silence. Modern composers use patches of silence as plastically as they use sound. But music itself, Dr Steiner seems to imply, is a species of silence: it is the art that begins when words leave off. How much of a musician Dr Steiner is, I do not know: he seems to have a thorough acquaintance with the score of *Moses und Aron*, on the significance of which—in the context of his main theme—he writes very eloquently. But I don't think his thesis would greatly commend itself to a practical composer. Anyone who has ever written music knows all too well the charlatanism which is inherent in sheer sound. Sit down at the piano and improvise a sequence of slow secondary ninths, and your unwise auditors will murmur 'How lovely'. But such loveliness is a step down from the loveliness of a tender steak. It is ear-tickling only; it totally lacks nutritional value. And, on the higher level of formal organization, there are plenty of elemental siren-voices in silver oboes and silken violins. The silence Dr Steiner is perhaps feeling towards is the silence of the orchestral score: there's the true music, eternal, above accidents, self-electedly virginal, safe. And yet, of course, emasculated. But the sound of music, with its key to the zones of darkness and halls of pre-articulate speech, is—if we accept the Steinerian philosophy—far more dangerous than any concentration of words. Hitler rode to power on waves of upper partials. Who could resist Nazi choirs and military bands? One swooned in a Valhalla of harmonics.

And yet one can love *Die Meistersinger* even though it was Hitler's favourite opera. Art is outside human history: it is a god or an animal, but it is not made in man's own image. It has no value as an interpreter of human motives or inhuman actions; fingered by gross men, its virtue remains intact. In bringing together art and the agonies of our time, Dr Steiner has done a daring thing whose implications he has not, because of the limitations of his own literary forms, pursued to the limit. The limit would inevitably be the explosion of his thesis. As it is, all his eloquence cannot convince us. The final image is of a scholarly man, with taste and capacity for suffering equally pitched to a hardly tolerable exquisiteness, puzzled and angry at the oldest mystery in the world—man as a split personality, able to maintain his precarious balance only because of the equal tug of incompatibles.

A Very Tragic Business

'I DON'T want comfort,' says the Savage in Brave New World. 'I want God, I want poetry, I want real danger, I want freedom, I want goodness. I want sin.' And Mustapha Mond, the Controller, sums up for him: 'In fact, you're claiming the right to be unhappy.' He is, and he's also claiming the right to find Sophocles and Shakespeare intelligible, for, unless life is tragic, there can be no art of tragedy. We don't have to go to AF 632 to find a world whose rulers have settled for the liquidation of the raw material of Oedipus or Hamlet; ask any good union man today, or psychologist or new-wave religious apologist, and he will probably say that society ought not to need tragic heroes or victims.

As for progressive dramatists, we have the words of Brecht: 'The sufferings of this man appal me, because they are unnecessary.' Meaning the tragic victim-hero-scapegoat, the necessity for whose sufferings—in the pre-Brechtian dispensation—was taken for granted. This seems to be where the modern and the traditional views of tragedy part company. The Hellenic and Renaissance conceptions of man saw what Raymond Williams calls in his new study* 'a fixed position—an abstract condition'; in Brecht we meet

* Modern Tragedy (Chatto & Windus, 1966).

'the new tragic consciousness of all those who, appalled by the present, are for this reason firmly committed to a different future.' The human condition as a permanency; the human condition as changeable history—take your choice. Your choice will depend on those convictions that have shaped, among other things, your politics.

It is not necessarily typical of Mr Williams's own political position that he should be prepared to see the term 'tragedy' spill over from art into life, taking as his subject-matter the area where all roads meet—'It is an immediate experience, a body of literature, a conflict of theory, an academic problem.' We are all past the time when the academic pundits could flail with impunity the broadening of a technical term to enclose meanings unratified by etymology or classical tradition. This is an age of semantics, and it is the scholar's task to discover the common root of diverse modes of usage. Moreover, the term 'comedy' has, unimpeded by guardians of terminological propriety, long been allowed to describe true events, not merely artistically contrived ones; in addition it has never been a very precise term even in literature (*The Divine Comedy*; *The Comedy of Errors*; Graham Greene's *The Comedians*).

But perhaps because Aristotle laid down rules for tragedy, and in consequence the academicians have been strict in the dramaturgical application of the term, there has been a resistance among the educated to its loose application to sad or shocking events. Some will not accept 'Jobs Tax Split with Labour a Tragedy' (*Daily Telegraph*, May 31st, 1966), though they may agree with the newspapers in finding Dylan Thomas's death tragic (great man driven to self-destruction by flaws of character; poet-scapegoat—*tragos*, a goat; life-enhancer still enhancing life posthumously, etc.). A child may be cured of a deadly disease only to be run over and killed on leaving the hospital. Tragic? Too much there (vide *The Anti-Death League*) of the nasty joke dealt by God in the guise of chance, the black border of comedy. I knew a man who, having been engaged for seventeen years, died on his wedding-night. It would require great boldness to admit publicly the comic element in that, though let one start to smile and the rest will. Mr Williams, I think, would not smile.

Mr Williams's point is that tragedy is not a fixed classical form but an impulse that is re-shaped by an ever-changing sensibility. He recognizes the dangerous alienation of the traditionalists, their deliberate refusal to engage the power of human sympathy beyond certain frozen limits, so that a man of rank can die tragically, but not a slave or retainer. And (this is where art and life meet) there is an undue limitation in that theory which, seeing no tragic significance in 'everyday tragedies', holds that 'the event itself is not tragedy, but only becomes so through shaped response'—in other words, the event is a mere 'accident' if it cannot bear a general meaning. This, says Williams, might be in order if 'the event chosen for argument was a death by lightning', but 'the events which are not seen as tragic are deep in the pattern of our own culture: war, famine, work, traffic, politics'.

Despite the Aristotelian pedants, tragic drama developed, as Williams reminds us, into forms capable of accommodating middle-class heroes (not merely citizens but apprentices as well) and views of the universe highly sceptical about Providence. So now we can corral practically all the 'serious' dramatists and novelists of the last hundred years and give them the tragic brand: Ibsen and Miller (Liberal Tragedy); Strindberg, O'Neill, Tennessee Williams (Private Tragedy); Tolstoy and Lawrence (Social and Personal Tragedy— we're given a very good account of the probable influence of *Anna Karenina* on *Women in Love*); Chekhov, Pirandello, Ionesco, Beckett (Tragic Deadlock and Stalemate); Eliot and Pasternak (Tragic Resignation and Sacrifice); Camus, Sartre (Tragic Despair and Revolt). Readers sympathetic to the extension of a category once chillingly narrow may still feel dubious about the width of this embrace.

Eliot called *The Cocktail Party* a comedy. Was he mistaken or was he being ironic? Celia Coplestone, rejecting the ginny chatter of the world of illusion, elects for reality, which for her means martyrdom. 'Sacrifice', says Mr Williams, 'is what saints are for, but we, we go on with the cocktail party.' If Celia has died to sustain the life of a group which cannot rise above the unconscious— unsaintly—level of subsistence (as Oedipus suffered to restore his kingdom to health), then the play is tragic in that all its personages are involved in a sacrificial act—sacrifice not only done but seen to be done. But Eliot seems to intend here a background of reality—of which mankind cannot bear very much—to contrast with the ordinary messy world; the symbol of the latter is a failing marriage which, given the right medicines, can be reorientated to a mildly happy rehabilitation—the best of a bad job, as Eliot poetically puts it. A little life getting into a mess and then clearing it up is comic, but the larger comedy springs from the contrast of that with the bigger life, whose end looks like a mess but isn't.

The danger is that, if we loosen the term too much, we shall find comedy itself a tragic form (Malvolio as tragic victim: discuss). Doesn't Socrates in the *Symposium* tell Aristophanes that the qualities required for writing tragedy and comedy are the same, and that a tragic genius must also be a comic genius? The special use of the word 'absurd', bequeathed to us by Camus, represents a significant pivot. Man's lot is an absurdity, for the gap between the aspiration and the potency can never be bridged, man is an alien in the universe, etc. etc. (the existential slogans are already becoming clichés).

If man is a tragic figure (or 'absurd', or comic), all his art is the same, and hence it is inappropriate to talk of tragic art as a separate category. So we have to start all over again, and we might as well use 'tragedy' for a narrow compartment of art, one which sees the human dichotomy as terrible rather than ridiculous, accepts the need for sacrifice to the power that has cursed man by making him what he is, and knows that *hubris* must be punished. Delimitation is no bad thing. Up to the time of Elgar, everybody knew what a symphony was—a work for orchestra in three or four movements, sonata-form in at least two of them, the hegemony of a key. Now all that people expect of a symphony is that it should be something 'serious' for orchestra. We don't want tragedy to end up as something 'sad' for the stage.

Sir Philip Sidney wrote of the 'sweet violence' of tragedy, an oxymoron pointing the mystery of our taking pleasure in the sight of enacted horror and suffering. Mr Williams leads us expertly through the mazes of traditional theory—the privy relief of catharsis,

Bradley's 'self-division and self-restitution', Nietzsche's metaphysical delight in the momentary identification with 'the primal Being', which manifests its 'extravagant fecundity' in creating phenomena (the Hero being the highest of these) only to destroy them. The modern age has produced better comic theory than tragic, but perhaps it has concluded that the older aesthetics of tragedy was really so much humbug, and that our pleasure in watching people enact self-destruction needs no explanation. Our joy in lying in bed is intensified by knowing that other people are going to work; our safety is defined by other people's danger and, more keenly, by their untimely deaths. Somebody has to die; let it not be us. The enactment of the death of one of our group is apotropaic, a magical ritual which averts the thunderbolt from ourselves. We find the greatest physical pleasure in voiding—either seed or excrement. The greatest non-physical pleasure is the voiding of fear. When the tragic hero contrives the purgation for us, we can afford to repay him with a measure of pity.

What reaction Mr Williams expects from us in the third part of his book, which consists of his own play *Koba*, cannot, I think, be defined in terms of innocent entertainment. It is political, didactic, prosy, but its being there at all is something of an embarrassment. He seems to say: I have taught you all I can about the modes of contemporary tragedy; now I have cooked up a sample for you. What he actually says, disarmingly, in his Foreword, is: 'If any reader is good enough to find one kind of work useful, but not the others, he is welcome to use the book accordingly.' But so evidently unified a treatise has to be eaten entire. It is very tough eating, heavy, unleavened by joy or humour. It makes tragedy a very tragic business.

Fleurs du Mal

REVOLUTIONS lead to steel whips, salt mines, and great writers in prison. Nevertheless, the term 'revolutionary' continues

to carry only the noblest connotations; 'reactionary' has the monopoly of the bad. Mr Harrison's thesis* is that at least five of the
greatest of our modern writers—namely, Yeats, Wyndham Lewis,
Pound, Eliot and Lawrence (not Joyce; Joyce is safe)—belonged to
an anti-democratic intelligentsia, and that there is an intimate
connection between their politics and their art.

All except Lawrence, so Mr Harrison tells us, probably derived
their view of life from T. E. Hulme, that *éminence grise*, who taught
that 'the humanist's belief in the perfectibility of man is wrong ...
and the reason for this is a failure to recognize original sin. Life is
essentially tragic and futile ... ' I should have thought there were
older teachers of pessimism than Hulme—the *vanitas vanitatum*
patriarchs, for instance, and St Augustine and Jansen and Schopen-
hauer. And it is hard to see what this traditional, pre-liberal, view
of life is reacting *against*. Presumably Eliot and the rest were vouch-
safed the benison of the Progressive Vision (being luckier than the
fathers and William Shakespeare) and sinned by rejecting it. That
their rejection was somehow linked with the greatest literature of the
century is one of those puzzling and infuriating things that WEA
classes find hard to explain away, though it is to the credit of WEA
instructors that they recognize a problem. M. Sartre, who pronounced John Dos Passos the greatest modern novelist, and those
large optimists beyond the Iron Curtain, who exalt Alan Sillitoe
above William Golding, have no such difficulty.

Mr Harrison is really very good and very fair about the seeming
paradox. He states where the reactionaries went wrong, and—if we
regard the politics of men of letters as of any interest at all—we
shall not be unhappy to find him right. These writers believed
passionately in art as a vision of order (unlike Orwell, who merely
saw it as a mode of political communication), and they did not
see how art and *demos* were compatible. Art must decay without
a sustaining elite or aristocracy, they thought; therefore they must
lean, in politics, towards authoritarianism. They were, no doubt,
misguided in thinking that one type of society must necessarily
breed better art than another, since art has its own authority and is

* *The Reactionaries* by John Harrison (Gollancz, 1966).

197

altogether parallel to the political order. And, conversely, they had no right to wish to impose the hierarchical structures of their art on a society that (*pace The Waste Land*) was no more a nasty welter of brutish values than any segment of the Golden Age it pleases poets to invoke.

It was, of course, very painful in the 'thirties to see Evelyn Waugh pro-Franco and Eliot on the fence, though I think it may seem more painful in retrospect than it really was. But can a writer be blamed if his Christianity makes him find republicanism on the Spanish pattern antipathetic? Yeats was silly to dream in print of Vandyke-bearded aristocrats with the poor clamouring at their gates, but he had, after all, seen a domestic revolution turn rotten. Lawrence was bitter at a bloodless England; *demos* had rejected the god in the loins; the voice of the mob reviled him and he retaliated. We all know that Pound was wrong to give comfort to Mussolini (it was minimal comfort anyway), but it seemed at the time the logical thing to do for a man who hated American *usura*. History shows all these men to have been politically misguided, just as—after the horrors of the gas-chambers—it exacerbates their mild anti-Semitism into a major crime. But there is a sense in which Eliot's Sir Ferdinand Klein has no power to revolt or hurt, since he is a convenient symbol of a truth that has nothing to do with racial or sectarian intolerance.

If one wished to get nasty about the activities, as opposed to the implicit ideologies, of writers whose politics mean as little to reading posterity as their moles or ingrowing toenails, one could say that Eliot at least firewatched in London while Auden scampered off to America—just as Edward Heath and Enoch Powell fought the Fascists while Harold Wilson directed economics and statistics and George Brown promoted the cause of the unions. This would be silly and pointless, but it is perhaps silly and pointless to look for a nexus between misguided political beliefs and supreme works of literature (remember that *New Statesman* Wodehouse competition, with Bertie Wooster saying, 'Cheeriheil'?). The alleged pro-fascism of these dead writers touches their art at no vital point: the forms they chose were no emanation of political conviction—any more than the Hopkinsian devices of the early poems of Auden and Day Lewis showed the great Jesuit to have been a crypto-Communist. And though I agree with Mr Harrison when he says 'to have sympathy for one's fellow human beings ... seems to me to be an eminently desirable human quality', I can't accept that 'the writers here discussed were lacking in this quality'. There are other modes of sympathy than those provided by the democratic forms—the sad patriotism of Yeats, Lawrence's anger over a traduced and debased England, Eliot's prayers for the single party of the dead.

I don't wish to imply that Mr Harrison's book is anything but decent and compassionate. What puzzles me is that he should think it necessary to survey ground neither arable nor suitable for building. It's waste land; it doesn't matter. There is an introduction by a man whom the dust-cover calls simply 'Empson'. Speaking of Joyce, he says that here was one example of an 'original and rigorous author' who 'could avoid these political and religiose fashions'. Alas, not so. He had indeed 'escaped from a theocracy such as many of the authors examined in this book were recommending', but the penultimate episode of *Finnegans Wake* presents the modern world in terms of sexual impotence; a thunderclap is needed to recall a theocratic age. Of course, to Empson the important or salvatory statements may be such *obiter scripta* as 'I am afraid poor Mr Hitler will soon have few friends in Europe apart from my nephews, Masters W. Lewis and E. Pound', but why should these be more significant than the *obiter dicta* of a dustman? It is the work, it is the work that counts. Empson, after another slam at Milton's 'sacrificial theology', finds comfort in the neo-Wellsianism of the Cambridge School of Divinity. I don't think any such ethos is likely to produce a new Hopkins or Eliot, but one never knows. Literature is disconcertingly autonomous.

The Triple Thinker

T. S. ELIOT said that Dr Johnson was 'a dangerous person to disagree with'. Of only three literary critics of our time may this also be said—Eliot himself, F. R. Leavis and Edmund Wilson. I must, in the instance of Mr Wilson, make it quite clear that his near-infallibility applies only to literary judgments: like the rest of us, he is capable of silly pronouncements on politics and income tax. But, from *Axel's Castle* on, no man has done more to show how exciting literary criticism can be, and no man has had a profounder influence on the capacity of a couple of generations (including my own) to form its own judgments on a very large and important sector of European literature—that one in which France meets and modifies the Anglo-American tradition.

Polymathy and the cosmopolitan outlook—these were never characteristics of pre-Eliotian criticism, but, since Eliot, we have all been expected to take Sanskrit as seriously as Greek, to read Garnier as well as Kyd, and to compare Dante's cosmology with Milton's. Wilson has, if anything, gone further than Eliot in calling for wider reading and even deeper linguistic study: he has seen, for instance, how the examination of the phenomenon of languages can stimulate purely literary inquiry, and he takes it for granted that we can argue about no book unless we know it in the original. The essay 'Legend and Symbol in *Doctor Zhivago*' makes the writings on that book of some British critics—unblessed by a sense of the need to know Russian—look very shabby. It is gloriously typical of Wilson to find something of *Finnegans Wake* in *Doctor Zhivago*, 'and something of the cabalistic Zohar, which discovers a whole system of hidden meanings in the text of the Hebrew Bible'. And if we ourselves cannot read Pasternak in the original? Well, we'd better get down to learning Russian, hadn't we? One of these days, I look forward to reading Edmund Wilson on 'Fantasy and Fact in the *Hikayat Abdullah*'.

In this compilation* there is a good wad of writings on linguistic matters—an appreciation of Eric Partridge (and some very privy fault-finding), a long essay called 'My Fifty Years with Dictionaries and Grammars', and some uncomfortable examinations of current clichés and solecisms. Wilson is not, however, one of the professional American linguists, able to talk about phonemes and taxemes, but a kind of very large Ivor Brown: 'I have always been greedy for words. I can never have enough of them. I love Elizabethan plays, dictionaries of slang and argot, lists of Americanisms.' His amateurism, admirable in so many ways, robs his attack on verbal slipshodness ('Words of Ill-Omen') of much of its force. He says: ' ... *womanizer* seems sometimes in England to have come to be used simply as a derogatory epithet for a man who likes women. The word has, in fact, become disgusting.' This emotive condemnation can frighten no one. We hear shrill crankiness rather than calm objectivity. And, if Wilson is so concerned to keep language pure and sharp, what are we to make of this Churchillian image (from 'Is it Possible to Pat Kingsley Amis?'): ' ... it is a world that, even imitating America, still carries, in an eroded and degraded form, the skeleton of its class stratification'?

These are small matters, however. Some of the longer literary essays are superb, especially the two on the Marquis de Sade:

I am in the habit of reading at breakfast, but I found that *Les 120 Journées* was the only book I could not face while eating. The almost exclusively anal interests of Sade, which extended to the excremental, figure here, as even his admirers have been obliged to confess, on a scale which is very discouraging from the literary point of view and from the scientific, disproportionate ...

After breakfast the task of examining the Sade documents is taken up with scholarly relish, and some of the judgments find almost aphoristic expression: 'The freakishness of Sade consists in his combining a voracious sexuality with some stubborn and infuriating

* *The Bit Between My Teeth: A Literary Chronicle of 1950–1965* by Edmund Wilson (W. H. Allen, 1966).

obstruction to having it gratified.' The essay on 'Swinburne's Letters and Novels', which finds great merit in the prose-writer and is severely critical of the poems ('We become exasperated with Swinburne for not knowing that too much brightness will make things dim'), is, to me anyway, an eye-opener. I am delighted to know that Swinburne wrote a cod French drama called *La Sœur de la Reine*, in which Queen Victoria confesses to her mother 'a humiliating love affair': '*Ce n'était pas un prince; ce n'était pas un milord, ni même Sir R. Peel. C'était un misérable du peuple, un nommé Wordsworth, qui m'a récité des vers de son 'Excursion' d'une sensualité si chaleureuse qu'ils m'ont ébranlée—et je suis tombée.*' I am even more delighted to know that Swinburne wrote a couple of cod reviews for the *Spectator* (on French writers of his own invention) and that one of them got into proof, though no further.

Doubtless one could get all this strange information, and so much more, from other sources, but one always seems to be learning new facts from Edmund Wilson, as well as being drubbed intellectually and enlightened with conclusions that, so well are they stated and so logically arrived at, appear inevitable and hence obvious. The range of his fifteen years of explorations is very wide, and nothing is dull. The Wilsonic image is still frightening, though there is great good humour, simple warmth, grumpiness, largeness of heart, and something very like schoolboyish ludibundance. He is, finally, so generous to modern British novelists that when he mentioned the 'Warwickshire burgess Shakespeare' I felt that this was too much of a good thing. But then I spotted the lower-case letter and breathed again.

8

Graves and Omar

FITZGERALD'S *Rubaiyyat* was a piece of Victorian naughtiness that got away with its godless hedonism by passing the buck. Darwin has exploded the Bible and there is no after-life, therefore drink wine and enjoy your regret at the dying of the roses. Such a philosophy cannot, however, be thrust direct at the corresponding societies and working-men's clubs, nor can it be plonked naked on to a parlour table. Dished up as quaint Oriental fatalism, it will shock, but not too much: here is the Eastern Mind, and there, thank God, is the British Empire. And here is the paynim heart that rightly expresses its disenchantment with Islam, which means we cannot altogether condemn the mode of the expression.

It has been known for a long time that Fitzgerald traduced Omar Khayyam, misrepresenting his philosophy through ignorance and, when his ignorance was shown up by M. Nicolas, the French Consul at Resht, persisting obstinately in his traduction. 'M. Nicolas', he said, 'does not consider Omar to be the material epicurean that I have literally taken him for, but a mystic, shadowing the Deity under the figure of wine, wine-bearer, etc., as Hafiz is supposed to do; in short, a Sufi poet like Hafiz and the rest.' And he tried to confute Nicolas with the judgments of scholars like Von Hammer, who pronounced Omar 'a free-thinker, and *a great opponent of Sufism*'.

Omar Ali-Shah, a Sufi poet of today and a classical Persian scholar, confirms that Nicolas was right and the Fitz-Omar cultists not merely wrong but immoral: 'I feel outraged by such wilful ignorance combined with the crooked manipulation of verses to make them fit alien patterns of thought.' Fitzgerald and his followers have been responsible for spreading in the West a false but highly seductive interpretation of Omar Khayyam. Despite the long European tradition of allegory, they have insisted on a crude literalism, reading the themes of wine and drunkenness as themselves and not as symbols. Moreover, their Persian scholarship has combined complacency with insufficiency. Of Fitzgerald and Cowell, Fitzgerald's Persian teacher, the Muslim divine Molvi Khanzada has said: 'Both scrawled badly like small children.' The time had come, considered Omar Ali-Shah, for a correct English verse translation of the *Rubaiyyat*, and he honoured Robert Graves with the commission: 'the greatest poetic compliment', says Graves, 'that I had ever been paid.'*

Fitzgerald worked from two Persian texts—the Ouseley manuscript No. 140, in the Bodleian (written down by Shaikh Mahmud-i-Jarbudaki at Shiraz in A.H. 865, or A.D. 1460), and a copy of the Bengal Asiatic Society's manuscript in their library at Calcutta. Neither of these, according to Graves (which means Omar Ali-Shah), is sufficiently authoritative. There has been a twelfth-century text 'available to Sufic students in Afghanistan since shortly after Khayaam's death more than eight hundred years ago', and this manuscript belongs to the family of Omar Ali-Shah. Omar Ali-Shah provided Graves with a literal crib, well-annotated, and it was from this that the poet—who presumably knows a good deal less Persian than either Fitzgerald or Cowell did—made his translation.

As the rest of us do not know this early manuscript, we have to take everything on trust, but the two quatrains reproduced in this volume, in both Arabic and romanized scripts, do not seem to differ from the Ouseley text. Readers who do not know the Arabic alphabet will gain some sense of the form and music of the original Omar from the following:

> Khurshid kamandi sobh bar bam afgand
> Kai Khusro i roz badah dar jam afgand
> Mai khur ki manadi sahri gi khizan
> Awaza i ishrabu dar ayam afgand.

* *The Rubaiyyat of Omar Khayaam. A New Translation with Critical Commentaries by Robert Graves and Omar Ali-Shah (Cassell, 1967).*

You will see that Fitzgerald reproduced the rhyme-scheme of the Omar quatrain exactly, though he rarely permitted himself a trisyllabic rhyme, as here. Such classical Persian as I know I learned when I studied Malay: having cut the barbed wire of the Arabic alphabet, which all Islamic peoples use, I was delighted to find that Persian was much easier than Arabic. Persian, in fact, belongs to the Indo-European family, though this is obscured by the large number of Arabic loan-words. Diffidently, since my Persian is rusty and I have no dictionary at hand, I offer this prose translation of the above stanza:

'The sun hurls the noose of the dawn on the roof, and the Cyrus of the day pours wine into the cup. Drink wine, for the muezzin who rises at dawn cries "Drink ye" to the world.'

This will be recognized as corresponding to Fitzgerald's

> Awake! for Morning in the Bowl of Night
> Has flung the Stone that puts the Stars to Flight:
> And lo! the Hunter of the East has caught
> The Sultan's Turret in a Noose of Light.

There is no reference to wine here, but Fitzgerald must not be blamed for an inept translation. In the Calcutta manuscript, it is a pebble, and not wine, that goes into the cup, and this Fitzgerald follows. Because of the long browsing time required by a camel after a day's march, caravans had to start before dawn. As a signal for loading, the caravan-master would put a stone into a metal vessel, cover the mouth with his hand, and then shake the thing as a rattle. Now here is Robert Graves's translation:

> While Dawn, Day's herald straddling the whole sky,
> Offers the drowsy world a toast 'To Wine',
> The Sun spills early gold on city roofs—
> Day's regal Host, replenishing his jug.

One regrets immediately the lack of rhyme. It's useless for Graves to protest the difficulty of matching the Persian form in English while at the same time retaining the whole meaning: the poet's job is to overcome such a difficulty. Fitzgerald may strike us as a minor

Victorian jingling camel-bells, but he has dared to try to transmit the music of the Persian. Graves is closer in meaning, but he is very pedestrian.

But, diffidently again, I submit that, since he is unhampered by the exigencies of a difficult rhyme-scheme, he might perhaps have got closer to Omar than he seems to have done. *Bam*, in the first line of the original, means 'roof'; *jam*, in the second, means 'cup'. Light catches the roof like a noose, but it is the roundness of the roof that suggests that image. The *bam* is a dome. Once caught, it can be turned upside down and changed into a *jam* or cup; then King Cyrus can pour the chilled white wine of the dawn into it. It is a startling image—typically Oriental, we like to think, remembering our Old Testament. And we are startled in another way. We expect day to begin with the first *waktu*—the muezzin from the minaret calling thinly that there is no God but Allah. What we hear instead is a kind of cock-crow—*ishrabu*, meaning 'Drink!' This, taken as blasphemy by Fitzgerald and his followers, may be regarded merely as a new and forceful way of representing the muezzin's message: 'God is wine; drink Him.' The poetic charge is considerable.

There is a regrettable lack of such magic in the Graves version. It's hard to see the spilling of gold *on* city roofs as a replenishing: the correct preposition is *in*, and the *bam* must somehow be turned into a *jam*. Also, there's too much pleonasm. Dawn can be nothing but Day's herald; the dawn gold is bound to be *early* gold. And 'Day's regal Host' is surely inferior to the *Cyrus* of the original, with its associations derived from a real king.

The other stanza reproduced as part of the appendix to this volume is one of those, not infrequent, which make the third line rhyme:

> Gar dast dihad zi maghzi gandum nani
> Az mai kadui zi gusfandi rani
> Wa angah man wa tu nishasta dar wairani
> 'Aish buwad an na haddi har sultani.

In Fitzgerald's First Edition, this is rendered as:

> Here with a Loaf of Bread beneath the Bough,
> A Flask of Wine, a Book of Verse—and Thou
> Beside me singing in the Wilderness—
> And Wilderness is Paradise enow.

A little-known version by Brigadier-General E. H. Rodwell (Kegan Paul, Trench, Trubner, 1931) gets closer:

> If fortune favours me with bread of wheat,
> A gourd of wine, sufficiency of meat,
> With beauty sitting by me in the wild,
> Kings in my happiness may not compete.

(Fitzgerald moved too far away from that *sultani*.) Here is Mr Graves:

> Should our day's portion be one mancel loaf,
> A haunch of mutton and a gourd of wine
> Set for us two alone on the wide plain,
> No Sultan's bounty could evoke such joy.

A literal translation would run something like this:

'Should I be lucky enough to have a loaf made from the kidneys of wheat, together with a gourd of wine and a leg of mutton, and should I be sitting on the plain with one whose face is beautiful like the moon, then that would be bliss beyond the reach of a Sultan.'

Fitzgerald seems to have got the singing from the mention of a lute in the preceding quatrain of the Calcutta version. The substitution of the book of verse for the leg of mutton is excusable only when we remember that grosser food than bread and wine is apt only for Victorian humorous verse. This wishy-washy water-colour idyllism of Fitzgerald won't really do, but it has a certain music and is myopically picturesque. Graves has everything except the magic: even that 'mancel' fails to lift the loaf off the ground. He badly needs rhyme.

One further example. Here is Fitzgerald, in his fourth edition:

They say the Lion and the Lizard keep
The Courts where Jamshyd gloried and drank deep;
And Bahram that great Hunter, the Wild Ass
Stamps o'er his Head, but cannot break his Sleep.

And now Graves:

A Palace gorged in by gigantic Bahram—
The vixen whelps there and the lion nods.
Bahram, who hunted none but onagers,
Lies tumbled in a pitfall called the grave.

Neither can render the paranomastic irony of Omar's use of the word *gur*, which means both 'wild ass' and 'grave'. 'Bahram', says the original, 'was continually hunting the *gur*, but now the *gur* has caught Bahram.' Both poets succeed equally with association, but identity is beyond the resources of the language.

As poetry, the Graves version is lacking. But his insistence that we view the *Rubaiyyat* as an entity, and not as a bundle of disjunct stanzas, is of some value: a new dignity is given to the Omar we thought we knew. And Graves has the 'controlled tenseness' proper to a religious poem; the austere accuracy of his verses justifies his inveighing against Fitzgerald's 'slip-shod sense, faulty grammatic construction and neo-romantic affectation'. Nevertheless, his work is neither one thing nor the other: it is not quite a poem, and it is not quite a crib. The task of achieving a true glamour that will drive out Fitzgerald's false is evidently still there for some poet's undertaking. Or it may just be a matter of deblanking the Graves verse, turning (for instance)

Ah me, the book of early glory closes,
The green of Spring makes way for wintry snow,
The cheerful bird of Youth flutters away—
I hardly noticed how it came or went

into

I see the book of early glory close,
The green of Spring make room for winter snows.

The cheerful bird of Youth flutters away—
I hardly notice how it comes or goes.

Something like that, anyway.

On English in English

THE term 'philologist' is becoming old-fashioned. To study language is no longer a legitimate spare-time activity of those who use language. But, in the period covered by Professor Bolton's compilation* it was only the literary men who concerned themselves with the broader issues of the growth and control of language; the makers of penny grammars and spelling-books and elocutionary readers represented a mean and niggling specialization, but the only one there was. Reading what Caxton, Camden, Hobbes, Defoe and Johnson had to say about English, one is heartened by a humanism that is now pretty well dead in what has come to be a highly technical study. One is also, and perhaps one should not be, surprised at how much they knew. There is a tendency nowadays to regard all linguistic scholarship coming before, say, 1890 as highly suspect. But William Camden, in *Remaines Concerning Britain* (published 1605), has the instincts of a good language historian, though some of his conclusions are false. Thus, he recognizes the importance of Scaliger's discovery that certain Persian words are cognate with their Germanic equivalents ('*Fader, Moder, Bruder, Band* &c ... in the very sence as we now vse them'), but finds in that not evidence of a common ancestor but a possible proof 'that the *Saxons* our progenitors, which planted themselves heere in the West, did also to their glorie place *Colonies* likewise there in the East'.

Let them take the languages of this country—as William Harrison also does, twenty years earlier than Camden, in *The Description of*

* *The English Language: Essays by English and American Men of Letters, 1490–1839.* Selected and edited by W. F. Bolton (C.U.P., 1966).

Britaine—and they seldom go very far wrong. Speaking of the languages of Devon and Cornwall, Harrison sees, rightly, 'more affinitie with the Armoricane toong than I can well discusse of' (nowadays we would say Breton, not Armorican), but, again rightly, he says, 'they are both but a corrupted kind of British' (nowadays we would say Welsh). These old scholars described well, though they could not keep out phony aesthetic judgments (Harrison calls Anglo–Saxon 'an hard and rough kind of speech, God wot'). What they lacked chiefly was an ability to gather the materials for a larger view of the languages of the Indo–European group: they did not, for instance, know any Sanskrit. And perhaps the area where we would disagree with them most is that in which they seem to shake hands with the framers of Newspeak: they believed that English could be limited and controlled.

In the preface to his translation of *Eneydos* (1490), William Caxton gives prototypical expression to the classical worry about the excessive variety of English. He tells the story of the mercer 'named sheffelde' who went to buy eggs from a 'good wyf' and was told 'that she coude speke no frenshe. And the marchaunt was angry, for he also coulde speke no frenshe, but wold haue egges and she vnderstoode hym not. And thenne at last a nother sayd that he wolde haue eyren / then the good wyf sayd that she vnderstod him wel / Loo what sholde a man in thyse days now wryte, egges or eyren'. English then was still, rather painfully, moving towards a standard or received dialect. Two hundred years later, Daniel Defoe—in his remarkable *Essay upon Projects*—is still concerned with the tendency of English to spend its strength in wanton proliferation of words. He wants 'Purity and Propriety of Stile'; he abhors 'Irregular Additions'. What he is after is an academy on the French pattern, an oligarchical linguistic authority trail-blazed by a dictator: 'We want indeed a *Richlieu* to commence such a Work: For I am persuaded, were there such a *Genius* in our Kingdom to lead the way, there wou'd not want Capacities who cou'd carry on the Work to a Glory equal to all that has gone before them.' Swift, who despised Defoe, agreed with him on the need to limit and fix the language: 'The Fame of our Writers is usually confined to these two Islands, and it is hard it should be limited in *Time*, as much as *Place*, by the perpetual Variations of our Speech.'

Ben Jonson (also represented in this book as an amateur philologist) said of Shakespeare: '*Sufflaminandus est*'—keep him down, control him, cool his extravagance. The classical attitude to Shakespeare is also the classical attitude to the language he helped, more than any writer, to enrich. English is so various and creative that it must be rejoiced in; at the same time, for the same reasons, it must be feared. English writers have envied French its cool capacity for logical statement; try setting out a close argument in English, and its chimes of ambiguity, as well as the poetic conflict between its native Anglo–Saxon and imported Latinate elements, will over-colour the white enlightenment. It is hard for an English writer to use his language: he tends to be used by it. The English poets, who want to be used, or possessed, are luckier than the practitioners of didactic prose. Great Augustans like Gibbon achieved control only by artificial balance or deliberate irony.

In Sartre's novel *Nausée*, the hero Roquentin is sickened by the sight of a chestnut tree in a park—an excessive mass of being-in-itself, a cancer of self-proliferating *yin*. The English rational mind is similarly nauseated by the luxuriance of the language it tries to work in, and it is perhaps no accident that empiricism—which mistrusts words—has made such an appeal to the philosophers of these islands. David Hume, who is not represented in this volume, was scared of any word that did not assert either mathematical quantity or 'matters of fact and existence'; John Locke—Professor Bolton gives us a large slice from *An Essay Concerning Human Understanding*—insisted on the purely arbitrary connection between a word and its meaning. The logical empiricists of our own day have so mistrusted 'natural language' that they found it necessary to hammer out a purely logical syntax and to limit statements to the mathematically or experimentally verifiable. The problem of making our own natural language submit to the needs of rational communication is implied, where not directly stated, throughout this compilation. And yet, even when Dr Johnson himself brings his weight to the taming of it, English insists on having its own way.

For one of the small joys of watching these philologists at work—from Caxton to de Quincey—lies in seeing the continued autonomy of what they would all like to control. We are given not only a history of linguistic ideas but a history of East Midland English. 'The comyn termes that be dayli vsed ben lyghter to be vnderstonde than the olde and auncyent englysshe' is the same language as 'In every word of extensive use, it was requisite to mark the progress of its meaning, and show by what gradations of intermediate sense it has passed from its primitive to its remote and accidental signification'. Caxton's 'eyren' eventually passed out of currency, which then admitted only 'egges', but it was not because Caxton, or any other pundit, wanted it that way. At a level below the consciousness of even the most authoritative linguist, the English language followed its own laws. One thing we can learn from all these pleas for academies, imposed uniformities, the enactment of stasis, is their utter hopelessness.

One of the American contributions to this book is Noah Webster's plan—published in 1789—for the rationalization of English spelling. He had in mind, in that year of revolution, only the 'American Tongue', and he thought, by the use of 'a correct orthography', that a general uniformity of pronunciation could be achieved throughout the United States. His proposals—with the exception of such forms as *laf* for *laugh*—are still applicable to British English, and there are many who still wonder why we have not yet established *meen* for *mean*, *blud* for *blood*, and so on. The answer is, I think, pretty obvious. The pronunciation of English, both here and there, continues to resist uniformity, and the printed word remains a compromise between a phonological notation and a semantic counter. If we are to give *blud* to a Northern English man, we must also give him *wul*; an Irishman maintains the traditional distinction between *sea* and *see*. The orthographical rationalizers, of whom Bernard Shaw was the last of the great ones, all fell into the amateur's trap of thinking that change could be imposed, that there could be legislation for English, that the language had only one acceptable dialect, and that a phonemic spelling really mattered. Webster's aspirations fit all too neatly into the general pattern of a control to be wished but not

attained. Professor Bolton is well aware of where the literary legis-
lators go wrong: they assume 'that the writer is an influence on, but
is not influenced by, the habits of the linguistic community. Caxton
drew heavily on French and Latin when he attempted to emulate the
syntactical systems of those languages, but he was limited by the
actual clausal conventions of fifteenth-century English. He could no
more mould the language by extension than Johnson or Franklin
could mould it by restriction'.

That the writer does influence language is undeniable. He gives
it idioms, images, new coinages. By working, as Chaucer did, in the
dialect of that geographical area where the capital and the senior
universities are situated, he was able to give a kind of sempiternal
authority to it, help to consolidate its hegemony as the standard
language. But writers are the children of language: the mother-
tongue takes their gifts of adornment indulgently. We are understanding better the nature of the relationship nowadays, and it is
doubtful whether we should read, with much hope of enlightenment, an anthology of speculations on language compiled from the
writings of literary men of today. This is the age of the Two
Cultures: lang and lit are becoming ever more irreconcilable studies.

English as an America

TERMS like 'The American Language' or 'The Australian
Language' or, for that matter (and we may expect this soon), 'The
Rhodesian Language' have more to do with politics than linguistics.
When colonies turn themselves into sovereign powers, it is natural
that they should wish to confer a national status on their versions of
the mother tongue. But a national language is not like a constitution:
it cannot be fabricated. Crown a dialect and decorate it with flags,
and it still remains a dialect. English as spoken by the Tamils of
India has drifted further from metropolitan English than the language of either Milwaukee or Alice Springs, but nobody hails the

emergence of a new tongue; one is inclined rather to talk disparagingly of a perverted English. Preston (Lancs.) has locutions like *'Oo's getten eed-warch'* and *'Art wichet?'*, which are phonetically and morphologically remote from anything we hear in London, but 'The Preston (Lancs.) Language' is an absurd concept. To stress minor differences between U.K. English and U.S.A. or Australasian English, elevating these into signals of radical divergence, is the task of the patriot rather than the dialectologist.

The irony is that the writers of books on the liberated daughters of the tyrannical mother tongue are rarely qualified to deal with that aspect of language where the differences really show. I receive letters from America, and only the address and stamp indicate that I am being written to in The American Language. Admittedly, a polite correspondent will temper his usage to my British taste, perhaps taking a cosmopolitan's pleasure in avoiding *gotten* or *atop* or *sidewalk*; I will perhaps reciprocate by deliberately (with the same pleasure) employing these forms. What we do is to meet in the same linguistic area, and this has more to do with the Queen's English than with that putative American Language. The true difference comes out when I meet my correspondent: my phonemes and intonations are not the same as his. There is also the matter of slang, but the transatlantic two-way traffic is pretty vigorous, and he will be as inclined to say 'It's not cricket' as I will be to talk about taking a rain-check. In terms of educated usage (as opposed to *phones*, which is what American linguists call the sounds we make) there seems to be a genuine Anglo-American community.

Is it then necessary to produce a book like the late Wilson Follett's *Modern American Usage** when we (meaning members of the Anglo-American community) already have Fowler? Apparently yes, since where British and American speakers and writers diverge is chiefly in the forms their solecisms take. What Follett and his successors are doing is precisely what Fowler did—to promote a clear, dignified, unambitious expository standard of English which has little to do

---

* *Modern American Usage* by Wilson Follett. Edited and completed by Jacques Barzun and others (Hill and Wang; Longmans, 1966).

with art but much to do with journalism. They are as stringent as Fowler, though more rational and less pigheaded. What many readers of the book may feel, however, is that there is a purging from the language of those elements which make it American, an elimination of American herbs (pronounced *erbs*) from the joint cuisine.

Take the split infinitive, for instance. One had always assumed that the British used it guiltily and the Americans with glee. Follett invokes two British pundits—Shaw and Fowler—in its defence and says: 'It should be used when it is expressive and well led up to.' That goes for the whole language community: Americans can lay no special claim. Follett finds it rare in speech: 'the voice supplies the stress needed by the unsplit form or conceals by a pause the awkwardness of the adverb placed before or after it.' I doubt the accuracy of that, and I don't like the whimsy of this:

> It is in written work that splitting is called for, and desk sets should include small hatchets of silver or gold for the purpose.

We need examples, not hatchets. And we ought to be told why a double standard may be assumed for usage, as well as why the stream of English has always rejected the form. Comparing it to consecutive fifths in harmony won't do. Consecutive fifths implied bitonality before music was ready for it: they weren't an irrational bugbear. The rhythm of Germanic languages has never been able to take easily to the split infinitive: *schnell zu gehen* admits the buffer of a mere synsemanteme (or mortar word) between two autosemantemes (or brick words); *zu schnell gehen* is clotted; *zu gehen schnell* opposes the tendency of subordinate verb-forms to move to the end of the phrase. Something of this still adheres to English.

Of course, none of that kind of Emily Post stuff really matters: do what you like with words so long as you're intelligible. The ear is the best guide, whether in speaking or writing. But there was always something charming about the opposition of British non-splitting prissiness ('definitely to do something') to American what-the-hell punch ('to definitely do something'). It's a pity *Modern American Usage* is so woolly about it. It's not so woolly about another traditional solecism which, having early gained general currency in

America, has now received the blessing of a British public utility: 'Due to snow on the line trains will be running late.' Follett and his successors (who include not only Jacques Barzun but Phyllis Mc-Ginley and Lionel Trilling) say: 'Can someone complain that *due to worry* he sleeps badly? The answer of everyone who cares about workmanship is a flat no.' I fail to see what workmanship has to do with it. If we can make one conjunctive phrase do the work of two, we have made some progress along the track of formal economy. The great thing about English has always been its tendency to enlarge the lexicon but at the same time jettison dead structural wood.

If, from this example, the reader gains the impression that *Modern American Usage* is somewhat conservative and pedantic (rather like Fowler, but not quite so dogmatic: the tone is rather of donnish regret), then he will not be far wrong. Thus, the back formation *enthuse* is less acceptable than its fellows *reminisce, donate*, and *convalesce* probably because 'no verb lurks in its past history, whereas Latin verbs do exist for the other three'. But *enthuse* is a useful form, and this question of history is bunk. So *bant*, a back formation from *Banting*, had a shakier grammatical provenance, but the instinct that made it was sound. To take over the name of the first great reducer as a gerund or present participle was both economical and witty, but—on the usual ground of 'rationality' (which really plays little part in linguistic processes)—the purists had to disapprove.

Modern American Usage disapproves of so much that one is impelled to a kind of vicarious defiance: if Americans are not to say 'I figure he is likely to get the appointment' (they should use *suppose* instead), let us say it for them. Then there is this term *togetherness*, which is called a 'dreadful word'. It first appeared, apparently, in Kahlil Gibran's *The Prophet* in 1923—'a publisher's dream of the inspirational gift book—a work for which limp leather would have to be invented had it not existed'—and its *locus classicus* remains the statement 'Let there be spaces in your togetherness'. Now it seems to me that summary condemnation is not enough. I dislike the word as much as anyone, but I want to know why. Morphologically, it's as legitimate a formation as anything in the long roll of German

zusammen compounds; evidently, to judge from its excessive popularity, it fulfilled a semantic need. But perhaps the 'sensible men' of
Follett's article on the word were revolted by the sheer existence
of that need; there are some things (and marital togetherness is one of
them) that must either never reach the verbal surface or be cocooned
in some such Latinate generality as *sodality* or hybrid like *companion-
ship*. *Togetherness*—a pure Teuton—gets too close to unveiling
intimacies.

One cannot quarrel with Follett or Barzun or anyone when the
charge is sounded against 'the general diffuseness of aim that is
weakening many words'. It is obviously healthier to prefer the con-
creteness of 'The readers of this magazine are adults' to the abstract
'The readership ... is adult'. And the barbarians or *barbaroi* or
babblers ('the same imitative word is related to Babel, the well-
known institution which today would be called a General Confusion Center') have doubtless to be put down. Out, then, with the
tautology of *guidance counselor* (whose inventor 'had barbarism in
him by birthright') and the dollie-fringed *fun activities* and the
bureaucratic *leisure-time preoccupations*. But turn everything over
carefully before consigning it to (or putting it in) the dustbin (or
refuse container): don't just take the word of the Follett academy
that this or that is junk.

For these people have no more authority to legislate for usage
than you or I or anyone. Hemingway, a great writer, talked about
'writing good'. How finicking are the rules of 'correctness' of the
Fowlerians and Follettists when seen in relation to the *insouciance* of
literary artists, or that mysterious general will which drives the
language community at large to determine the forms and sounds and
structures of the future. If we go to Fowler or Follett for guidance,
it should be guidance in the narrow zone of linguistic etiquette, on
which—in our superstitious way—we are always ready to be
instructed, as in the movements of a religious ritual. But all the
fulmination, scorn, querulousness and cold reason of the pundits can
do nothing to stop the current of language from going its own way.

★

Modern American Usage promotes, with Bostonian rigour, the virtues of the Queen's English. A dictionary which purports to be of the 'English language' turns out to be very American.* American in its generosity as well as in the angle of approach to the total vocabulary which our Atlantic communities share.

We're given more than we want—atlas, gazetteer, summary of world history, Declaration of Independence, and—more defensible, as genuinely lexical superfetations—concise French, Spanish, Italian, and German dictionaries. Great names as well as baptismal ones peer from among the common nouns (I'll come to this in a moment). The unwillingness to distinguish between the functions of a dictionary and an encyclopedia, common as late as Dr Johnson and justified by Noah Webster in terms of the pioneering urge to educate the Union, becomes somewhat embarrassing here. If there was space to spare it should have been planted with Onions—I mean an etymological lust seeking (like the recent fine *Oxford Etymological Dictionary*) the deepest possible penetration. Take *shit*, for example, which only goes back in Random House to Old English *scitan* (a long *i* giving *shite*) and *scite* (dung) and *scitte* (diarrhœa). C. T. Onions makes poetry out of it by suggesting that we end up with Indo-European **skheid-* (split, divide) and consider, on the way, the etymology of *schism*. And, while I have the two books open before me, let me grumble at the Random House pronunciation guide, which is as old-fashioned as old Webster—all loops and diacritics. The Oxford Dictionary uses the International Phonetic Alphabet in its broad form, the only system of sound-indication which (broad or narrow) the 1960s should be willing to accept.

My choice of *shit* as a first sample doesn't spring from scatomania or scatophilia (words which Random House doesn't give, preferring to hand you the do-it-yourself pieces *scato-* and *-mania*—though not *-philia*—and let you make up your own learned terms); I have an old habit of testing a dictionary through its treatment of borderline taboo words. It dates from childhood, when I was delighted to find *bum* (appropriately) in my school Chambers and from then on

---

* *The Random House Dictionary of the English Language.* Editor in Chief: Jess Stein (Random House, New York).

approached dictionaries with the exhilaration proper to banned books. *Fuck* and *cunt* are not in Random House, but *cunnelingus* is. For *arse* we are directed to *ass* and there given:

1. *Slang.* the buttocks. 2. *Slang (vulgar).* rectum.
3. *Slang (vulgar).* coitus; a woman considered as an object of coitus.

And then a pretty full etymology, going back—through Middle English *ars, ers*—to Old English *aers, ears*, and finding cognateness in Greek *orrhos*. Very strangely, the Modern English form, which has a long and honourable ancestry, is not given at all. Follett gives no guide to Americans on the use of the term, but I feel sure that he would have recommended the British form. *Arse* is in Ben Jonson and *Hudibras* and Urquhart's Rabelais, but *ass* is in *Last Exit to Brooklyn* and *An American Dream*.

A really American dictionary then, on this count, and, if we look further, American in its occasional inaccuracies over British idioms. The American use of *cup of tea*—as in 'Chemistry, not art, is my cup of tea'—is surely the British use; I have not yet met—despite the dictionary's assurance that these are Britishisms—either 'He has a sad life, but that's his cup of tea' or 'The investment seems secure, but be careful of that cup of tea'. And certain relics of the British Empire do badly. A *stinger* is 'a highball of whiskey and soda,' but only because the Malay word for a half (in this context a half measure of whisky) is *stĕngah*: STING + -ER doesn't come into it. Onions is right in making *tiffin* a light midday meal in India; Random House are wrong in generalizing it into 'British'.

On the other hand they are with-it, switched on to the contemporary scene and so on. A *rocker* is '(in Britain) a teenager who is devoted to motorcycling, typically wears a leather jacket, tight pants, and boots, and strives to attain a tough, unsentimental personality'. Etymology? *Mod* is: 'a teenager who strives to attain a sophisticated, aloof personality and affects an ultramodern version of Edwardian dress and manners.'

Every dictionary that strives to attain up-to-dateness must pay the penalty of soon seeming out-of-date. Were phenomena so transient worth recording? A *Teddy boy* was 'a rebellious British youth affecting the dress of the reign of Edward VII'. He could, from that, be a sort of Shelley, full of high ideals. How waxwork they all look set there (along with the *stilyagi*). Dictionaries always cleanse and statify things (*statify* is not given): where are the razors and boots? The *Beat Generation* is, I think, well defined: 'members of the generation that came of age after World War II who, supposedly as a result of disillusionment stemming from the Cold War, espouse mystical detachment and relaxation of social and sexual tensions.'

Beatles and their derivatives are not to be found. *Jazz* is presented at some length, but its origins are left to Raven I. McDavid Jr's introductory article on *Usage, Dialects, and Functional Varieties*: 'a Southern term meaning to copulate.'

As for the proper names which are sprinkled among the common ones, their choice seems pretty arbitrary, especially when they are the names of writers. I don't object to the only two literary Burgesses being Frank Gelett and Thornton Waldo, but, if Louis Golding is to be admitted, William should be too; the whole Waugh family is there, but not Anthony Powell; Kingsley Amis, but neither Iris Murdoch nor Muriel Spark. Vladimir Vladimirovich Nabokov (a complicated symbology brought to the phonetic representation of his name) is not credited with the introduction of *nymphet* ('2. a sexually attractive young girl'; etymology—Middle French *nymph-ette*), and *Lolita* is merely a 'girl's given name, form of *Charlotte* or *Dolores*'. Now, in a dictionary as up-to-date as this, *Lolita* ought to be given common-noun status ('That kid's a real Lolita') like *Pooh-Bah* ('a person who holds several positions, esp. ones which give him bureaucratic importance').

But no more carping, or very little more. This is expert lexicography which neglects no aspect of the contemporary scene, synthetizing the functions of many of the special dictionaries. As a compulsive dictionary-reader I welcome it, but I'm dubious about its usurping the lectern in my workroom occupied by the 1926 Webster.

I cannot like, however much I may admire, a dictionary that cuts itself off so thoroughly from literature. Random House define *sprung rhythm* and list Gerard Manley among the Hopkinses (though there's no cross-reference, no indication that GMH invented the term); they tell us what a sonnet is; a huge library-list can be plummed out. But no literary citations illustrate usage; one misses the blank-verse lines and heroic couplets that humanize Webster. This is a hard, efficient, utilitarian dictionary, short-haired and contact-lensed. It is undoubtedly what the age demands. But Johnson's quirky pioneering masterpiece should be kept near to it, just to remind us that there was once a time when a man could contain a language. Present-day English exists somewhere *out there*: a foreign country with familiar features, a sort of America. One's hopelessness about ever knowing it all is, of course, a reflection of one's resigned ignorance in the face of so many of its referents. Accept the big sleep, then, noting that the final Random House entry is ZZZ ('used to represent the sound of a person snoring').

Word, World and Meaning

WE MAY as well (clinging to the rags of the liberal, whimsical, Fosterian tradition) begin with a slice of pidgin:

Long time ago ole feller Donkey him bin big feller boss longa country. Alright. By an' by another feller—him name ole Muckbet—bin hearem longa three feller debbil-debbil woman: them feller debbil-debbil woman bin tellem him straight out— 'You'll be big feller boss yourself soon.' Alright. Him bin havem lubra, ole Lady Muckbet.

That, as the reader will at once recognize, is part of an attempt to tell the story of Macbeth to a primitive people: the native word *lubra* pins the people down to Australia, Northern Territory. Most readers will probably be amused, even touched, and want to hear more. Few will be outraged, as T. G. H. Strehlow is outraged: 'The whole account is an inadequate, untruthful, and malicious caricature of a great story ... Yet this is the medium in which most native legends have been noted down in the first instance by white scientists!' To be outraged, even minimally, is to have the glimmerings of a concern with both linguistics and anthropology and the growing area where these two sciences meet. To be tolerantly amused is to wish to perpetuate the fiction of the uncomplicated 'native' with his 'primitive' tongue and his 'infantile' thought-processes, who does not deserve to know about the eclipse of the sun but instead must put up with 'him kerosene belong Jesus Christ him bugger up, him finish'. How quaint, how charming.

The technological hegemony of the West has been reponsible for the fallacy that western languages are somehow superior to those of less well-developed communities. It is not clear in what the fancied superiority consists—logicality of form, ability to generalize? Certainly not the former, since Greek and Latin, with their intolerable batteries of irregularities, continue to be accorded great reverence, while Chinese and Malay, which have neither declensions nor conjugations, are regarded as too naked to be decent. But a capacity for forming abstract terms must, to science-worshipping societies, seem more desirable than that alleged 'over-particularity of primitive speech' which Archibald A. Hill, with other primitive language scholars, refutes. One of Hill's specialities is Cherokee, which, ever since an unfortunate statement by Otto Jespersen, unchecked by serious inquiry and perpetuated in book after book, has been taken almost as a type of the primitively inefficient language.

Jespersen was shocked to find that the Cherokees had no general term meaning 'to wash'. His source was A. H. Sayce, whom Jespersen misunderstood, and who in his turn misunderstood his own sources. What is most disturbing is that the original source (the pioneer Americanist, John Pickering) was making his observations as early as 1823, and that a book by Professor Ullmann, published as late as 1951, should speak of the 'savage' (meaning the Cherokee) as having 'special terms for "wash oneself" ... "wash someone else" ... but none for the simple act of "washing" '. Professor Ullmann has been caught out before, dishing up the tired old myth (taken from Professor Conklin) about the Malay language having no particular words for denoting relationship but having to make do with some such general term as *saudara*. (The 'primitive' language, it seems, can never win; it does everything to excess, whether generalizing or particularizing.) There was nothing to prevent Professor Ullmann from buying a copy of *Teach Yourself Malay*.

And, says Hill, there is nothing to prevent philologists from getting the facts about Cherokee from contemporary specialists who are still working in the field. He shows that Cherokee has its general terms like any other language, and that it is 'possessed of order and system, no matter if that system is different from our own'. The linguistic approach to anthropology is disposing very nicely of the old fallacies, but there are still too many scholars unwilling to listen. To be told that no language is superior to any other language may be a shock to the racialist, but it should please those who are promoting the notion of human unity, the common dignity of man.

But neither the anthropologist nor the specialist in linguistics is directly concerned with such humane slogans, nor should he be. The task of the anthropologist is to study 'that larger whole which is the common property of all groups of men and which distinctively sets off mankind from all other animals' (the late A. L. Kroeber's words) — this we call culture. But within the totality of culture language is revealed as a satisfying self-contained and self-ruled unit, though its very autonomy may make it suspect to the anthropologist — a product of culture, it may nevertheless not always be a reliable index to it. Yet culture and language do share a single body of phenomena, the one we term 'meaning'. Linguists, as Kroeber reminds us, equate culture with the lexical element in their studies: a dictionary tells us little about the structure of the language, but it tells us a great deal about the culture in which the language operates.

This whole question of 'meaning' remains a difficult one, and it is significant that the study of linguistic sounds and structures (phonemes and morphemes) is further advanced than semantics, the science of meaning. Once we start admitting the semantic element into the study of forms we find the laboratory door torn from its hinges, life, like a gang of louts, rampaging in. Anthropology is the humanizing force that linguistics needs, since it is impatient with those aspects of language that are not lexical. But it recognizes well enough that there are shadowy regions in linguistics which will enable the anthropologist to dig deeper than observed patterns of behaviour—regions that lie between meaning and form.

One thinks, for instance, of those untranslatable 'numerical coefficients' which are a feature of languages like Chinese and Malay. A Malay–English dictionary tells us that *satu* means 'one' and *rumah* means 'house'; the grammarian tells us that the Malay words are invariable. The tyro may go confidently ahead and render 'a house' as *satu rumah* but he will have committed a small solecism. The Malay says *sa-buah rumah* (*sa-* is an apocope of *satu*). The dictionary gives *buah* as meaning 'fruit', but it is evident that the clear light of lexical meaning is to be excluded from *sa-buah*: we are in the shadowy zone. The Malay mind, in fact, finds it necessary to classify objects according to shape and size—*buah* suggests something vaguely round, vaguely large. And so he will render 'a car' as *sa-buah kereta* and even 'a country' as *sa-buah negeri*. He has a whole battery of coefficients, most of which relate to shape and size (*sa-biji*, meaning literally 'a seed', introduces words denoting small objects), though one— *sa-ekor* ('a tail'), used for animals—denotes a characteristic feature of the class of objects. The interest here, it would seem, is less linguistic than anthropological: light is thrown not just on a pattern of behaviour but also on a mode of thought. Benjamin Lee Whorf shows how the language of the Navaho Indians possesses an even subtler classificatory system. The Navaho world of inanimate objects is divided into 'long' and 'round', but this is not indicated by noun coefficients, nor (on the analogy of gender) do the words form morphological groups. It is the verb-stems that are affected: 'a different stem is required for a "round" or a "long" subject or object'.

It is conceivable that the gender system of the Indo-European languages—including English and the other languages we learn at school—has its origin in a view of the world more meaningful to the anthropologist than to the linguist. A. Meillet notes that the feminine gender designates not solely animate females but inanimate objects that, through a kind of personification, may be thought of as possessing female life. The earth bears things and lies open to the sky; it is feminine. A tree gives fruit and hence is feminine, but the fruit—the thing borne—has to be neuter. The hand receives and is feminine; the foot is aggressive and is therefore masculine. This, as Meillet recognizes, must not be taken too far. 'The grammatical machinery compels all animate nouns to be either masculine or feminine', and arbitrary apportionment—based more on fancy than on animistic conviction—tends to creep in. But linguistic anthropology can attempt to read the signs, clarifying the picture of the prehistoric Aryans.

All science prefers the light to the shadows, and it is on the wide plain of semantics that the great work waits to be done. The nature of the problem of meaning in its anthropological context is well indicated by Eugene A. Nida's article 'Linguistics and Ethnology in Translation Problems', where the task of the Bible-bearing missionary (traditionally the pioneer in anthropology) is examined. 'At times,' says Nida, 'the problems of translation which involve social practices become very complex.' There is this matter, for instance, of 'a bill of divorcement' (Mark x. 4) and how to put it over to the Totonacs of Mexico. When the Totonacs require a divorce they pay the town-secretary to strike their name from the civil register. If divorce is by mutual consent, the fee is small; if only one party wants a divorce, the fee is considerably higher. But the whole process is regarded as legal, and the Totonac term for 'divorce' has, as its root-meaning, 'erasure of one's name'. To translate 'bill of divorcement'—as a cybernetic engine might—into 'a letter stating that a man is leaving his wife' would induce strong passion among the Totonacs: they would all wholeheartedly condemn the ethic that the text seemed to reveal. Translation, then, cannot be a matter of Nabokovian fidelity. When the Totonacs read, in Mark xiv. 3, about a man carrying a pitcher of water, they are greatly amused—water-carrying being woman's work—and 'are astonished at the man's ignorance of propriety'. Ignorance of ethnology led one translator into African tongues to render 'Holy Spirit' as something like 'a spirit (probably an evil one) which has acquired a tabu by contact with some other spirit (undoubtedly evil)'. The moral is clear for all linguistics scholars. The referent (that is, the extra-linguistic datum to which a word refers) is not just in a vague 'outside world': it is in a narrow closed world hemmed in by laws, codes, and traditions. No wonder that linguistics is happiest in the safe world of sounds and structures.

Language, Culture and Society, however, is not primarily—if at all—concerned with prodding the linguistics men into doing more about semantics. Its aim is to show the anthropologist a wider field. If, as the editor, Dell Hymes, says, 'it is the task of linguistics to co-ordinate knowledge about language from the viewpoint of language', it is the job of linguistic anthropology 'to co-ordinate knowledge about language from the viewpoint of *man*'. So many characteristic human activities—play and ritual, for example—are conducted in the medium of speech that the student of culture is impelled to examine language at a level deeper than that of mere denotation. To say something useful about Hanunoo linguistic play (as Harold C. Conklin does) or, for that matter, about Cockney rhyming slang, requires the full apparatus of descriptive linguistics, but mere description is not enough. The Hanunoo (pagan jungle farmers living in southern Mindoro in the Philippines) have, as a common salutation, an indirect request for betel: 'Ba: rang may bu: nga qa: san sa kanta katagbuq' ('Perhaps the people we've just met have some areca nuts'). Quite frequently the phonemic elements of the polysyllabic forms are deliberately transposed: 'ra: bang may nga: but sa: qua sa tanka kabugtaq'. It is, of course, morphemically analogous to the ludic tropes of English double-talk (comic mystification) or Cockney traders' back-slang (the deadly serious mystification of the customer). Conklin sees in this play, however, a positive correlation with *layqaw* status position (*layqaw* refers to a category of 'marriageable but unmarried youth'). Mastery of phonemic substitution is one of the prescribed skills of courtship—

* A Reader in Linguistics and Anthropology. Edited by Dell Hymes (Harper & Row).

like serenading with an instrument, preparing betel quids, reciting from a vast repertory of traditional verse. It is the element of disguise in this word-play that is of most significance, however. Hanunoo settlements are linked by 'close bonds of cognatic kinship' and there is a growing tendency to exogamy. But endogamy is not forbidden at a certain social level, though it is hedged round with ritual. The young courter follows a pattern of disguise (blanket over the head, speaking in an unusual manner) if the young courted is known to be closely related to him. Hence the phonemic substitution.

The cultural implications of language have, in our own society, been almost totally neglected. The class-elements in British English have been desultorily studied, but rarely by linguists and never by linguistic anthropologists. The U and non-U parlour-game of a few years back could hardly be dignified by the term linguistico-social inquiry. Meanwhile the professional linguists avoid value-judgments and are frightened of speculation; linguistics remain a descriptive craft and nothing more. And yet such phenomena as the Great Vowel Shift, which moved English pronunciation out of the Middle Ages and into the modern period, cry out for elucidation—whether social or psychological. The vowel of, say, 'shine' ceased to have its 'Continental' value and changed towards the diphthong we use today. Why? It is not enough to answer: 'because English long vowels tend to instability and hence to diphthongization'. Why that particular kind of diphthongization, why at that particular period? There ought to be 'human' answers to such questions.

Linguistic anthropologists are at least asking questions about language which pull that phenomenon down from its cold noosphere back into the warm current of social living. 'Whatever else language does,' says A. L. Kroeber, 'one of its patent uses is to convey information.' In other words, meaning ought to be enthroned as the central concern of linguistics, however important the phoneme or morpheme may be. We cannot doubt that it is through the type of inquiry exemplified in Dell Hymes's monumental reader that the next great advances in linguistic science will be made.

The Proper Study of Literary Man

THE Bookman's guilt about the Two Cultures can easily be palliated. After all, was it not science that deserted humanism, rather than the other way round? Dr Johnson conducted home-experiments in chemistry, but science found that it needed more than a corner of the sitting-room, a penny table of logarithms and a five-shilling telescope. The man of letters pretends to be outraged by this. Science has become expensively specialized, but the study of aesthetics costs no more today than it did in the time of Longus, Horace or Lessing. We can shatter the casuistry by reminding practitioners and students of literature that there is a science far nearer home than nuclear biology and that its study has less to do with the full Snovian man than the minimally equipped *littérateur*. Linguistics ought to be the primary science of the lover of language, since love presupposes understanding. The other sciences can come after. Not even Lord Snow can claim an exemption here.

Linguistics, like the other sciences, draws on specialized equipment such as the sound spectograph and cybernetic brains, but we carry the essential laboratory around with us. Our only excuse for not seeking a better understanding of the basic material of literature resides still in the failure of university courses to demonstrate the latent unity in the parallel studies of language and literature. Ever since *The Muse in Chains*, the Lang–Lit dichotomy has remained a grim joke. The recent gathering together of Bernard Shaw's writings *On Language*, as well as the success of *My Fair Lady*, will remind us that only one great literary artist took phonetics seriously, though not seriously enough. He was aware that the dramatist's first concern was with setting down patterns of speech-sounds, and that conventional English orthography was not competent to render these accurately. His greatest act of daring was, in the revised edition of *Pygmalion*, to introduce pretty consistently the inverted 'e' symbol for *schwa*—the 'er' sound of 'father', one of the many snakes in the

Eden of 'good English', fangless when a legitimate syllable, pure poison as an intruder. Shaw did not go farther since, though he knew the International Phonetic Alphabet, he was not himself a phonetician, only the creator of one. The question for post-Shavian dramatists and novelists is this: should Shaw's pioneer example be followed, not with amateur timidity or hobby-horse quirkiness but scientifically, all the way?

Music is not just crotchet-and-quaver calligraphy, and phonetics is not just 'rational' transliteration: it is a study of sounds and their organic formation, and a phonetic notation presupposes this study. Every dramatist and novelist is concerned with the representation of idiolects, some of them dialectal. Is amateur observation of speech-sounds quite enough? And, a corollary to that, can we put up much longer with an amateur alphabet? This is not to advocate the substitution of the International Phonetic Alphabet for our modified Roman one (Shaw calls it Phoenician): rather we should be prepared to bring in 'scientific' notation when it is needed—for Eliza Doolittle's glottal stops as well as her *schwa*, and for that 'bilabial fricative' of Sam Weller which Dickens heard sometimes as 'v' and sometimes as 'w' but never as something in between the two. Ida Ward presents, in an appendix to her *Phonetics of English*, phonetic transcriptions of passages from both *Pygmalion* and *The Good Companions*: the words leap up from the page; there is an enrichment of literary experience.

The study and scientific representation of phonemes or speech-sounds is only part of the story. *Systems of Prosodic and Paralinguistic Features in English** shows what serious work there is to be done on 'non-verbal phonology'. Characters in novels and plays utter words, but words are not the beginning and end of meaningful utterance. Categories of paralanguage include 'voice qualities'—whisper, breathiness, huskiness, creak, falsetto, resonance—and 'voice qualifications'—laugh, giggle, tremulousness, sob, cry. The terms concede to non-scientific habits of description; the tables of 'articulatory components' make no concessions. Thus, the five voice qualifications can be compared and contrasted under the parameters of pulsation

* By David Crystal and Randolph Quirk (The Hague: Mouton).

type, pulsation speed, oral aspiration, vocal cord vibration frequency, volume of supraglottal cavities, and so on. None will question the value of this, nor of any scientific analysis of the elements of speech, but its relevance to the work of the literary practitioner is yet to be seen.

It begins to show itself during the section on prosodic features—tempo, prominence, pitch range, rhythmicality, pause. There are four 'marked terms' for tempo in polysyllabic utterances—allegrissimo, allegro, lento, lentissimo, 'the unmarked term being of course the norm'. Prominence can be pianissimo, piano, forte or fortissimo. We approach, in fact, a scheme of description analogous to that of music, and we are not surprised to end up with a notational system that takes us beyond Eliza Doolittle's mere phonemes and cold-blooded murder of the English tongue to her rhythms, tempi, and creaks. The aim of Messrs Crystal and Quirk is, of course, totally scientific—a summary of the facts of non-verbal phonology and a consistent symbology for indicating the non-lexical elements of the speech continuum. Nevertheless, the literary implications are important. Gerard Manley Hopkins, a pioneer in so many things, was a pioneer here too. He saw that his poetry could not lift itself from the page without the boosters of new marks and symbols: conventional typography was not enough. But the inertia of custom sets out his 'Harry Ploughman' as if it were an orthodox Wordsworth sonnet. And that same inertia will exclude scientific 'barbarities' from the representation of spoken dialogue in the drama and fiction of the future so long as the Lang–Lit dichotomy is maintained.

The shame is that the linguistics men are interested in literature, since literature develops out of the speech-continuum, while the literature men dismiss linguistics, shooing it away as horrid 'science'. Mr Priestley will continue to make a character palatalize his sibilants by 'putting an h after every s', and Mr Ivor Brown will write of the magical juxtaposition of 'the letters o and r' in the verse of Shakespeare. Even though there is no immediate hurry for the introduction of strange auxiliary signs into our printers' cases (the chapels may pray their relief), the need for writers and critics to understand the nature of words could not be more urgent. It would also be a move in the direction of healing the cultural rift. We look forward to hearing from Lord Snow on this matter.

Snow White and Rose Red

WALT DISNEY put some things in, but he also left some out. The huntsman, ordered by the wicked queen to kill Snow White, is ordered also to bring back the child's lungs and liver as the token of a job well done. As we know, he lets Snow White run away. As we forget, he takes to the queen the dripping viscera of a young boar. 'The cook had to salt these, and the wicked Queen ate them, and thought she had eaten the lungs and liver of Snow White.'

The intention of cannibalism is there, and that's quite as bad as the fulfilment. At the end of the story (which comes after the riding off, with a smile and a song, into the sunset) the queen is invited to the young prince's wedding. 'And when she went in she recognized Snow White; and she stood still with rage and fear, and could not stir. But iron slippers had already been put upon the fire, and they were brought in with tongs, and set before her. Then she was forced to put on the red-hot shoes, and dance until she dropped down dead.' Charming. We have to imagine our winsome princess helping to get the iron slippers ready and then, presumably, grinning sadistically from her throne. It is not at all Disneyesque. It is, for want of a better term, decidedly grim.

The English connotation of the name of the brothers who compiled all that tough folklore—was it not confirmed in all our childhood nightmares? I used to wake up screaming: I was a sparrow flapping around inside a man's head; I was a thumb-sized dwarf imprisoned for a whole winter in a blood sausage. And yet the next morning I was drawn back, fascinated, to the thick, worn book and to fresh enormities. There was charm as well, of course, and gentler morality than in the story of Snow White. Also humour—as in the fine tale of Gambling Hansel (which I told the other night to an

Irish pub audience much given to poker and slot machines; they listened to the end). But my earliest image of the brothers Grimm was of a couple of hunchbacked manikins hugging each other in nasty glee, the emissaries of some witch who loved to frighten children. Grim, decidedly. And the German meaning of their name intensifies rather than diminishes the English connotation. *Grimm* means rage, anger.

The Grimm brothers were, as we shall see, capable of rage and anger, though in the best of causes. But it is as well to discard the Gothic caricature, which, being formed in childhood, is hard to extirpate: gnomes working by candlelight with scratching quills. The brothers are revealed, in the one engraved portrait I have seen, as good-looking, with fine eyes, well-shaped mouths, sensitive noses, Byronic hair styles. They were products of the Byronic age, born a few years before the French Revolution, and they have as much claim to be thought of as romantic heroes as, say, storm-swept Beethoven or exophthalmic Keats.

But the true romantic hero is a solitary figure, and the brothers Grimm were inseparable. Were they thinking of themselves when they transcribed the story of Snow White and Rose Red? 'The two children were so fond of one another that they always held each other by the hand when they went out together, and when Snow White said: "We will not leave each other," Rose Red answered: "Never so long as we live," and their mother would add: "What one has she must share with the other." '

Jacob was born in 1785 and Wilhelm a year later. Their town was Kassel—undistinguished, a solid bourgeois gobbet of a Germany that was still a parcel of disunited states. They went to school there, but moved on to Marburg to become law students. In everything they were together. Having played together as children, as undergraduates they studied together, sharing the same room for sleep and the same table for work. They conceived a common devotion to the jurist Friedrich Karl von Savigny, their professor, and through him were inspired to pursue studies that had little to do with law. For Savigny had a passion for German literary antiquities; it was in his library that Jacob Grimm, browsing, discovered the old poems of the minnesingers and was at once hooked on the potent drug of medieval language and literature. Wilhelm was quick to become an addict, too. While hardly more than boys, the brothers saw in a flash what their life's work had to be, though not even two life-times would be sufficient for its fulfilment. They had dedicated themselves to something that had hardly been thought of before: Germany's folk heritage.

This must sound dull to some of us. What is the use of studying weird dialects that nobody speaks any more, and groping, unhandy apologies for literature? No use at all, unless it can be conceded that pure knowledge has a use. But Charles Darwin uncovered the probable origins of man, and nobody will deny that the excitement of the theory of evolution is still with us. The Grimm brothers were looking for the origins of a language: where did German come from; what slow process or sudden explosion produced a German-speaking people? And how did that people use its language for bodying its primitive dreams and ancient myths? The brothers were, if you like, in search of an ethnic soul.

This, remember, was the romantic age. The eighteenth century had been all for reason and elegance, the calm surfaces of a stable civilization. But the French Revolution had shown how precarious such a rational order can be, and the new poets and thinkers, follow-ing Rousseau, were exalting the wild, the natural, the untutored. In England Wordsworth made a hero out of the peasant and a religion out of mountains and sunsets. Coleridge, the opium taker, dredged his unconscious mind and found magic. There was a new passion for the primitive, which meant the anonymous *Volk*. In poetry, ballads were collected, read, and imitated. Sir Walter Scott made a book of the ballads of the Scottish border, and Coleridge's *Ancient Mariner* was deliberately and artfully archaic—the work of a sophisticated poet trying to dream back to the style and tone of nameless folk singers. A lot of this new simplicity failed because writers themselves were no longer simple: it is not easy to throw off centuries of complex civilization by a sheer act of will.

Thus the two friends who compiled volumes of early German folk songs—Clemens Brentano and Ludwig Achim von Arnim—were not content merely to transcribe. The primitive was fascinating but it must not be too primitive. Anybody who knows the symphonies and song cycles of Gustav Mahler will know also that *Des Knaben Wunderhorn* (the name that Brentano and Von Arnim gave to their compilation) has a kind of false simplicity about it. Mahler drew again and again on the songs sounded by the boy's wonderhorn, but he was not going back to the beginnings of German poetry, only to a sophisticated editing of it. The old ballads and folk songs were mere raw material—irregular, simple, shocking—to be worked up by cultivated artists.

But the Grimm brothers were not artists. They were scholars, and they were after truth, not beauty. They loved the old language, and they would not harm a hair of its head; they were after folk, not folksiness. This is not to say that they had nothing of the aesthete in them. They enjoyed the stories they collected, and they delighted in giving shape to them and imposing economy. It seems that Wilhelm's gift for doing this was greater than Jacob's. Jacob was something of a plodder, happier with the hard work of philology— grammars and dictionaries and laws of sound-change—than with the dangerous exercise of the imagination. Six months after Wilhelm's death, Jacob summed up the difference between them pretty succinctly: Wilhelm, he said, had a vein of silver in him, while he, Jacob, was pure iron.

He had an iron constitution as well as an iron devotion to work. Jacob was never ill, while Wilhelm was never really well; during the years of the collection of the tales he suffered from a severe heart disorder that kept him in bed for days at a time. There was about Wilhelm the kind of wistfulness that sometimes goes with chronic ill-health. He was gay, but gently so; he liked children and music. Jacob remained a bachelor, but Wilhelm married a girl named Dorthchen Wild, one of six sisters who had, among their other attractions, a large fund of inherited folk tales. Marriage did not interfere with the brothers' inseparability: Uncle Jacob lived in Wilhelm's house, though one presumes he now had a bedchamber of his own, and, says Richard Cleasby, the Icelandic scholar, 'one might almost imagine the children were common property'.

Happy days, then, and plenty of hard study, but we would be wrong to think of a couple of dull and cloistered lives. In the postgraduate days in Kassel, while the foundations of the huge folk edifice were being laid, Napoleon was shouting his way through Europe. In 1806 his armies overran Kassel itself. The town, recalled Wilhelm, was infested with 'foreign persons, foreign manners, and a foreign, loudly spoken language ... and poor people staggered along the streets, being led away to death'. The brothers tried to drown their spiritual depression in Old German, but the library was no mere escape. They felt that their conservation of the German past might somehow contribute to 'the return of a better day'. In a sense, they were helping to forge a German national consciousness. If Martin Luther gave the German language a Bible, the brothers Grimm went deeper and gave it a dictionary and a grammar. And, of course, they drew its myths out of the darkness of the past.

The brothers rode the storm. They had posts in the Kassel library, where they stuck to their worktables, though in 1805 Jacob saw the libraries of Paris and in 1808 was appointed librarian to Jérome Bonaparte, new-made puppet-king of Westphalia. The year 1812 brought Napoleon's retreat from Moscow and, like a quiet fanfare of German rejoicing, the first volume of the *Nursery and Household Tales*. But the iron Jacob had to use his iron in more than scholarship. In 1814, the year before Waterloo, he was sent to Paris to demand restitution of Kassel's library, which the French had stolen. And the next year he was secretary of the Hessian legation at the Congress of Vienna, presenting—among the uniforms and ball gowns—the sharp, tough image of an uncompromising intellectual, learned in law, history, national rights. And then he was off to Paris again, demanding the return of more filched books. The French librarians feared and hated him: '*Nous ne devons plus souffrir ce Monsieur Grimm.*' The other Monsieur Grimm—gentle, unassertive—stayed at home, wandering through the villages around Kassel and listening quietly to folk tales. Nobody ever said that *he* was insufferable.

Much of the rest of their story is of academic appointments, hard work, the slow amassing of honours. They were in Göttingen in 1830, burrowing in the libraries there. Jacob was made a professor

235

and, in recognition of his services to scholarship, a *Hofrat*, or coun-
cillor, at the court of Hanover. Wilhelm, always a little slower,
received the same honours a short time after. Work, publications,
learned discussions, beer, games with the children: it was a good
quiet life. But in 1837 both brothers showed that they were not
called Grimm for nothing. The new king of Hanover, Ernest
Augustus, had dictatorial dreams; he decided that he would abrogate
the constitution. The Grimms joined five other professors in protest-
ing with eloquence and vigour. They lost their posts and were
banished from Hanover.

But Kassel was glad to have them back, and so were the villages
crammed with folklore. Then Berlin called them to the most exalted
of professorships and the final dignity of the Academy of Sciences.
There they stayed, accumulating honours and reputation till they
died. Wilhelm succumbed to heart trouble in 1859; Jacob followed
four years later. In Berlin they lie buried side by side. Snow White
and Rose Red had had a good life: 'they divided between them the
great treasure which the dwarf had gathered together in his cave.'
The rose trees that were their totems stand before the window, 'and
every year bear the most beautiful roses, white and red.'

There are no roses without thorns, and Jacob's tree is thornier than
Wilhelm's. I mean that Jacob pricks us more sharply with the grim
science of philology. Most people respond with smiles to Grimm's
fairy tales but with shudders to Grimm's law. And yet one achievement is relevant to the other. To probe into the dark forest of German folklore meant also to examine the trees, root and branch, leaf
and bark: no lore without language. Jacob was the first grammarian
of German to look at the language as a process working through
time, not as a static museum filled with fixed and immutable words.
He started his *Deutsche Grammatik* in 1819 and finished it in 1822, the
year of Grimm's law.

What is Grimm's law about? It is about language as a changing,
living thing, and it is about the patterns of linguistic change. To
Jacob Grimm, as to other language scholars of his time, the term
'German' did not mean just the tongue spoken in Berlin or Göttingen
or Kassel. It meant everything that could be recognized as a dialect of

German, and it moved to the borders of languages that were not German at all—English, Dutch, Danish, Swedish. English, after all, is a kind of German: 'My father is a good man' is demonstrably of the same family as '*Mein Vater ist ein guter Mann*'.

It seemed that there had once been a parent language, now long dead, that had had many children—some of these themselves dead (the tongues of the Goths and the Vandals among them). Others—like English and Dutch and High German—were much alive. You could see that all these Teutonic languages were brothers and cousins: they all ate butter or *Butter* and drank beer or *Bier*. They had diverged somewhat from each other, and words that must have had a common origin had grown apart. Thus, German used the word *Zahn* and English preferred 'tooth'. But if you compared ancient enough writings in both languages, you would find that the German *z* (pronounced 'ts') was once *t*, just as in English, and that there had even been a *th* after what was now the final *n*; the German word had been *tahnth*. And once upon a time English had had the word 'tanth'. In England this word had changed by a quite natural process to 'tooth': first of all, get rid of the *n* and, as compensation, nasalize the preceding *a* (as French nasalizes the *a* in *danser*); then get rid of the nasalization; then change the *a* to a good long *o*, giving *tòth*; then push the back of the tongue higher, giving the 'tooth' we have today. By examining the history of sound-changes in reverse, you end up with German and English as pretty much the same language.

There was a time, then, in prehistory, when the children—English, Dutch, Norwegian, and so on—had not been born: only the original parent existed. This parent had left no written records; you could only discover roughly what he had been like by comparing his children one with the other. The earliest language of the Teutonic family that had left any records was Gothic, the tongue of the barbaric invaders of Rome, but it gave some idea of the character of the great dead Germanic father; the grammar was complicated, and there were endings somewhat like Latin (the Gothic for 'tooth' was *tunthus*). Jacob Grimm's grammar book caught a shadowy, conjectural image of the *Urvater*, the original primitive Germanic

237

tongue. And it asked the question, how did this tongue come into existence?

You will be aware here of the probing, adventurous spirit that wanted to push farther and farther back in time; it is the spirit that dug for ancient myths and fairy tales, the gold of the dwarfs in the forest. For farther back than primitive Germanic, farther back than Greek and Latin and Sanskrit (that great Indian tongue whose first records date from about 1500 B.C.), was the mother of all Western (and some Middle Eastern) languages—the speech of the ancient Aryan tribes, once called Indo-Germanic and now called Indo-European. Jacob Grimm recognized that the Latin and Greek tongues must have been close relatives of primitive Germanic; all three, as well as Sanskrit, were children of the lost Indo-European language. But Latin, Greek, and Sanskrit were closer to each other than they were to primitive Germanic. You had only to look at the various words for 'father' to see this. All the Germanic words for 'father' begin with an *f* sound, sometimes disguised as a *v*—German *Vater*, Dutch *vader*, Old Norse *fathir*—while Greek and Latin had *pater*, and Sanskrit had *pitar*. Primitive Germanic had broken away from the old 'classical' languages, and one of the banners of its revolt was inscribed with the slogan 'Initial P is dead. Let's have an F instead.'

There were other ways in which Germanic words differed from words in Sanskrit, Greek, and Latin, and Jacob Grimm drew up tables of these differences, searching all the time for a pattern. He saw, incidentally, that English had preserved some of the features of primitive Germanic better than Modern German had: it had kept the *th* in 'father', for instance, while Modern German had lost it. English, then, is a worthy representative for the entire Teutonic group in the following confrontation:

CLASSICAL	ENGLISH
Greek, Latin *pater*	father
Latin *pulex*	flea
Latin *frango*	break
Latin *tenuis*	thin

CLASSICAL	ENGLISH
Greek *kard-*, Latin *cord-*, }	heart
Latin *octo*	eight (German *acht*)
Latin *hortus*	garden
Greek *thugater*	daughter
Latin *fero*	bear (*i.e.* carry)

The pattern at length showed itself, by dint of much hard work, unenlightened by the kind of sudden imaginative shaft that was to give Einstein the formula $E = MC^2$. Those noises—clicks and bangs and buzzes—called consonants, said Jacob, were the only sounds worth paying attention to in examining the shift from the 'classical' to the primitive Germanic phase. Vowels were always variable, very feminine, and their caprices had best be ignored. But three areas of the mouth where consonants are made—the lips, the teeth, and the back portion of the palate—were the courts of a very strange game in that period when primitive Germanic was trying to emerge. You can explode a consonant on the lips—as in 'pop' or 'bib'—or you can rub it, giving some such sound as *fffff*. You can explode on the teeth ('teat', 'dead') or you can, with the help of the tongue, rub out a sound like *th*, as in 'thick'. You can explode at the back of the palate ('kick', 'gag') or you can get a rubbing noise like our *h* or the German *ch* in *Bach*. Now here, at last, comes the law.

The law states that the consonants of primitive Germanic keep consistently to the same mouth areas as the corresponding consonants in the older Indo-European languages: what is a tooth-sound in Latin or Greek remains a tooth-sound in primitive Germanic. But, and it is a big but, where you get a classical explosion you get a Teutonic rub; where you get a classical rub you get a Teutonic explosion. There is a total consistency in this exchange. If the word for 'brother' in Latin begins with *f*, so must the word for 'break' (see table). Conversely, if the Latin word for 'carry' is *fero*, there must be a Teutonic word of identical meaning beginning with a *p* or a *b*. And so there is: 'bear'. The whole thing can become a mildly fascinating game. The Latin word *hortus*, which gives us

239

'horticulture', begins with a rubbed sound made at the back of the palate. It ought to oppose a Teutonic word beginning with an exploded sound made in the same area; namely, with *k* or *g*, and so it does: 'garden' (*Garten* in German). And if we have the Latin *pater*, *frater*, and *mater*, what ought we to expect in the corresponding early Germanic forms? Certainly a *th* in the middle, and here it is: 'father', 'brother', 'mother'.

But occasionally things went wrong, and Jacob Grimm could not understand why. Take the Latin *centum*. The initial *k* sound corresponds, in accordance with the law, to the initial *h* sound in the English 'hundred' and the German *hundert*. But why doesn't that middle *t* correspond to a *th* in the English word? If we oppose *pater* to 'father' we should oppose *centum* to something like 'hunthred'. Something was not quite right: Grimm's law had broken down.

But about ten years after Jacob's death, a Dane named Karl Verner explained the irregularity. Grimm's law only applied when the accent was on the same syllable in both opposed words. If the old Indo-European language had stressed its word for 'hundred' on the first syllable—giving the Latin *CENTum*—then primitive Germanic would have had something like 'hunthred'. But the old stress was on the second syllable, giving *centUM*, and primitive Germanic, like its modern derivatives, preferred the stress on the first syllable: 'HUNdred'. So an explosion in the older language confronted a rubbing or buzzing consonant only when the stress lay in the same place; otherwise (and Verner made his own law out of this) you had the same sort of consonant. Grimm's law held, then, and it has never ceased to hold. But Jacob died unsure and a little puzzled.

This world of remote sound-changes may seem totally irrelevant to the 'real' world of getting and spending and, for that matter, reading fairy tales, but any man who widens the vistas of knowledge deserves our homage. Jacob Grimm asked a big question: how did the speech of the Teutons (the speech of the Americans and British, as well as of the Germans) emerge from the lost language of the ancient Aryan wanderers? He got an answer, and he was able to encapsulate that answer in the nutshell of a law. All students of Teutonic languages are in his debt. Germany itself, of course, owes him most. His huge dictionary of the German language, whose first volume appeared in 1854, never got finished in his day, nor even in his century. The final volume was published in 1960, thanks to the combined efforts of scholars from both East and West Germany. Only a Grimm could blow up the Berlin Wall.

The first edition of the Grimm folk tales appeared during the last years of Napoleon's imperial career. It was called *Kinder- und Hausmärchen*—'Children's Tales and Household Tales'—and its reception was mixed. In Vienna the book was banned as a work of superstition; the aesthetes complained of a lack of style and grace (they were barking up the wrong tree); the staid complained of horror and impropriety; the newspaper reviewers were either condescending or frigid. But ordinary people seemed delighted: here, in an era of high and often pretentious literary contrivance, was a return to the very wells of literature—the tales told in the dim light of village evenings (in dim light or none at all), with work done and the fowls roosting. Moreover—and this was where Jacob the uncompromising scholar came in—the language of the tales had the freshness of well-water; it was honest dialect, with no High German sophistication. It was a vision of a good old innocent Germany.

What nobody saw was that it was not Germany or any other land, no matter how old: it was all lands and all people. The Grimm brothers, who had dared to watch primitive Germanic arise out of ancient Indo-European, had reached in this compilation—by way of German rivers—the sea of universal myth. The stories are in various forms of German peasant language, and they contain German properties, like sausages and cheeses and beer, but there is nothing about them that we can call *echt deutsch*, 'essentially German'.

'Among people who follow the old ways of life without change,' wrote Wilhelm Grimm in 1815 (the year of the second volume), 'attachment to inherited patterns is stronger than we, impatient for variety, can realize.' He mentioned one of his story tellers, Frau Katherina Viehmann, who lived in the village of Niederzwehren, outside Kassel, and he emphasized her delight in accurate transmission of her ancient tales: 'how close she always keeps to her story and how zealous she is for its accuracy; never does she alter any part in repetition, and she corrects a mistake herself, immediately she notices it.'

Conservatism is of the essence in the old agricultural way of life; even the minimal innovation is resented. It is easy to accept that there is a parallel between the German language and the tales told in it: both sprang out of a culture far older than Germany's. The migrating Aryans brought their myths and gods and charms to north-western Europe where they were conserved in the tales of the folk. Names changed, devils became goblins, locales became familiar localities, but the stories remained the same.

But how do we explain why so many of the Grimm tales can be found, with appropriate differences in dress, all over the world? When I lived in Malaya and Borneo I heard, or read in transcription, stories of the little mouse deer called Sang Kanchil that outwits tigers and elephants; or of humble kampong youths who, through virtue helped by magic, attain the hand of a sultan's daughter; or of the eternal opposed brothers, one good and the other bad; or of a greedy crocodile (like Red Riding Hood's wolf) that beguiles succulent children with seductive eloquence. Freud said of folk tales that they contain 'the dreams of the human race'. One of these dreams is about the simple good prevailing over the subtle wicked. Most of the stories that the Grimm brothers collected are lay moral sermons.

This fact probably justifies the nightmare element that troubles so many teachers, parents, and educational publishers. Some terrible things happen in the tales, but there is a severe moral logic in them. Evil itself is not just vague malevolence but an actively destructive impulse that is pushed on to the ultimate enormity of cannibalism; nevertheless, there is no gratuitous dwelling on violence or horror: the reports are abstract, the hacked bones and pools of drying blood are mere emblems that do not quite belong to the world of true sensuous experience.

And sometimes the horrors are reversible, so that we cannot take them seriously. The maiden who goes to the evil house to find her sisters cut to pieces has only to set limb to limb, like the bits of a jigsaw puzzle, and the girls come back to life again. It is manifestly impossible for the wolf to swallow Red Riding Hood and her grandmother whole, so that they may be taken out of his belly—in shock but otherwise little the worse—by a sort of Caesarean operation. The evil is not quite the photographed iniquities of the Nazis: it is a potential realized in symbols, and it is often enclosed in ritual. But it is frightening enough, recounted by a guttering candle or in the owl-haunted dark. Ought children to be protected from it?

I go back to my own screaming in the night. If I had not had the Grimm tales to trigger my nightmares, undoubtedly there would have been plenty of other gruesome doors into the Gothic wings of my dream-house. Indeed the picture on my bedroom wall—called *Beware* and depicting a fortune-telling gypsy—caused more horror than can easily be explained. I would dream that the picture swung open like a door to disclose a pleasant-looking world of trees and flowers with smiling human faces. I used to rouse the house in terror, and eventually the picture was taken down. And the hospital opposite our house was, I was often told, a place where people had their insides removed. That was another, and pretty regular trigger of nightmares. Children, and adults for that matter, will always find something to have nightmares about. A much more important question is this: are the Grimm tales corruptive, are they likely to whet day-dreams of violence? I think not; I think they are far more likely to instil a profound sense of the moral order.

It is, for the most part, a pre-Christian moral order, with an inexorable apparatus of punishment. A man allows a cart to run over a dog. A sparrow, the dog's friend, pursues retribution to the limit, pecking out the horse's eyes, pecking the bungs out of the cartload of wine casks. Finally the man swallows the sparrow whole, but the bird flutters back into his mouth. 'Wife,' says the man, giving her an axe, 'kill the bird in my mouth for me.' The woman strikes, misses, hits her husband on the head, and kills him. The bird, its rhadam-anthine duty done, flies away. Perhaps the punishment goes too far, but the lesson is bound to get home to a juvenile audience. Better the odd nightmare than a boyhood dedicated to cat-torturing and pulling wings off flies. When, as a child, I said 'I don't care', I got the ritual response:

> Don't-care was made to care,
> Don't-care was hung,
> Don't-care was put in a pot
> And cooked till he was done.

That, when you come to think of it, is grim enough. I never took the prospective punishment seriously, but the rhyme has a ritual force about it, like a liturgical execration, and it plants a certain uneasiness. No child hearing or reading the sterner of the Grimm stories can remain wholly innocent any longer. He has been introduced, through delicious rites of terror, into the horrible but necessary world of experience.

Not all the stories are moral. Some of them seem to encapsulate ancient myths of spring and winter: Snow White is a vegetation goddess like Persephone. And those tailor-dwarfs who get inside thimbles are surely Priapus in disguise. Some stories are just sophisticated nonsense—surrealism, if you like: 'There were two crows which were mowing a meadow, and I saw two gnats building a bridge, and two doves tore a wolf to pieces; two children brought forth two kids, and two frogs threshed corn together. I saw two mice consecrating a bishop, and two cats scratching out a bear's tongue.' Others provide privy warnings for young and foolish wives—like the tale of Frederick and Catherine. Catherine, when she drops a cheese down the hill, sends another cheese after it to bring it back. And another. And another. And sometimes we touch the fringes of true German sentimentality, as in the story of the poor peasant boy who goes to church and believes he is in heaven ('next Sunday, when the host came to him, he fell down and died, and was at the eternal wedding').

But the stories are all very firm, confident, sure of themselves. Once started, they travel to the end by the shortest route, wasting no time on decorative fripperies, Jamesian qualifications, or depth psychology. 'There was a man who had three sons, the youngest of whom was called Dummling, and was despised, mocked, and sneered at on every occasion.' We're off, and we stay till the finish. If anybody cavils at the improbable, grumbles about too much magic, laughs in the wrong place, he will be told to hold his tongue or receive a salutary slap.

An ancient crone is telling the story, toothless, parchment-skinned, very vigorous, vibrant with authority. Having listened to her voice through eight hundred pages of rereading Grimm, I've become restive at the slow-moving, tentative, groping, unsure techniques of the contemporary novel. 'Once upon a time there was a boy who was brought up among goats, and he believed himself to be a goat.' That's how Mr Barth's masterpiece ought to begin. And it could learn something about brevity from these old tales, told after work or on a holy day of obligation. 'Once upon a time there was a man called Rojack, and he hated his wife so much that he had to kill her.' That's Norman Mailer's *An American Dream*. 'There was once a man who was always writing letters to people, but he never sent any of these letters off.' We all know Saul Bellow's Moses Herzog. One of these days the Grimm brothers will be seen to have started something.

9

The Good Companion

WHO collaborated with W. S. Gilbert on *The Happy Land*?
Which great novel-sequence is based on a metaphysical conception
of the unreality and reversibility of time? What is the Hebrew name
of Apollyon, angel of the bottomless pit? Which rivers of Damascus
did Naaman consider better than all the waters of Israel? Which
Scythian priest of Apollo rode the air on an arrow? To which
dynasty of Caliphs did Haroun-al-Raschid belong? What new theatre
opened on 18th July, 1966?

The answers are on the first page of the fourth edition of *The
Oxford Companion to English Literature.*★ It is not a question of those
who need them (Gilbert Arthur à Beckett; *A la Recherche du Temps
Perdu*; Abaddon; Abana and Pharpar; Abaris; Abbasides; Abbey
Theatre, Dublin) needing the book. There are plenty of genuine
encyclopaedias about, and these will tell you about the aardvark,
aardwolf, Aaron (his beard and rod) and the abacus as well. The
curious and irresistible quality of this compilation is its mode of
selection and the resultant strangeness of its juxtapositions. Thus,
Eppie, who comes in *Silas Marner*, is followed by *Eppur si muove*
('see Galileo'), which, with *Er the son of Armenius, The Myth of*,
makes a sandwich of Sir Jacob Epstein, who 'carved and modelled
large figures, often of religious subjects'. In other words, we miss,
and are glad to miss, the impartiality and impersonality of the
encyclopaedia, but the alphabet is there to impose the most piquant
patterns. It's more like reading a Michel Butor novel than a cold
work of reference.

One entry that Dorothy Eagle could have given us might have

★ Edited by Sir Paul Harvey, revised by Dorothy Eagle (O.U.P., 1967).

told us all about Sir Paul Harvey, whose child this *Companion* was (her job has been to bring the work up to date, though—following the Harvey cautiousness—not aggressively so). Harvey's aim was to help ordinary readers of literature, whatever that is or was, to follow up references and clarify allusions. But he evidently had an Autolycan, or Kinbote-Nabokov, mind and liked oddities for their own sake. Of what use, for instance, is it really to know the names of all those 'Dogs, famous in History, Myth, and Fiction'? It's pure 'Round Britain Quiz' stuff, yet (or should that be 'hence'?) totally seductive. Who, then, owned the following: Keeper, Crab, Math, Music? That's right—Emily Brontë, Launce in *Two Gentlemen of Verona*, Richard II (according to Froissart, Math deserted his master when his deposition was imminent and attached himself to Bolingbroke), Wordsworth. For completeness, there ought to be a section on cats, but Harvey was evidently no cat-man. Admittedly, Hodge, Dr Johnson's cat, is mentioned, but (it seems to me) rather grudgingly. Horses, on the other hand, are so important that Arion, Bayard, Black Bess and the rest of them have solus entries. How do I find out the name of Cowper's pet hare? I don't; I have to know it (Puss) already.

Then there's the matter of the very full synopses of the novels that Harvey evidently admired. I've never been able to read Trollope with any pleasure, but Harvey makes the task unnecessary. Thus, just above *Ayenbite of Inwit* and Ayer, Alfred Jules, is a loving summary of *Ayala's Angel*: 'Lucy and Ayala Dormer, after having been brought up in an artistic and luxurious home, are left penniless orphans ... ' But for *Awkward Age, The*, we're merely told that it is by Henry James (q.v.) and was published in 1899. *Ambassadors, The*, does all right, though: ' ... Sadly disillusioned, but still insisting on the necessity of Chad's loyalty to Mme de Vionnet, Strether from a sense of duty turns his back on Paris.' Pages 22 and 23 are, in fact, pretty good. You get, as well as *Ambassadors, The*, a save-work synopsis of Meredith's *Amazing Marriage, The*, a brief summary of Meinhold's *Amber Witch, Mary Schweidler, The*, and a useful examinee's guide to *Amelia*. You also get a full account of John Wilson's Ambrose's Tavern, where the *Noctes Ambrosianae* had their setting:

247

this is real Harvey country, which a more swinging companion-compiler would not wish to visit. Scott, too, comes in for the most adoring of expatiations. There's a cosy, dated, tobacco-smelling, worn-leather bookishness about Harvey, and it's one of his charms.

The task of bringing him up to date had evident dangers. How far should a bow be made to the scientists, who had so little space in Harvey's library? Boldly, Mrs Eagle has admitted a pretty full entry on Einstein, including an account of the Lorentz Transformation, complete with mathematical formula; but other revolutionaries of thought do not do so well. Bertrand Russell has about one sixth of the space allotted to Ruskin, and Rutherford gets less than Mrs Gaskell's *Ruth*. Existentialism has a very sound entry, as does Sartre himself, but there is no reference to Lévi-Strauss, and Marshall McLuhan seems not to exist. The non-literary arts are very strangely served—a little article on Benjamin Britten, but nothing on either Elgar or Vaughan Williams; Picasso, but not Stravinsky; no film-makers at all. I suppose the answer to my objections about such omissions must be that anything not directly literary is, so to speak, *ex gratia*: we have no particular rights. This is the quirky book that Harvey made, and these are additions in the same quirky style.

But with the post-Harvey literary entries we can, perhaps, be less indulgent. Some of these are excellent—the ones on Joyce, Heming-way, Mann, Beckett, for instance—but the principle of selection, when it comes to the not quite great, is very odd. John Osborne is here, presumably because of the angries, but the influence of Pinter—not here—has been more considerable. Charles Snow gets in, and so, for some reason, do Gerhardi and Lawrence Durrell, but Amis—whose *Lucky Jim* is as important a myth as Jimmy Porter—is absent, though *Amis and Amiloun* continues to celebrate a noble friendship. No Golding but Arthur (translator of Ovid, 1536?-1605?), no Angus Wilson, Murdoch, Spark. And if it be argued that there are no settled reputations here, how long do we have to wait? Presumably we've waited long enough to know that *Rab and His Friends* is no longer even of historical interest and that William de Morgan is only a master to the man who called himself Oliver Edwards. As for Anthony Burgess, I am reconciled now to seeing the name survive only as that of a seventeenth-century divine who wrote too many sermons on the one text from St John.

Perhaps all these objections are beside the point. The point for me has been chiefly the fructifying value, on a practising writer sometimes desperate for ideas, of a casual browsing through any two facing pages. I open at random: pages 446 and 447. These take me from Kennedy, Margaret (author of *The Constant Nymph*) to Kierkegaard, Soren Aabye. Good, I shall write a novel about an Anglo-Dane called Soren Kennedy, who lives in Kensington and is doing research on St Mungo (who is also St Kentigern). Discovering that this saint probably sojourned for a time on the Isle of Man (Keys, House of), he goes to Douglas, where he meets a beautiful Arab divorcée called Khadijah, after the first wife of the Prophet. She is very interested in Khusrau I, King of Iran (531–79), and they argue a great deal, despite an evident and inescapable physical attraction, about their irreconcilable faiths. A man called W. P. Ker, a fellow of All Souls on holiday, tries to heal their breach, urging that they see how ridiculous religious bigotry is by reading the episodes about the fanatical covenanter Kettledrummle in Scott's *Old Mortality* (q., inevitably, v.).

Khadijah falls for Ker, and Kennedy becomes violently jealous. But Ker is in love with a certain Ebenezer Balfour (*Kidnapped*), whom he is expecting to come to Douglas in a day or two. Balfour duly arrives, along with a certain Alan Breck, a con-man who pretends to weary for the heather and the deer, but whose Scots accent is suspect. But Balfour is under his power, and it is left to Khadijah to show the greatness of her love for Ker by exposing Beck as a mere adventurer who, when she pretends to wealth, at once starts to woo her and, when deliberately made drunk on a local whisky called Jack Ketch (or Captain Kettle), speaks in an American accent and proves to be a penniless descendant of Francis Scott Key of Frederick, Maryland, author of 'The Star-Spangled Banner'. The dénouement brings in learned discussions on St Kentigern's miracles (it was on the Isle of Man that he revived St Serf's favourite robin-redbreast) and on proto-existentialism.

The *Companion* has 961 pages, so no writer, especially a novelist, need ever be short of material. At a pinch, he can always refurbish a plot by Meredith, Scott or Hardy. When the work is complete, he can check on the copyright position in Appendices I and II. And if any of his characters says that Easter Day fell on April 12th in 1088 (first regnal year of William II), he can at once be put right by another character, who will tell him (Appendix III) that it was actually April 16th. There is no end to the uses of Harvey, as I know. As I very well know. As I know as well as any literary man living.

The Modicum is the Messuage

I MAKE no apology for that title, especially as Professor McLuhan will, if he goes on as he is going on, be forced to use it himself sooner or later. A messuage is legally defined as a house with outbuildings and garden. Professor McLuhan has created a very commodious messuage, productive of a most satisfactory rent, with a modicum of raw material. Good luck to him.

There are various approaches to Professor McLuhan and, during the recent McLuhan season marked by the publication and reissue of four of his books, most of them have been tried. I diffidently suggest a new one. McLuhan started his academic career as an engineering student at the University of Manitoba, but then changed to English. This is an interesting example of the influence of a hot medium, linear alphabetical arrangement leading McLuhan ineluctably from *Engi* to *Engl*. He went to Cambridge, where he came under the influence of I. A. Richards and, one presumes, must have at least been touched by the terrible magic of F. R. Leavis and *Scrutiny*. In 1939 he wrote a thesis on Thomas Nashe, an Elizabethan notable for highly auditory prose and an appeal to the entire sensorium. It may or may not be relevant to add that in 1937 he was converted to Catholicism and was thus enabled to leave teleological matters in hands other than his own. No need to speculate about the purpose of life: from now on the epistemological would be enough.

The important thing, though, is the Cambridge aesthetic. *Scrutiny* taught that, in an acceptable work of literature, it was not possible to separate content from form. You couldn't talk about the *meaning* of a poem: to explain it in terms of a prose paraphrase was not merely heretical but destructive of a highly wrought artefact. In a work of art the form is the content, the medium is the message. But *message* implies intellection—the reading eye of the mind. And so, through a pun that Thomas Nashe would have approved, suggest through *massage* the laying on of pummelling hands, the beneficent attack on the skin and the nerve-endings. It was all there in Eliot, a *Scrutiny* darling, who complained about the dissociation of sensibility in the (hot medium) Romantics and not only taught but demonstrated the need for modern poets to submit to the massage of (the 'twenties man's mechanical bride) the internal combustion engine.

McLuhan's gimmick has been to push an aesthetic doctrine to the limit. Nobody denies that a piece of music represents the condition to which all works of art must tend—a condition of unparaphrasability, a total identification of form and content. Painting and sculpture became non-representational; literature became symbolist or surrealist: they were trying to be like music. But what makes one art different from another is, of course, the medium. The painter loves squelchy pigment, the sculptor loves intractable stone. The old baroque way was to ignore the character of the medium, so that stone became ridiculously plastic, losing its stoniness, and orchestral instruments were made to behave like each other and like the human voice. The medium must be allowed to have its own way: the artist resists its tyranny at his peril.

But McLuhan is concerned with society more than art (though art, being something that just 'happens', has no hieratic status in social patterns). Applying the Cambridge aesthetic to all the communication media, he is led to distort it in a very interesting way. He deliberately refuses to distinguish between a medium as the determinant of an art-form and a medium as a transmissive device. I watch, on television, a film of a man reading a poem. Now obviously there are separables here—three media of communication concentrically set about the thing that is being communicated. But, to

251

McLuhan, there are really four things of the same order. A medium has to have a content, but the content is always itself a medium. Nor is any medium transparent: it modifies our perception of the medium which is the content. Thus, an old film seen on a TV late show is a different experience, and hence a different art-form, from the original performance in a cinema.

McLuhan is absolved from the need to get to the core of a communication-process by his deliberate identification of the artistic 'message' with the purely informative or didactic one. Ends are not his concern; indeed, they may not really exist. It seems to me that his doctrines have progressed from (as in *Understanding Media*) an insistence on our accepting the importance of knowing what the massage is doing to us, to an elevation of the massage-machine to the rank of demiurge. His adoration of the Beatles (always, to me, an index of intellectual unsoundness) is based presumably on their having become priests of electronics. That they have to refuse a million dollars for a live concert in the United States (their new electronic medium being unable to accommodate the protoelectronic one) must be, to McLuhan, a sign of ultimate grace.

But he is very good and suggestive when he tells us of, say, the influence of the typewriter on the art, not just the craft, of authorship. Henry James became a new kind of writer when he began to dictate to a stenographer. The *vers libre* and typographical tropes of e. e. cummings owe, thinks McLuhan, everything to the machine (how much more this applies to the admirable work of Don Marquis). I myself, humbler but still an author, know that my prose, such as it is, has been determined by a lifelong devotion to the typewriter: coming to the end of a line, unwilling to split a word with a hyphen, I will often use a shorter word than the one I intended. This is utter slavery to the machine. And McLuhan is right to insist on the *worthiness* of such commercial media as the advertisement. A special edition of an American magazine, compressed for airmail transmission by the elimination of advertisements, was promptly rejected by its GI recipients: it was the advertisements that they primarily wanted. They wanted them, says McLuhan, because advertisements are always by far the best devised feature of a periodical. (True, and because of the urgency of their aim, which McLuhan does not mention—to sell goods.)

McLuhan is at his most Cambridge when he preaches the repressive and limiting force of our western visual culture and our failure to maintain the richer auditory and synaesthetic traditions of tribal societies. Alphabetic writing he calls a 'hot' medium: it is explicit and authoritative and it doesn't invite participation: it imposes a linear way of looking at the universe; it attacks one sense only. Ideograms and syllabaries he regards as functioning quite differently. Thus, the ideogram of Chinese writing does not impose meaning with the explicit brutality of a quasi-phonetic script: it is 'cool', the meaning is suspended airily between you and it. All this strikes me as a lot of nonsense. To read Chinese and a western language involves much the same process of instant recognition: we take in a word whole, as a Chinese takes in an ideogram. To present the traditional East–West difference in terms of irreconcilable modes of writing will not do. Islam is as alphabetic as Christendom, and Islam's history went, for centuries, in an opposed direction to that of the West. It is ideas, not scripts, that change cultures. Ultimately, all scripts function in the same way. We do not take in the word *not* as a collocation of three sounds; the Chinese do not take in *pu* (which means *not*) as a graphic representation of a little plant prevented from growing (a metaphor of notness): the semantic signal flashes in a split second. And yet on the factitious notion of radical differences of function McLuhan erects a whole historiography.

Perhaps he is right—though I'm not at all sure—when he says that the West is being dragged by the new electronic media out of the Gutenberg or Caxton age. Children, he says, brought up on the cool medium of television (a medium which invites participation) find difficulty even in the visual adjustment required when reading is forced on them. The straight-line chronology symbolized by a book belongs to the pre-Einsteinian era. Television is a norm we have to accept, not an upstart deviant that hypnotizes the young. There is nothing sacrosanct about a medium that hasn't changed since the fifteenth century, despite the halo that all books, however bad, borrow from the good one. But in refusing to accept that ideas are stronger than media, that the influence of media is (appropriately: I'm thinking of my typewriter prose again) marginal, McLuhan is perhaps guilty of a heresy worse than the aesthetic one that thought the message was all. I say 'perhaps': I'm not sure. That McLuhan should shake our minds up and make us powerfully aware of the pressure of media is probably enough. But he wants more than that.

What is Pornography?

AFTER the devaluation announcement and those threatening words about England being a proud country, after the *Daily Mirror*'s dollifying of thinned sterling as the 'perky mini-pound', I knew what the verdict on *Last Exit to Brooklyn* would have to be: it was just one of those weeks. I had hoped, even after the Marlborough Street magistrate's wonder that post-Zola novelists were not satisfied with the reticence of *Vanity Fair*, that sense would prevail in the higher court, and that eminent men of letters would not be dismissed as fools or smuthounds. But a man of God and former Test captain testified that *Last Exit* had injured him to an extent he could not yet assess (this presumably means *corrupted* him), and mere *littérateurs* knew the cause was lost.

Despite David Sheppard's evidence, the question whether fiction can morally corrupt a normal mind still seems to me to be an open one. To say that a book can have no moral influence at all is probably nonsense, but the moral influence of works of literary art, as opposed to didactic works, must be regarded as very much in doubt. Arguments addressed to reason or to prejudice—*Il Principe*, *Das Kapital*, *Mein Kampf*—have radically determined the moral beliefs of whole nations, but there is little evidence that a book which merely represents life, however one-sidedly, can change the code of behaviour of a healthy mind. We must remember, when using this term, that behaviour is of social or legal import only when it concerns more than one person. The law, if not the Scout Code, permits onanism, solitary bondage and self-flagellation.

A pornographic work represents social acts of sex, frequently of a perverse or wholly fantastic nature, often without consulting the limits of physical possibility. Such works encourage solitary fantasy, which is then usually quite harmlessly discharged in masturbation. A pornographic book is, then, an instrument for procuring a sexual catharsis, but it rarely promotes the desire to achieve this through a social mode, an act of erotic congress: the book is, in a sense, a substitute for a sexual partner. A pornograph can be either verbal or visual, but the visual stimulus is generally more intense than the verbal one. If anything that encourages sexual fantasy and leads to onanistic discharge is a pornograph, then pornographs lie all about us—underwear advertisements, the provocative photographs in the non-class Sunday papers. Etymologically (*porne* is Greek for 'whore') any depersonalized picture of a possible sexual partner represents the purest pornography you can get; how much more stimulating, though, is a real girl in a miniskirt. Women cannot help moving, and men cannot help being moved.

A pornographic work and a didactic work (like Smiles's *Self-help*) have this in common; they stimulate, and expect the discharge of the stimulation to be effected in real-life acts—acts of masturbation or acts of social import. They differ from a work of literature in that the purpose of literary art is to arouse emotions and discharge those emotions as part of the artistic experience. This is what Aristotle meant by his implied doctrine of catharsis (the full explication of this has been left to his commentators). If we read a book or see a play or film and are then driven to discharge the aroused emotion in some solitary or social act, then we have experienced good pornography or good didacticism but very bad art. Where *Last Exit to Brooklyn* possibly fails as good art is in its arousing of our social conscience to the extent of our wanting to do something charitable to people whose tragic lives arouse Aristotelian pity and terror. The book is over-didactic, then. In that it does not conduce to a desire for sexual discharge it is not pornographic. Twelve good men have made an error of classification.

Pornography, as I have indicated, is harmless so long as we do not corrupt our taste by mistaking it for literature. But it has been

255

alleged, most recently by Lady Snow in her book on the Moors Murders, that a pornographic work may induce unstable minds to carry over the fantasy element, particularly when it involves element, of cruelty, to real life. Brady apparently read the Marquis de Sade, and his crime was nauseatingly sadistic. It is, I think, all too likely that Sade helped to stimulate a nature already perverse, but a perverse nature can be stimulated by anything. Any book can be used as a pornographic instrument, even a great work of literature, if the mind that so uses it is off balance. I once found a small boy masturbating in the presence of the Victorian steel-engravings in a family Bible. Blood-drinking murderers have admitted to the stimulation of the sacrifice of the Mass. One multiple child-murderer in the United States was, on his own confession, haunted by the Abraham–Isaac episode in the Old Testament. Ban the Marquis de Sade and you will also have to ban the Bible. No more Academy nudes, no more stocking advertisements, no women (except if Islamically shrouded) in the streets of cities. No *Hamlet*, no *Macbeth*. There would then, because of the outlawing of the reasonable catharsis of art, be far more Moors Murders.

This sounds like a total rejection of the arguments for censorship, and, so far as the State is concerned, it is meant to be. Only a fool would inflame an unbalanced personality with books and pictures of sexual violence (a fool or someone absolutely—theologically—evil). A reputable publisher will not put his business at risk by selling books which are recognizably—to the normal, anyway—instruments of erotic stimulation: his list is limited to the artistic and the didactic. Hard-core pornography is normally censored by price. The reasonable elements of the community (I mean the community, not the State) contrive to preserve the weaker from excessive stimulation. The evil and unbalanced are in a minority, and the culture of the majority may not be emasculated because of a few aberrants.

Sometimes pornography gets through even the most refined net. This, I believe, happened with a novel called *The Night Clerk*, which won, inexplicably, the last Prix Formentor. One's anger at this had nothing to do with the danger of corruption: it was the categorical anger that saw an instrument of stimulation masquerading as a work of art. The publishers of *Ulysses*, *The Well of Loneliness*, *Lady Chatterley's Lover*, *The Image and the Search* and *Last Exit to Brooklyn* are reputable, and always were: it is at least conceivable that they are better qualified for the exercise of censorship than jurymen who may know nothing of literature, or even magistrates whose idea of a daring modern yarn is something by Marie Corelli.

The best argument against external censorship by church or state is still Juvenal's: '*Quis custodiet ipsos custodes?*' Why should a grocer-alderman consider himself qualified to prevent a student of Joyce from seeing the film of *Ulysses*? Why should a non-specialist and perhaps even only partly literate jury, directed by a judge untrained in aesthetics, prevent an honest inquirer from learning about the sexual mores of Brooklyn perverts? Why should a Maynooth priest seek to protect Irish morals by proscribing the novels of Edna O'Brien or, for that matter, Anthony Burgess? Our souls are ultimately our own, and it is only to God that we pray not to be led into temptation.

The recent judgment on *Last Exit to Brooklyn* is a sorry and disquieting affair. It is not only a question of the inability of the law to encompass matters of aesthetics—a question, incidentally, which Sinyavsky made the basis of his defence in the trial of himself and Daniel in February 1966. It is a matter of the law's apparent inability to cope with the semantics of its own terms of reference. The act under which the book was tried condemns whatever is conducive to concupiscence and lewdness; the judgment seems to confuse such conducement with what can only be termed an appalled and near-Swiftian representation of sexual violence and perversion. The book is what the enlightened American judgment on *Ulysses* called 'emetic'. To be sick may not be pleasant, but there is no law against making people sick. And there is not much common sense at work when a dose of mustard-and-water can be confused with a pinch of cantharides. Our would-be censors ought to try a little common sense when the next honest work of literature comes up to earn suppression through excess of human concern. All novelists must feel uneasy now. It might be anybody's book. It might be mine.

If Oedipus had read his Lévi-Strauss

IN HIS inaugural lecture as a newly appointed professor of the Collège de France—a lecture given as long ago as January 5th, 1960, but only now made available in English as *The Scope of Anthropology* —the anthropologist Claude Lévi-Strauss recounts a fascinating piece of folklore common to both the Iroquois and the Algonquin Indians. A young girl is plagued, every night while in bed, by the amorous importunities of a young man she is convinced is her brother. Formally accusing her brother in full daylight, she is very dubious when he tells her that her visitant was not himself but a double—a kind of non-familial twin with whose destiny his own is linked. She accepts his story only when he summons the double and punishes him for his attempt at a sexual crime by killing him.

Now, since the brother and his double are sympathetically related by the fact of physical identity, the murder cannot be committed with impunity: the punishment, though just, is a kind of self-condemnation. The brother realizes that the mother of his victim—a powerful sorceress, the mistress of magic owls who ask difficult riddles under pain of death—will come to avenge her son. But the last thing in the world she will think of is the breaking of the incest taboo by any member of the tribe, so the brother marries his own sister and is thus able to pass himself off as the man he killed. Only the magic owls see through the hoax, but the brother and sister evade punishment by running away.

One interesting thing about this legend is that it is a very close parallel to the Western myth of Oedipus. One of Lévi-Strauss' doctrines is that territories far separated share archetypal myths. His kind of anthropology insists on the universality of *structures* of social beliefs and taboos. But the similarities between this tale and that of Oedipus are not just summed up in Lévi-Strauss' statement, 'The very precautions taken to avoid incest in fact make it inevitable.' In both legends there are riddle-asking half-human creatures: owls, the sphinx.

Exposed on a hillside, a spike driven through his foot to ensure immobility, the infant Oedipus ('Swellfoot') is left to die: the prophecy made at his birth—that he would kill his father and marry his mother—is thus, think his parents, thwarted of fulfilment. But the very inhumanity of the device to obviate incest is bound to shock somebody and arouse pity. So Oedipus is saved by his father's shepherd, grows to manhood and sets out on the travels that are destined to end in the two worst crimes known to man. On his way to Thebes he meets the sphinx who, like the Indian owls, specializes in asking lethal riddles. Oedipus has no difficulty in identifying the creature that walks on four legs in the morning, two at noon, and three in the evening: the sphinx, humiliated, slays herself.

If Oedipus had read his Lévi-Strauss, he would have known that incest was on its way. The man who solves the insoluble puzzle has, symbolically, disrupted nature. Since incest is the ultimate perversion of nature, nature is shocked to death. In the Indian legend, there is no record of the punishment that has to be visited on a pair who commit incest: apparently the brother got away before having to submit to the riddling owls' inquisition. It seems that if you avoid the riddles you avoid the penalty for incest. If Oedipus had failed to answer the riddle of the sphinx, the sphinx would have killed him: dead, he would not have been punished for incest. If he had skirted the Theban territory where the sphinx was at its work, he would have avoided both incest and death: the crown and queen of Thebes wouldn't have been offered to him as a reward for overcoming the riddling killer.

Apparently this conflation of word-puzzle and incest is common among the American Indians. The Pueblo nation had the institution of a group of ceremonial clowns who set riddles on festal occasions and who, according to legend, were always the product of an incestuous union. To the 'primitive' mind, the puzzle and the sexual taboo have an essential factor in common—the knot that it is dangerous to untie since, untying it, you are magically untying the knot that holds the natural order together. It is doubtful whether an incest-puzzle correlation can be found in our own culture, however far back we go. In England, certainly, incest only became a crime in

1908: there is no long history of the deep-seated horror that found expression in the myths of the Greeks and the Indians. But sophisticated literature, which so often digs below the level of history, can sometimes provide toothsome bones for the anthropologist.

Take James Joyce's *Finnegans Wake*, for instance. This is an attempt at presenting the dream of a man who has, though he will not consciously admit it, an obsessive passion for his daughter. Even the word *incest* is too terrible for direct articulation: the dream-censor changes it to *insect* and makes the dreamer abandon his real name of Porter for the more suggestive one of Earwicker. The language in which the dream is expressed is the language of riddles, and the riddles are never solved: thus the commission of the terrible sexual crime is never fulfilled. The desire for the daughter is transmitted by Earwicker to his two sons, Shem and Shaun, so that both are faced with an Iroquois-Algonquin taboo. In one chapter, Shem—who is clearly to be identified with Joyce himself—is tempted by his sister, who says: 'Stop up, mavrone, and sit in my lap.' The temptation at once coincides with the asking of riddles by a chorus of girls who are not quite human—angels rather. One of the riddles is a sort of phonetic mime of a colour. The other is totally insoluble: 'Find the frenge for frocks and translace it into shocks of such as touch with show and show.' Shem's bafflement is his salvation: he is told 'Get!' and removed from the scene. Humiliated as he is, he is rendered safe from incestuous sin.

I don't think Lévi-Strauss has read *Finnegans Wake*. Certainly Joyce never read Lévi-Strauss, who first published seven years after Joyce's death. Here, then, we seem to have a gratuitous confirmation of the proposition that the riddle-incest nexus is deep in human culture. I think I can provide another literary confirmation—this time from my own work. When, in 1965, I wrote my novel *Tremor of Intent*, I had not yet come across this lecture by Lévi-Strauss. Now I see that, quite innocently, I had contrived a riddle-incest correlation. My hero, a spy, receives a message he cannot decode; almost immediately he becomes attracted to a girl who is a kind of daughter-substitute. Later, falling in love with her, he recognizes the nature of his passion. 'The love he proposed, still marvelling at himself, was the only genuine kind: the incestuous kind.' Meanwhile, the girl's brother has decoded the message, but my hero refuses to listen. This saves him from incest. When he sleeps with the girl, he sees that he is merely a teacher or initiator, and she is only too eager to learn. The sexual encounter ends sourly. The girl's brother, almost as soon as my hero has got up from the bed, brings in the coded message again. This time it has dissolved: the ink was disappearing-ink; the paper is blank. The riddle is nullified, and this strikes all incestuous elements from the record.

This Lévi-Strauss is obviously no fool. I feel now somehow that I've been manipulated by him. I want to find that other authors, as well as Joyce and myself, have been manipulated too. Let's start digging into 'Tis Pity She's a Whore and The Cenci. Anyone searching for a brand-new subject for a doctoral thesis is welcome to this one. Lévi-Strauss will be neither pleased nor displeased to receive a carbon copy. He doesn't need confirmation. *He knows.*

Why All this Fuss about Libraries?

'THE FIRE has spread from your ships,' cries Theodotus to Caesar. 'The first of the seven wonders of the world perishes. The library of Alexandria is in flames.' But Caesar, though his own war books are in libraries, is unmoved by the destruction of 'a few sheepskins scrawled with errors'; if what is burning out there is the memory of mankind, it is 'a shameful memory. Let it burn.' Such a sweeping dismissal of the records of the thought and action of the past goes too far, but on the whole I am with Caesar and against Theodotus. People make too much fuss about the sacrosanctity of libraries. Look at the passion aroused by Mr Gordon Walker's decision to push the proposed new British Museum Library out of Bloomsbury, in response to the housing claims of the local borough council. A great megalith of a monument to the memory of mankind is not to usurp the space that the living want. It will be somewhere, but it will not be a central metropolitan glory, complementary to that more tangible horde of memories that is the museum itself. Theodotus is outraged.

When Mr Gordon Walker does something, it is axiomatically to be deplored. The Government's own attitude to the concept of a National Library undoubtedly springs from an unacceptable motive (probably something to do with the virtues of microfilm). I'd better make it clear now that I dislike great libraries for highly personal reasons which I'm quite ready to erect into a bibliothecal philosophy. I was frightened by a library as a child, and I've never got over it. When I was in the fourth form, I was told to give a lecture to the rest of the class on James Elroy Flecker, getting my material from the Manchester Central Reference Library. When I got there I didn't know what to do. A sort of blindness prevented me from finding the alphabetical index: all I could find was the Dewey decimal one. The librarians were tough men in good suits. When I filled in an order form, I noticed that it required my address as well as my name. I thought this meant that I had to take the book home (I'd found a title that would do, quite by chance, in the 820 section). Taking it home, I was stopped. Everybody stopped reading to listen. Then, of course, I perceived that nobody was taking books home. It was a nightmare experience.

But there was something else that made big public libraries anti-pathetic—my own agoraphobia. At five, I'd run screaming from the attic, where I'd found a map of the heavens in an old astronomy book of my father's. I still feel sick at the sight of a really large geographical atlas. The thought of millions of books, the sight of some of them, similarly brings on a kind of desperate panic—all those brains set in cloth or leather, flashing like items in a galaxy. That some libraries should actually house such millions is monstrously unnecessary, like the stars. I don't, like Caesar, despise 'a few sheep-skins scrawled with errors': I could put up with those. I can't accept that all those books should, like the universe, make a claim on me, demand not merely to be noticed but to be deferred to. I've never been able to think of a library as a thing to be used, nibbled or eaten piecemeal. A library encloses, and any one of its items seeks to possess the brain that approaches it: the things are alive and malevolent.

I have used small libraries and even built some myself, but I'm never happy in a public one. The books I seek are always on the bottom shelf, and bending brings on palpitations. When I go to look at my own books, just to comfort myself with the reminder that I, in my own small way, have become a part of the fearsome galaxy and that this, in consequence, cannot be so fearsome after all, I always find scrawled insults in the margins. On the title page of one of my novels somebody had inked neatly 'BLOODY RUBBISH'. The book that I want is never there, and when the librarian repeats the title it always sounds suspect. When a book of mine comes out, I usually present a copy, signed, to my local library—a weak joint act of assertion and propitiation. The librarian accepts it warily and invariably opens it at a page with a dirty word on it or a scene of loveless passion. Trying to insinuate pornography in, eh?—gratuitously seeking to corrupt those decent ratepayers with string bags and copies of Barbara Cartland.

Nothing ever goes right. The other week I entered the local library with a small cigar in my mouth: it had gone out, so I wasn't really smoking. A sort of rough caretaker told me loudly that I was *ignorant*. There have been other humiliations. Some time ago a paperback was being made of one of my novels and there was the question of making some corrections in the original hard-cover edition. I didn't have a copy of my own, so I had to borrow one from the library. Taking it from the shelf, I was told by an old man it was a waste of time reading it: he'd tried it himself and had been thoroughly bored. I said I proposed borrowing it nevertheless, and he said: everybody to his taste, such as it is. Having borrowed it and used it, I forgot to return it and the library forgot to remind me it was overdue. When I took it back I was fined 3s. 6d. My own book, mark you. And this was during one of those periodical flare-ups in the long campaign to rectify the injustice done by the free borrowing system to living, and hence needy, authors.

Reference libraries won't do. You can't read a book seated at a table on a hard chair, without a smoke and without a drink. A book can be properly read only when lying down or slouched gracelessly. Books were never meant to have notes taken out of them; they should be smeared, dog-eared, scrawled on, underlined. Page references should be pencilled on the fly-leaves or inside covers: that's what they're for. What I suppose I mean is that one should always read one's own bought or stolen books, never borrowed ones (unless borrowing really means stealing). The real argument against the institutional library is that the books have to be treated with respect, like governesses. A book should be a whore, not a lady. Except, of course, that the place of a book is in the home: there the image breaks down. Let us say, then, that one's personal library should be a kind of harem.

Looking at plans of Norman castles, I always used to be moved to see that one room was set aside as a library. I thought of the winter and wolves outside, the siege of snow and, when the weather mended, of local enemies, and all the time there was a little citadel of culture—illuminated books of hours, *gestes*, devotional manuals. Yeats conveys the feel of the domestic library as a place of warmth and safety in his poem 'Mad as the mist and snow', though he ends with the breaching of the walls, or rather the fifth column, since Tully and Homer and the rest are themselves as crazy as the elements. But I prefer my library at home—and I mean a library, not just book-shelves in the sitting-room. I've bought these books, or, if they're review copies, neglected to sell them: they can be ravished, defaced, spent pagemeal in the privy, arranged in disorder, lost and found again, used. But there ought not to be too many of them: that way, the shelves mount to the ceiling, library steps have to be imported, a simple classification system begs to be given a trial. Soon you start filling gaps, hungering after completeness, throwing out tattered paper-backs, judging things you once loved unworthy. That way madness lies, or rather the horrible sanity of the institution.

The horror of the British Museum Library, which I take to be the ideal towards which all institutional libraries must strive, lies, for me, in its comprehensiveness—those millions of cells which make up the genuine memory of mankind. But the days of such comprehensiveness are over, and if the Government thinks that, then the Government is being, for once, irradiated by a certain progressive spirit. Decentralized specialist libraries are needed, and, in the major field of information, the very term 'library' must become a misnomer, since new facts will not wait on the snail-trail that stretches from author's typewriter to book publisher's warehouse. This is the day of journals, xeroxed monographs, the immediate transmission of ideas and their immediate supersession.

But who am I to talk, since I have vowed, so far as my trade makes it possible, to keep out of the great libraries? And this same trade will flourish best if I stop myself thinking of all those millions of volumes in the British Museum Library and the others that haven't yet caught fire from Caesar's ships or Caesar's fear of the honest spirit of inquiry of his subjects. The writer has to think of himself as a lone star. To know that he's a mere speck in the galaxies of Bloomsbury is dispiriting and inhibiting. No writer is great enough for the great libraries.

Epilogue: Conflict and Confluence

WHEN people ask me, as they sometimes do, for a nice, quick, easy, capsule definition of Art, I usually say something like this: 'Art is the organization of base matter into an illusory image of universal order.' Like most true statements, that sounds too slick to be true. I suppose the Ten Commandments and the Eight Beatitudes and the Seven Deadly Sins have sounded equally plausible and questionable in their time. Still, I maintain the belief that Art—whether it's music, painting, sculpture, dancing or literature—wouldn't exist if we were sure that the universe was really a universe and not a duoverse, a unity and not a duality. What, I'm afraid, sounds portentous is really quite simple. The thing we're most aware of in life is division, the conflict of opposites—good, evil; black, white; rich, poor—and so on. We don't like to live in the middle of this conflict (it's rather like trying to picnic in the centre of a football field) and we rush eagerly to any saint or pundit or prophet who will convince us that all this conflict is really so much illusion, that behind it all exists a great shining ultimate unity which is eternal and *real*. The trouble is that this ultimate unity, whether it be God or the Classless Society, is always presented as being a long way off or away or above. I like my pie here and now. That's why I trust the artist more than the Marxist or the theologian. That's why I regard the artist's trade as not merely the most honourable but also the most holy. The vision of unity, which is what the artist sells, is preferable to any mere religious or metaphysical manifesto.

We all have our different memories of the first incarnation of division or conflict. To some writers it first appeared as class, and with such writers it remains as class—Mr Sillitoe, for instance. I first met it as religion. I was a Catholic in a Protestant country, an Old Catholic who, as a young child, took my beliefs as self-evident and never for one moment imagined that they were the beliefs of an assailed minority. My birthplace was Manchester, and Lancashire did its best to resist the Reformation—sometimes, as you will see in Lancashire village pubs with statues of the Sacred Heart in the public bar, with a four-hundred-and-fifty-year success. I first met Protestants when going home from school. The children of St Augustine's, a Church of England foundation, called the children of my school 'cat-licks'. We, in our turn, called them 'proddy-dogs'. Harmless enough, as harmless as the mutual vilifications of the supporters of Manchester City and Manchester United. But, as I grew older, the sense not so much of conflict as of estrangement, of exile, grew deeper, more metaphysical.

There was the question of November 5th, for example. Guido Fawkes and Robert Catesby had tried to blow up Parliament on behalf of the English Catholics. Was it right for us children to enjoy the fireworks and the bonfire? Well, we could always imagine that the guy was really Henry VIII. And didn't even the Protestant children treat their guy with a sort of protective love until the actual hour of conflagration? We pushed our guys round in old prams, cosseting them, begging for pennies for them. The guy could be ambivalent and everybody, Catholics and Protestants alike, could see his burning as a ritual rather than a revenge. But when history ceased to be ritual and became allegiance, the problem could not be solved in terms of love-hate. There was this business of the Spanish Armada, that palpable sword of the Counter-Reformation. Thinking ourselves back, in the dream-engendering fug of the classroom, to 1588, we asked what role it was proper to take? Should we be hanged and eviscerated as Spanish spies, or else set our bulldog jaws against the invader, fierce and patriotic in the glow of the beacon on the hill? It was very difficult, and it continued to be difficult. Religion got in the way of friendship and, when the time came for love, love. Even language was a betrayer. If I wrote a poem or a story, which audience was I supposed to be addressing—the great Protestant one which Shakespeare and Milton had helped to make, or the smaller, despised, exotic one which was fed on the pamphlets of the Catholic Truth Society?

The creative impulse was strong in me as a child and an adolescent, but it never took a verbal form. I drew; I painted until I discovered I was colour-blind. I taught myself to play the piano and eventually to compose music. But I knew that my business was really with words. What I could not find was a means of conveying an image of unity through words—or, to put it another way, a Marxist way, the synthesis which art stood for trembling in both the thesis and the antithesis. What I lacked, in short, was something it was possible to write about. The two big converts to Catholicism had not yet delivered their message. Graham Greene had still to show that the human condition of conflict was resolved in a divine mystery; Evelyn Waugh was still to dream back to the vision of an aristocratic Catholicism that carried, like a tiny lamp, the faith to the days of broken chapels and the ultimate barbarism. Meanwhile, the war arrived and I became a soldier. And, as a soldier, I travelled towards the solution of my problem.

I went to the Gates of Hercules, the sundered lips of Europe and Africa, to Deucalion's flood and Noah's. In other words, I was posted to Gibraltar. This was 1943, and the ship docked on Christmas Eve. As if in celebration of Christmas, the lights were on all over the Rock —a revelation after four years of blacked-out England. But this luminosity had nothing festal about it: it was the natural condition of a pretended neutrality, since Spain was neutral and Gibraltar was,

267

geographically, part of Spain. It was a sort of dazzling camouflage. In Madrid the 'Ferdinand and Isabella' plan for the Rock's invasion was being considered (after all, the Nazis had helped to bring Franco to power); over the border, in La Linea and Algeciras, the German spies snuffled around. The neutrality was a musical-comedy sham on both sides. The lights that sparkled all over the Iberian peninsula were the spots and floats of fantasy, but the fantasy went deeper for me than the delightful palpitations of a paperback thriller. Here was, in a sense, the home from which I had been exiled: here was the Catholic Europe from which the whole of the British people had been exiled.

But, of course, my Catholic childhood had brought me closer to Ireland than to the great Catholic Europe 'out there'. The Lancashire Catholics married into Irish families, holy water being thicker than blood. Lancashire was, for me, a province of Ireland, the provincial capital being Liverpool; the Irish ambassadors were Father Casey and Father Dwyer and Father O'Shaughnessy. Here, though, in Gibraltar, the extremity of the great Catholic Europe fossilized a religious and cultural history far less insular than the one that had begun with Saint Patrick in A.D. 432. I had thought little about St Thomas Aquinas in my Catholic youth. Now I began to be reminded of how the subtle Arabs had caged the great beast Aristotle, and how cunning St Thomas found the key to the cage and let the beast out, and then made it roar through his *Summa Theologica*. Coming to Gibraltar, I became aware of the two old enemies, Islam and Roman Christianity, tussling in the sun.

But Gibraltar was, after all, and still is, for that matter, a British colony. Here was the ultimate in fantasy, all summed up in the architecture of the Anglican cathedral. What should it be—Romanesque or Gothic? Neither. It should be a mosque, and a mosque it is. The British at home are dull; to a person of my tradition and temperament they are not *sympathique*. Get them abroad, however; start them on the fantasy of colonization and they change. In Gibraltar my muse seemed to have found what it was looking for in the way of a subject-matter—a conflict that had turned into a confluence. Catholic baroque, the onion domes and the barley-sugar columns of the Moors, the soft and fictile humanism of the British. Could one imagine a stranger mixture? Yet it worked here; it contrived a harmony. I saw that I was falling in love, unbelievably, with British colonialism. But where did I, an English Catholic, stand in relation to its pattern? I was not quite an agent of colonialism, since I was a soldier. I was not quite one of the colonized, since I was English. But, being a Catholic, I had a place in the Corpus Christi processions of the Gibraltarians. The language of Andalusia slipped on to me as gently and as well-fitting as a coat. I was part of the colony and yet I would always be outside it. But I could resolve my elements of new and different exile in my art.

What art, though? The words would not come. Music still got in the way. I wrote a kind of Gibraltar symphony which has still not been performed, though I think it ought to be—a work in which flamenco wailings, zapateado stampings and solid British trumpet-tunes clash and ultimately combine. But more than music strangled the hopes of a verbal utterance. An artist needs more than a subject-matter; he needs his home and his wife. Words were the stuff of letters home, soaked in loneliness. They could not be cleansed of nostalgia and set to work in the joy of artistic creation. Music was different; music was marks on paper standing for sheer sound.

But the time came, belatedly, for the transplantation of the Rock to the pages of a work of fiction. In the late nineteen-forties I wrote my first novel, *A Vision of Battlements*, and found, to my surprise, that it was a comic novel. This I had not intended. I don't think any potential writer ever knows what sort of a writer he is going to be. We see ourselves ten times a day in mirrors and shop-windows, but we always carry an image of ourselves very different from the reflected reality. I see myself as a creature of gloom and sobriety, but my books reflect a sort of clown. And yet I believe that if I had written my first novel out of the experience of my early days in Lancashire, with the sense of exile, the taunts of 'cat-lick' and 'proddy-dog', I should not have been a comic writer at all. There was something in Gibraltar which drew out a sleeping comic talent, and that something was the confluence of cultures. Now, in the work of fiction, conflict is everything, but the aim of the work is to resolve the conflict through imagination. When the resolution of cultural, religious, racial conflict—in real life as opposed to fiction—is achieved through gentle colonialism, then fiction, as opposed to real life, can separate out the elements and allow them to touch in tiny electric shocks which tickle the imagination. I learned from Gibraltar that I would be happiest when writing about fantastically varied communities on which an alien but benign rule had been imposed. I found such communities in Africa, in Malaya and, strangely enough, in Russia, but Gibraltar was the prototype.

Yet I've been shy of publishing my novel about Gibraltar—not solely because it was a tyro work. My own personal, as opposed to religious and cultural, exile was embedded in it, and for too many years it recalled loneliness. And yet it was not possible to re-make Gibraltar in a dispensation of settled maturity: one can never go back. It was to be expected that, when I attempted a second novel, it should be full of Catholic gloom, the whinings of the disaffected. I saw, since my Gibraltar novel had established my character as a comic novelist, that I was not being true to myself. I needed the stimulus of a new Gibraltar.

In the very summer in which I finished my second novel I was summoned to my new Gibraltar. Its name was Malaya. There was a war going on there, and both my wife and myself had had enough of war, but the summons was an authoritative one and it had to be obeyed. We went, my wife, myself and our Siamese cat, to a town on the River Perak, in the very core of the Communist jungle war. There was a royal palace for the Sultan and his wives, there were mosques that looked just like Gibraltar's Anglican cathedral. There was heat and thirst and a weary community of colonial officers. But there was the Gibraltar image in excelsis. Instead of Spaniards and Moors and Genoese there were Malays, Chinese, Bengalis, Sikhs, Tamils, Eurasians. There were toddy-shops, Cantonese eating-hells, open-air *sateh*-stalls, *ronggeng*-dancers and musical gong societies. There was conflict turned by the British into a confluence. At last I could write. In the oppressive heat of the afternoon the sweat flowed. It flowed on to paper, along with words. At last I had become a novelist.

Underneath the flowering of my vocation, hidden under the thick foliage of the stirring mind, there coiled, like a benign snake, a conviction that the gardener ought perhaps to have crushed. I was a writer at last, and all writers are radical. But here I was as a colonial officer, implicit supporter of a sort of *raj*, trying, as all creative artists try, to get the best of both worlds. I drank cocktails at receptions in the Sultan's Istana, sweating in my white tuxedo; I stood to attention on the Queen's Birthday parades. It was an act, of course; it was deliberate self-mockery; my place was in the kampongs and the coffee-shops, talking Malay with the people. But soon it was not an act and the self-mockery melted in the sun. Was not this colonial image of order itself a kind of work of art? Had not the British, in bringing together this scarcely imaginable mixture of races and faiths and cultures, already half-written my novels for me?

I suppose that my brief life as one of the colonizing British was salutary for me as a writer because it was salutary for me as a human being. The British have, throughout history, evinced two main talents, seemingly opposed and irreconcilable. They have produced the greatest literature the world has seen; they have produced an idea of empire. I think it's only the sweet stay-at-homes who vilify colonialism. Those who, like myself, have helped in the maintenance of the *pax Britannica* are more ready to admire than condemn. The literary talent and the colonizing talent are cognate in that they both forge an image of unity in a world split like an abscess. Back home for good in England I see myself as both colonizer and colonized. I remain, as an English Catholic, a subject of an alien *raj*. I can talk of an era of past oppression with the fire of any babu or West Indian lawyer or pub-crawling Dubliner. But I am reconciled now; the *raj* no longer seems alien.

The bigger *raj* is very nearly dead. It's the duty of novelists to record its obsequies. But without that dispensation of tolerant order I doubt if I could have become a novelist at all. Geographically the Empire once began at Gibraltar, and historically it's likely to end there. Go to the Rock now and you will find a certain blurring of colour, a diffusion of the television-and-bingo mind, a money-loving smugness. But you will also find the vestiges of what first set my creative imagination smouldering: the apes that have leapt over from the Barbary coast, the ruined Moorish castle, the baroque processions and the dark skins. I have been back myself, very recently, but I doubt if I shall go back again—the one fertilization was enough.

And yet I sometimes think that if I had continued to regard Manchester as my home, if I had been patient long enough, if there had been no war and no posting to Gibraltar, then perhaps fertilization would have come in a not very different form. I went back recently to the district where I lived as a schoolboy and found that it had turned itself into a Crown colony, full of shebeens, turbans and temples. The British withdraw from their colonies, but new colonies follow them home. We old colonial servants retire, but we find that we no longer have to yearn for the richness of a multi-coloured, multi-cultured society: it's growing here all about us. So, no longer an exile, I hope to be able to look forward to a few more years of recording in fiction the kind of human community I love best— shark's fins and chillis and cabbages all in the same shop.

But what about that first novel? *A Vision of Battlements* has, after twelve years, purged itself of the overtones of loneliness, and the time has come to publish it. In it I see a little funeral of old ambitions: the hero is a young composer who fails to write great music; he is also a Catholic who sought emancipation from his faith but sees daily in the huge crouching Rock a palpable image of the inescapable numen. His story, like all my stories since, is a slow and cruel stripping-off of illusion. But this background is alive with the current of opposing traditions. Where he strips I clothed myself—in the varied colours of the history of that sea, the strong boots that Catholic Europe gave me, the Mediterranean sun as a helmet. But over the Joseph's coat fell the drab but durable cloak of the community-forging British, able to stand all weathers, possessed, despite all changes in fashion, of a glum but sempiternal elegance.

H MAY 6 1969

BUFFALO AND ERIE COUNTY PUBLIC LIBRARY

This book is due on the last date stamped
on the card in the pocket.

7 Days